GUARDIANS
OF THE
BOARDROOM

GUARDIANS
OF THE
BOARDROOM

A Strategic Guide to Boardroom Excellence, Ethical Leadership, and Risk Oversight

DR TANIA DEHURY

Cursive

Published by
OakBridge Publishing Pvt. Ltd.
934, Tower B3, Spaze i-Tech Park, Sector 49, Gurugram, 122018, Haryana, India
Tel.: +91 124 4305970, E-mail: info@oakbridge.in
www.oakbridge.in

ISBN: 978-81-993052-0-5

Printed and bound in India

Dedication

To the Almighty
the unseen force behind every step, the light in confusion, and the calm in the storm.

To my Gurus/Mentors
the guides who opened my mind and awakened my purpose.
With deep gratitude to Dr. Prabir Kumar Mohanty and Prof. Pabitra Kumar Jena,
whose wisdom, belief, and example continue to shape my path.

To my grandmother
who laid the foundation with love, resilience, and quiet wisdom.

To my mother, father, and uncle
for everything, the values imparted, the sacrifices made, and the unwavering belief that shaped my journey.

To my elder brother
a steady pillar of strength, always there, always solid, always sure, and forever standing by my side.

To my wife
my early warning system and my engine, whose insight, energy, and love fuel every endeavour.

To my daughter
the rebel director of tomorrow, whose questions keep me sharp, and whose presence is my daily dose of joy and purpose, my living vitamin.

To my best friends and all family members
for their constant motivation and invaluable insights.

And to all my dear friends and my extended family
your love, laughter, and faith have sustained me in ways words can never fully express.
With deep gratitude and love.

Praise for the Book

Guardians of the Boardroom by Dr. Tania Dehury is an insightful guide to modern corporate governance. The independent director is portrayed as a guardian of ethics, a sentinel of accountability, and a guide to strategic foresight. Regulatory clarity is seamlessly blended with practical, real-world wisdom, defining governance as a balance between conscience and competence. A must-read for professionals aspiring to be directors and for promoters committed to building transparent, responsible, and resilient organizations.

Radhakrishnan Nair
Independent Director, ICICI Bank; ICICI Prudential Life Insurance Company; ICICI Securities; Axis Mutual Fund; Geojit Financial Services, etc.
Retired Member (Finance & Investment), IRDAI
Former Executive Director, SEBI

"I found Guardians of the Boardroom to be a lucid and insightful guide for today's independent director. What appealed to me most is how Dr. Tania Dehury connects the dots between the past, present, and future of corporate governance. This book is a must-read for anyone seeking to understand the purpose and practice of responsible board stewardship."

Sarita Bahl
Independent Board Director
BharatRohan Airborne Innovations / Thrive India / Etherwire.Ai

"Guardians of the Boardroom beautifully bridges theory and practice, providing a nuanced understanding of the challenges and responsibilities that independent directors shoulder in today's complex corporate environment. Dr. Dehury's reflections remind us that true governance begins with integrity, courage, and foresight."

Jyoti Prakash Mohapatra
Joint President
Grasim Industries Limited, Aditya Birla Group

"Guardians of the Boardroom" is a thoughtful and timely work that reimagines the role of independent directors as custodians of conscience, not merely of compliance. Dr. Tania Dehury blends strategic insight with ethical clarity, demonstrating how wisdom and vigilance can elevate corporate governance from procedure to purpose. With its lucid prose and evocative metaphors - especially *The Owl in the Boardroom* - this book is a must-read for anyone committed to building transparent, resilient, and responsible boards.

Amit Marwah, CFA
CEO, Fraikin Dayim Trucks GCC | Group Chief Investment Officer, Dayim Holdings

Preface

In an era where corporate scandals, investor activism, and regulatory scrutiny dominate the headlines, *Guardians of the Boardroom* offers a timely and authoritative exploration of the evolving role of Independent Directors (IDs) in shaping India's governance landscape.

Structured around eleven core chapters, each tackling a pillar of boardroom oversight, fiduciary duty, and ethical leadership, this book serves as both a practical handbook and a strategic manifesto for current and aspiring Independent Directors. From legal responsibilities and committee participation to culture-building, digital oversight, and ESG imperatives, the book equips readers with a 360-degree view of what it takes to be a trusted boardroom guardian in 21st-century India.

Central to the book are detailed case studies, including Satyam, Yes Bank, Sahara, Cognizant, Fortis, IL&FS, Kingfisher Airlines, and more, which provide real-world insights into successes, failures, and systemic lessons for directors navigating complex environments. These stories serve as cautionary tales and learning opportunities, showcasing the power and consequences of boardroom decisions.

Whether you're a governance professional, company secretary, legal advisor, or corporate leader, this book unpacks what it truly means to be "independent" in a landscape that often tests that very notion.

Key Themes Include:

- The evolution and legal framework of Independent Directors in India
- Board dynamics, conflicts of interest, and promoter challenges
- Risk management, financial oversight, and audit committee effectiveness
- Ethics, sustainability, digital governance, and whistleblower protection
- Case-based governance failures and corrective board action
- Future-readiness for directors in tech-driven, ESG-conscious companies

Why This Book Matters:

Independent Directors are no longer figureheads; they are the ethical anchors and strategic sentinels of modern corporate India. As regulatory scrutiny tightens and stakeholder expectations rise, the boardroom demands more than legal compliance. It demands independent judgment, moral courage, and informed oversight.

Guardians of the Boardroom addresses this call. It bridges the gap between regulation and real-world practice, offering a clear, actionable guide to what independence truly means in the Indian context. Through incisive analysis and powerful case studies from Satyam to IL&FS, it unpacks how decisions made (or avoided) in the boardroom can shape a company's future.

This book empowers directors to:

- Ask the right questions, not just tick the right boxes
- Navigate promoter influence with integrity
- Lead on risk, ethics, digital oversight, and ESG

It is a roadmap for those who believe that being an Independent Director is not just a designation; it is a duty.

> *"A seat on the board does not make one independent; courage does. In times of silence, it is the vigilant voice that protects, the questioning mind that shields, and the principled stand that defines true guardianship. For it is not compliance alone, but conscience in action, that shapes the future of governance."*

Dr Tania Dehury
06 November, 2025

Contents

Introduction

"Shaping Integrity, Accountability, and Trust in Indian Corporate Governance"

In the complex, high-stakes theatre of corporate India, the Independent Director (IDs) stands as both sentinel and steward-guarding against excess, guiding toward integrity. As boardrooms evolve into arenas where ethical judgment, regulatory compliance, and strategic foresight must intersect seamlessly, the role of the ID has never been more critical. Yet, beyond the statutory definitions and checklists lies a deeper truth: IDs are not mere observers or token appointees; they are the living architecture of good governance.

This book, *Guardians of the Boardroom*, explores the powerful yet often misunderstood world of IDs in India. It unpacks their evolving responsibilities, from watchdogs of shareholder interest to champions of sustainability, from risk sentinels to architects of corporate purpose. In doing so, it brings into sharp focus the moral and institutional backbone they provide to companies navigating a turbulent economic and regulatory landscape.

India's corporate governance regime has undergone tectonic shifts in the past two decades—triggered by scandals, shaped by reforms, and fuelled by rising public expectations. In this transformation, IDs are increasingly called upon not just for their detachment, but for their wisdom, agility, and moral clarity. They are expected to ask difficult questions, stand firm in the face of groupthink, and ensure that the boardroom remains a forum of accountability rather than a stage for complacency.

This book is not merely a legal or procedural treatise; it is a strategic lens, a governance manifesto, and a call to action. It is meant for current and aspiring directors, corporate leaders, policymakers, scholars, and all who believe that the strength of India's economy lies as much in boardroom ethics as in balance sheets.

At its core, *Guardians of the Boardroom* is about restoring trust. Because in a world where credibility is currency and transparency is power, IDs are the pillars upon which good governance must stand.

1.1 Setting the Stage: Why Governance Matters More Than Ever

In today's rapidly evolving corporate world, governance is not merely a regulatory checkbox – it is the very foundation upon which sustainable growth, trust, and accountability stand. Across the globe, and particularly in India, the importance of robust governance structures has been amplified by increasing stakeholder expectations, regulatory reforms, and heightened public scrutiny.

Corporate scandals, financial irregularities, and governance failures have demonstrated that strong boards are essential not only to safeguard shareholder value but also to protect the broader ecosystem of employees, customers, communities, and the economy. The IDs sits at the heart of this architecture – a guardian who balances diverse interests with impartiality and insight.

India's journey toward good governance is both unique and inspiring. The convergence of legal reforms, economic liberalisation, and rising investor activism has shaped a governance ecosystem where independent directors have emerged as pivotal players. Yet, the role remains complex, nuanced, and often misunderstood. This book seeks to unravel that complexity and illuminate the path forward.

Guardianship is not a ceremony; it is a commitment.

1.2 The Indian Governance Context: A Transformative Backdrop

India's corporate governance landscape has undergone a remarkable transformation over the past two decades. Landmark legislative enactments such as the Companies Act, 2013, and regulatory frameworks introduced by the Securities and Exchange Board of India (SEBI) have established a clear mandate for IDs. These reforms have aimed to enhance transparency, protect minority shareholders, and institutionalise the role of independent directors in safeguarding board independence.

However, India's governance journey is set against broader social, cultural, and economic dynamics. Family-owned businesses, promoter influence, varying levels of board maturity, and evolving regulatory compliance culture create a challenging environment. In this context, IDs must navigate competing demands, ethical dilemmas, and complex stakeholder landscapes. This book captures these challenges candidly while highlighting the profound opportunities for IDs to shape India's governance future and corporate credibility.

1.3 Why Independent Directors? The Pillars of Boardroom Integrity

IDs are the sentinels of the boardroom, entrusted with the critical task of ensuring that management acts in the best interests of the company and its stakeholders. Their independence – both in thought and action – is fundamental to balanced decision-making, robust oversight, and ethical leadership.

This role requires more than compliance or formal presence on the board. It demands courage, wisdom, emotional intelligence, and the ability to question assumptions without losing sight of the larger strategic goals. IDs must act as guardians who prevent groupthink, check undue promoter influence, and safeguard against conflicts of interest.

True guardians don't just watch the process they protect its purpose.

In India, the evolving expectations from IDs reflect a deepening recognition that governance excellence is essential for attracting global capital, fostering innovation, and enabling sustainable business models.

1.4 The Governance Architecture: Beyond Roles to Relationships

Good governance is often depicted as a structure – board committees, charters, and policies. Yet, the architecture of governance is more than frameworks; it is the relationships and cultures that enable boards to function effectively.

This book explores how IDs engage with promoters, executive management, regulators, and other stakeholders. It examines the subtle balance between oversight and partnership, vigilance and trust, and challenge and collaboration.

By understanding these dynamics, IDs can transcend transactional roles and become true architects of governance, driving cultures of accountability, transparency, and ethical decision-making.

1.5 Emerging Themes in Indian Governance and the Independent Director's Role

The governance landscape is continually evolving. New challenges and priorities, such as Environmental, Social, and Governance (ESG) factors, digital transformation, risk resilience, and stakeholder capitalism, have expanded the ID's remit.

This book integrates these contemporary themes, providing a holistic view of how IDs can lead through complexity. From overseeing ESG disclosures to understanding cyber risks, from ensuring ethical innovation to guiding strategy in volatile markets, the role is expanding and deepening.

The text is not only a manual of duties but also a guide to leadership in an age where governance is synonymous with long-term value creation.

The test of independence is not how you vote, but why you speak.

1.6 Bridging Theory and Practice: Case Studies and Real-World Insights

A central strength of this book lies in its blend of rigorous analysis and practical wisdom. Drawing from Indian corporate boardrooms, regulatory developments, and interviews with experienced IDs, it offers candid insights and actionable strategies.

Readers will find vivid case studies illustrating successes, failures, dilemmas, and best practices. These narratives humanise the role, highlighting how IDs grapple with ambiguity, exercise judgment, and influence outcomes.

This approach bridges the gap between legal prescriptions and boardroom realities, making the book a vital resource for practitioners, regulators, scholars, and students alike.

1.7 Why This Book Matters: For Whom and Why

"*Guardians of the Boardroom*" is intended for a diverse audience: seasoned IDs seeking to deepen their impact; aspiring directors preparing for this critical role; corporate executives striving to understand board expectations; regulators and governance professionals shaping the ecosystem; and academics analysing governance trends.

In a marketplace increasingly shaped by trust and transparency, this book provides a roadmap to navigating governance challenges with integrity and foresight. It aims to empower IDs to lead confidently, balancing rigor with empathy, and vigilance with vision.

1.8 The Architecture of This Book: Navigating the Chapters

The book unfolds in carefully structured chapters that progressively build understanding:

- Foundations of Indian corporate governance and the independent director's legal duties

Directorship is not about knowing the answer—it's about asking the right question.

- The interplay of power, influence, and independence in board dynamics
- Deep dives into committee roles, risk oversight, and stakeholder engagement
- Contemporary challenges such as ESG, digital governance, and ethical dilemmas
- Practical guidance on director skills, continuous learning, and governance leadership

Each chapter combines conceptual clarity with illustrative examples and thought-provoking reflections, designed to engage and inform.

1.9 A Call to Leadership and Stewardship

Ultimately, governance is about leadership – leadership that transcends transactions and embodies stewardship. IDs are entrusted not only with protecting the company from risks but also with shaping its future in line with societal values.

India's economic rise and corporate aspirations demand a new generation of governance guardians' directors who are knowledgeable, courageous, and committed to the highest standards of integrity.

This book is a call to action for those who answer this call, who understand that good governance is both a responsibility and an opportunity to build resilient, trusted enterprises.

1.10 Final Thoughts: A Journey Begins

Good governance is more than a system of rules and processes – it is the embodiment of values, trust, and stewardship at the highest level of corporate leadership. As the guardians of the boardroom, IDs carry the solemn responsibility of balancing diverse stakeholder interests while steering organisations toward sustainable, ethical success.

Leadership demands courage; stewardship demands conscience.

The role demands courage to question, wisdom to discern, and integrity to act in the best interests of the company and society. It is a role that is constantly evolving, shaped by economic shifts, regulatory reforms, technological advances, and rising expectations for transparency and accountability.

This book invites you to embark on a transformative journey – one that unpacks the complexities, celebrates the challenges, and illuminates the profound impact independent directors can have on India's governance landscape. Through a blend of insight, analysis, and real-world examples, it aims to equip you with the knowledge, perspective, and inspiration to lead with confidence and conviction.

The journey ahead is demanding yet rewarding. It calls for continuous learning, fearless leadership, and unwavering commitment to the principles of good governance. But it is also a journey of immense opportunity to build resilient boards, foster trust, and contribute meaningfully to the future of Indian corporate India.

As you turn these pages, may you find clarity in complexity, strength in stewardship, and vision for the road ahead. The path of a guardian is never easy, but it is essential, and the journey begins here.

"Independent Directors are not just sentinels of compliance - they are the architects of trust, the guardians of conscience, and the silent scaffolding upon which the edifice of good governance stands tall in India's corporate future."

CHAPTER 1

The Multifaceted Role of Independent Directors: Balancing Committee Duties and Board Responsibilities

"The boardroom is a mirror; the independent director reflects its integrity."

1.1 Introduction: Guardians of Oversight in an Era of Accountability

The role of the Independent Director (ID) in India has evolved from a statutory requirement to a cornerstone of credible and ethical corporate governance. In today's boardrooms, IDs are expected not only to bring an unbiased perspective but also to actively engage in shaping the strategic direction, monitoring risk, ensuring compliance, and safeguarding the interests of stakeholders. As boards face increasing expectations from regulators, investors, and the public, the spotlight on IDs has intensified, transforming their position into both influence and immense responsibility.

At the heart of this transformation lies a growing tension between two interconnected domains: committee duties and full board responsibilities. IDs frequently serve on and often chair key committees such as the Audit Committee, Nomination and Remuneration Committee (NRC), Risk Management Committee, and Corporate Social Responsibility (CSR) Committee. Each of these roles demands specialised knowledge, diligent oversight, and significant time for preparation. However, their responsibilities extend beyond committee walls; they are equally accountable for contributing to board-level deliberations on strategy, ethics, governance, and long-term value creation.

Balancing these twin demands requires agility, sound judgment, and deep commitment. IDs must pivot seamlessly between the granular review of financial controls in one meeting and high-level discussion on ESG integration in another. They must maintain independence while collaborating effectively with executive management and ask difficult questions without disrupting board cohesion. The role is as much about oversight as it is about foresight.

This section explores the multifaceted nature of the ID's role, examining how they can effectively navigate the interplay between committee responsibilities and boardroom leadership.

1.1.1 The Growing Importance of Independent Directors

In today's corporate governance landscape, IDs have become indispensable pillars, safeguarding transparency, accountability, and ethical stewardship.

By providing an impartial voice in board deliberations, IDs help balance the often competing interests of shareholders, management, regulators, and broader society, ensuring that decisions are both fair and forward-looking. In India, the prominence of IDs has grown steadily, driven by legislative and regulatory reforms such as the Companies Act, 2013, and SEBI Listing Regulations. These measures are designed not only to enhance governance standards and protect minority shareholders but also to build investor confidence and strengthen the credibility of the corporate sector.

A clean audit is not always a clear conscience.

1.1.2 Multifaceted Nature of the Independent Director's Role

IDs serve a dual function. First, they contribute to the overall strategic direction and oversight of the company as part of the full board. Second, they assume specific responsibilities on various board committees, such as Audit, Nomination and Remuneration, CSR, and Risk Management. The committee system enables the board to delegate detailed and technical oversight tasks. IDs plays a crucial role in these committees as their independence ensures objective scrutiny free from management influence.

1.1.3 Why Balancing Committee Duties and Board Responsibilities Matters

The challenge for IDs lies in managing these multifaceted roles effectively. Committee work requires focused attention to specialised areas such as financial audits, executive compensation, or social responsibility, while board duties demand a broad perspective on the company's overall health and strategy. Failure to balance these responsibilities can lead to oversight gaps, conflicts of interest, or inefficiencies. Conversely, well-balanced engagement empowers IDs to:

- enhance the quality of board decision-making;
- proactively mitigate risks;
- foster a culture of transparency and integrity; and
- build trust among investors and stakeholders.

1.1.4 Scope and Structure of this section

This section explores the evolving and multifaceted role of IDs with a focus on:

- Understanding their legal and fiduciary duties
- Examining their contributions to key board committees

Numbers don't lie, but they do hide; look deeper.

- Identifying challenges and best practices for balancing responsibilities
- Highlighting real-world examples and emerging trends

1.2 The Legal and Regulatory Framework for Independent Directors in India

The role and responsibilities of IDs in India are defined and guided by a robust legal and regulatory framework. This framework sets the standards for board composition, duties, disclosures, and accountability mechanisms to ensure IDs serve as effective guardians of good governance. Understanding this framework is essential for IDs to discharge their responsibilities with confidence and full compliance.

1.2.1 The Companies Act, 2013: Cornerstone of Corporate Governance

The Companies Act, 2013, introduced significant reforms to strengthen corporate governance in India. Key provisions relating to IDs include:

- **Definition and eligibility:** Section 149 defines IDs and lays down eligibility criteria to ensure they are genuinely independent from the company's promoters and management.
- **Appointment and tenure:** IDs are appointed for a term of up to five years, with the possibility of reappointment for a second term. They cannot serve for more than two consecutive terms.
- **Duties and responsibilities:** Section 166 outlines fiduciary duties, requiring IDs to act in good faith, exercise due care, and avoid conflicts of interest.
- **Role in committees:** The Act mandates certain committees, such as the Audit Committee and NRC, to include ID as members or chairs.

If you don't question the accounts, the accounts may question you.

- **Liability protection:** The Act provides limited liability protections for IDs, provided they act with due diligence and in good faith.
- **Code for independent directors:** Schedule IV prescribes a Code of Conduct that guides their ethical and professional behaviour.

1.2.2 Securities and Exchange Board of India (Listing Obligations and Disclosure Requirements) Regulations, 2015

The Securities and Exchange Board of India (SEBI) further strengthens the corporate governance framework through its Listing Regulations, which apply to publicly listed companies.

- **Board composition:** SEBI mandates that at least one-third of the board must comprise IDs, with specific provisions for certain categories of companies.
- **Independent director criteria:** SEBI's criteria for independence are more stringent and detailed, addressing issues such as financial relationships, family ties, and cross-directorships.
- **Board committees:** SEBI requires mandatory Audit Committees and NRCs to have IDs, enhancing oversight of financial reporting and executive compensation.
- **Annual disclosure and reporting:** Listed companies must disclose information about IDs, their attendance, and remuneration, promoting transparency.
- **Board evaluation:** SEBI requires annual performance evaluation of IDs, individually and collectively, to ensure effectiveness.

1.2.3 Regulatory Guidelines and Codes

- **Institute of Company Secretaries of India (ICSI) Guidelines:** ICSI has issued comprehensive guidelines and training modules for IDs, emphasising their evolving role and promoting best practices.

- **Ministry of Corporate Affairs (MCA) Initiatives:** MCA periodically issues clarifications, circulars, and training programs to raise awareness and enhance the competence of IDs.
- **International Standards and Practices:** Indian regulations are increasingly aligned with global governance frameworks such as the OECD Principles of Corporate Governance and the United Kingdom Corporate Governance Code.

1.2.4 Recent Developments Impacting Independent Directors

- **Enhanced Environmental, Social, and Governance (ESG) Responsibilities:** With SEBI's Business Responsibility and Sustainability Reporting (BRSR), IDs are expected to take a more active role in ESG oversight.
- **Increased Liability and Accountability:** Courts and regulators are holding IDs more accountable, emphasising active participation, diligence, and prudent decision-making.
- **Digital and Cybersecurity Oversight:** As technology-related risks rise, IDs are increasingly expected to understand, monitor, and oversee cybersecurity frameworks.

1.3 Core Duties and Fiduciary Responsibilities

At the heart of the role of IDs are a set of core duties and fiduciary responsibilities that ensure they act in the best interests of the company and its stakeholders. These duties serve as ethical and legal cornerstones, guiding their conduct, decision-making, and oversight. This chapter examines these responsibilities in detail, highlighting their significance and practical implications.

Every unchecked risk is a promise of regret.

1.3.1 Duty of Care and Diligence

IDs are expected to act with reasonable care, skill, and diligence in the performance of their duties. This entails:

- **Being well-prepared:** Reviewing board materials, financial reports, and committee documents in advance of meetings.
- **Active participation:** Contributing constructively in discussions, asking probing questions, and challenging management where necessary.
- **Continuous learning:** Staying updated on industry developments, regulatory changes, and governance best practices.
- **Monitoring:** Overseeing the company's operations, risk management, and compliance frameworks on an ongoing basis.

Failure to exercise due care can expose ID's personal liability and significant reputational damage.

1.3.2 Duty of Loyalty and Avoidance of Conflicts of Interest

Loyalty requires IDs to place the company's interests above their own personal or professional interests. This entails:

- **Avoiding conflicts:** Steering clear of situations where personal interests may conflict with the company's interests.
- **Disclosure:** Promptly declaring any potential conflicts to the board.
- **Recusal:** Abstaining from participation in decisions where a conflict exists.
- **Independence:** Maintaining impartiality from management and promoters.

This duty is fundamental to preserving the trust reposed in IDs by shareholders and other stakeholders.

Where volatility begins, governance must stand still.

1.3.3 Duty to Act in Good Faith and for the Company's Benefit

IDs must act honestly and in good faith, consistently prioritising the company's long-term success over short-term pressures or personal benefit. This duty forms the ethical backbone of directorship, ensuring that decisions contribute to sustainable value creation rather than opportunistic gains. Key elements include:

- **Upholding integrity:** Ensuring transparency, ethical conduct, and compliance with laws.
- **Protecting stakeholders:** Balancing the interests of shareholders, employees, creditors, and the community.
- **Avoiding misuse of position:** Refrain from exploiting the role for personal gain or to benefit related parties.

Good faith acts as a moral compass guiding decisions, even in complex or ambiguous situations.

1.3.4 Duty of Confidentiality

IDs have access to sensitive and proprietary information. Maintaining confidentiality is crucial to:

- **Protect competitive advantage:** Safeguarding trade secrets, strategic plans, and financial data.
- **Build trust:** Ensuring that management and fellow board members feel secure in sharing information.
- **Comply with laws:** Adhering to insider trading regulations and data privacy requirements.

Breaches of confidentiality can have serious legal and reputational consequences.

The best Independent Directors wear many hats;
but never lose their head.

1.3.5 Specific Fiduciary Duties in Committee Roles

When serving on committees, IDs take on additional responsibilities aligned with each committee's mandate:

- **Audit Committee:** Ensuring the accuracy of financial reports, the independence of auditors, and the robustness of internal controls.
- **Nomination and Remuneration Committee:** Overseeing fair and transparent policies for director and executive compensation.
- **Risk Management Committee:** Identifying, assessing, and mitigating enterprise-wide risks.
- **Corporate Social Responsibility (CSR) Committee:** Overseeing the effective and ethical deployment of corporate social responsibility initiatives.

In these roles, IDs are expected to bring specialised knowledge and heightened vigilance.

1.3.6 Personal Liability and Legal Implications

While IDs enjoy limited liability protections, they may still be held personally liable for:

- Negligence or wilful misconduct that causes loss to the company or its stakeholders.
- Non-compliance with statutory obligations.
- Failure to disclose conflicts of interest.

Therefore, it is essential for IDs to understand and diligently fulfil their fiduciary duties to safeguard both themselves and the company.

1.4 Understanding the Board and Its Committees

The corporate board is the apex governance body responsible for steering the company toward sustainable success. To manage its wide-ranging responsibilities effectively, the board delegates specific oversight functions to specialised committees. IDs play a crucial role at both the board committee levels, bringing expertise, independence, and objective scrutiny.

This chapter provides an overview of the structure, purpose, and significance of the board and its committees, setting the stage for understanding how IDs balance their multifaceted responsibilities.

1.4.1 The Board of Directors: The Apex Governing Body

- **Role and composition:** The board is entrusted with overall strategy, policy-setting, and oversight of management. It typically comprises Executive Directors, Non-Executive Directors, and IDs.
- **Collective responsibility:** The board collectively ensures that the company meets its legal obligations, manages risks, and creates long-term value for both shareholders and stakeholders.
- **Key functions:**
    - Setting the company's vision, mission, and strategy.
    - Approving budgets and major capital expenditures.
    - Monitoring financial performance and compliance.
    - Overseeing management appointments and succession planning.
    - Ensuring effective risk management.

1.4.2 Importance of Specialised Committees

Given the increasing complexity of businesses, boards establish committees to focus on areas that require technical expertise, detailed review, or regulatory compliance.

- **Delegation for Efficiency:** Committees enable deeper, more focused discussions on complex issues than is typically possible in full board meetings.

A good director sees the trees and still governs the forest.

- **Enhanced Oversight:** Committees bring specialised skills, allowing for the proactive identification and resolution of issues.
- **Compliance:** Certain committees, such as the Audit Committee, are mandated by law or regulation, highlighting their critical importance.

1.4.3 Key Committees: Purpose and Role

1.4.3.1 Audit Committee

- **Purpose:** The Audit Committee oversees financial reporting, internal controls, audit processes, and compliance with legal and regulatory standards.
- **Role of Independent Directors:**
    - Ensure the integrity and accuracy of financial statements.
    - Oversee the appointment, independence, and performance of external auditors.
    - Monitor the effectiveness of internal audit functions and risk management frameworks.
    - Review compliance with accounting standards and disclosure requirements.
    - Facilitate communication between auditors, management, and the board.
- **Why Independent Directors are Crucial:** Their independence allows for unbiased scrutiny of management's financial disclosures, helping to reduce the risk of fraud or misstatements.

1.4.3.2 Nomination and Remuneration Committee

- **Purpose:** The NRC manages board composition, the selection and appointment of directors, and the remuneration of directors and senior executives.

Balance comes not from doing it all but knowing what matters most.

- **Role of Independent Directors:**
  - Establish criteria for selecting qualified, diverse, and competent candidates.
  - Evaluate the performance and independence of directors.
  - Design fair, transparent, and performance-linked remuneration policies.
  - Ensure alignment of executive pay with company goals and shareholder interests.
- **Why Independent Directors are Crucial:** Their impartiality ensures executive compensation is reasonable, justified, and free from conflicts of interest.

1.4.3.3 Risk Management Committee

- **Purpose:** The Risk Management Committee identifies, assesses, and monitors risks across the company's operations and strategic initiatives.
- **Role of Independent Directors:**
  - Provide independent evaluation of risk management frameworks.
  - Challenge management's risk assumptions and mitigation plans.
  - Monitor emerging risks, including cybersecurity, regulatory changes, and market volatility.
  - Ensure that a strong risk culture is embedded throughout the organisation.
- **Why Independent Directors are Crucial:** Their objectivity ensures comprehensive risk oversight, protecting company value and stakeholders' interests.

1.4.3.4 Corporate Social Responsibility Committee

- **Purpose:** The CSR Committee oversees the company's CSR initiatives and ensures compliance with statutory CSR obligations.

To oversee well, one must first understand where oversight ends.

- **Role of Independent Directors:**
  - Guide ethical and impactful CSR strategies aligned with social and environmental priorities.
  - Ensure transparent allocation, monitoring, and reporting of CSR funds.
  - Evaluate the effectiveness, sustainability, and long-term impact of CSR programs.
  - Promote corporate citizenship and meaningful stakeholder engagement.
- **Why Independent Directors are Crucial:** Their independent voice ensures that CSR is not treated as a mere compliance exercise but as a strategic, value-creating commitment.

1.4.3.5 Stakeholders Relationship Committee

- **Purpose:** The Stakeholders Relationship Committee addresses shareholder grievances and ensures transparent communication with investors.
- **Role of Independent Directors:**
  - Monitor mechanisms for the timely resolution of investor complaints.
  - Promote fair and equitable treatment of all shareholders.
  - Enhance transparency in investor relations and disclosures.
- **Why Independent Directors are Crucial:** Their independent oversight helps uphold fairness, accountability, and trust in stakeholder communications.

1.4.3.6 ESG and Sustainability Committees

- **Purpose:** ESG and Sustainability Committees drive environmental, social, and governance initiatives in alignment with global sustainability standards.

Governance is not a checklist; it's a conscience.

- **Role of Independent Directors:**
    - Ensure ESG risks and opportunities are integrated into strategic planning.
    - Oversee sustainability reporting, disclosures, and compliance with relevant standards.
    - Promote responsible business practices that create long-term value for the company and its stakeholders.
- **Why Independent Directors are Crucial:** Their stewardship fosters corporate responsibility, strengthens ESG governance, and ensures alignment with investor expectations on sustainability.

1.4.4 Legal Mandates for Committees Involving Independent Directors

- **Companies Act, 2013 and SEBI Listing Regulations**: Prescribe mandatory committees for specified companies, ensuring governance and compliance standards are met.
- **Audit Committees**: Must have a majority of IDs, including at least one financial expert.
- **Nomination and Remuneration Committees**: Must be composed entirely of IDs.
- **CSR Committees**: Must include at least one Independent Director.

1.5 Balancing Committee Work with Board Responsibilities

IDs often juggle multiple roles, serving not only on the full board but also on one or more specialised committees. Successfully balancing these responsibilities requires strategic time management, clear prioritisation, and a strong understanding of their distinct yet interconnected functions. This chapter examines how IDs can effectively harmonise committee responsibilities with broader board duties, ensuring both detailed oversight and strategic contribution to maximise their overall impact.

1.5.1 Understanding Dual Roles: Board vs. Committee

- **Board responsibilities:** The full board is responsible for overarching governance, setting strategic direction, and making collective decisions. IDs must actively contribute to broad discussions on finance, risk, corporate strategy, and stakeholder engagement.
- **Committee responsibilities:** Committees provide detailed oversight in specialised domains such as audit, risk, remuneration, and corporate social responsibility. Within these settings, IDs engage in in-depth analysis, scrutinise management reports, and develop recommendations for consideration by the full board.
- **Interconnection:** Committee insights enrich board-level deliberations with granular perspectives, while board decisions shape the priorities and focus of committee agendas. This dynamic interplay ensures coherence between oversight and strategy.

1.5.2 Time Management and Preparation

- **Meeting attendance:** Consistent attendance at both board and committee meetings is essential. Absences not only diminish the Independent Director's effectiveness but also weaken accountability and the ability to influence outcomes.
- **Pre-meeting preparation:** IDs should thoroughly review agendas, financial reports, risk assessments, compliance updates, and supporting materials prior to meetings. Adequate preparation ensures meaningful engagement, sharper questioning, and informed decision-making.
- **Effective use of time:** Balancing in-depth committee deliberations with broader board responsibilities requires disciplined time management. Directors must allocate sufficient time for

committee deep-dives while safeguarding their capacity to contribute effectively at the board level.

1.5.3 Coordinating Across Committees

- **Avoid overcommitment:** Serving on multiple committees allows IDs to leverage their expertise, but overburdening can impair performance and effectiveness. Directors should carefully balance their commitments to maintain high-quality oversight.
- **Cross-committee insights:** Knowledge and observations from one committee can inform and enrich discussions in others. For instance, risk issues identified by the Risk Management Committee may have implications for audit processes or CSR initiatives.
- **Collaborative approach:** IDs should work closely with fellow IDs and management to ensure alignment, share insights, and avoid duplication of efforts across committees.

1.5.4 Communication and Reporting

- **Clear reporting:** Committees provide reports and recommendations to the full board. IDs should ensure these reports are comprehensive, accurate, and actionable, facilitating informed decision-making at the board level.
- **Raising issues:** Committees provide reports and recommendations to the full board. IDs should ensure these reports are comprehensive, accurate, and actionable, facilitating informed decision-making at the board level.
- **Stakeholder engagement:** Effectively balancing committee and board responsibilities also involves engaging with shareholders, regulators, and other stakeholders when necessary, maintaining transparency and trust.

A board without courage is an institution without purpose.

1.5.5 Leveraging Expertise and Continuous Learning

- **Specialisation:** Committee roles enable IDs to apply and deepen their subject-matter expertise, whether in finance, risk, sustainability, or governance oversight, thereby strengthening board effectiveness.
- **Ongoing development:** Continuous learning through training programs, workshops, peer exchanges, and regulatory updates enhances the quality and relevance of IDs' contributions across both committees and the board.
- **Adapting to change:** Effective IDs remain agile, adapting to evolving governance challenges, emerging risks, and stakeholder expectations at both the committee and board levels.

1.5.6 Ethical and Fiduciary Considerations

- **Maintaining independence:** IDs must ensure that their committee roles do not compromise their objectivity or create conflicts of interest, preserving impartial judgment in all deliberations.
- **Upholding confidentiality:** Information shared within committees is often sensitive and proprietary. Maintaining strict confidentiality is essential for fostering trust among management, fellow board members, and stakeholders.
- **Accountability:** IDs are accountable for their decisions and oversight responsibilities in both committees and the full board, underscoring the importance of diligence, integrity, and ethical conduct.

1.6 Developing Essential Skills for Independent Directors

The role of an ID is demanding, requiring a broad skill set that extends beyond business acumen to encompass governance expertise, strategic thinking, and strong interpersonal skills. Developing these essential capabilities enables IDs to contribute meaningfully to both the board and its committees, navigate complex challenges, and discharge their fiduciary duties effectively.

This chapter highlights the key skills that IDs must cultivate and outlines practical approaches for their development.

1.6.1 Governance and Regulatory Knowledge

- **Understanding legal frameworks:** IDs must be well-versed in the laws and regulations governing corporate governance, including the Companies Act, SEBI Listing Regulations, and other applicable rules, to ensure compliance and informed decision-making.
- **Boardroom best practices:** Familiarity with governance codes, frameworks, and ethical standards enables IDs to set and uphold high standards of board conduct and corporate integrity.
- **Continuous updates:** Staying current on evolving governance trends, regulatory requirements, and emerging risks is essential for maintaining effective oversight and mitigating compliance gaps.

1.6.2 Financial Literacy and Analytical Skills

- **Interpreting financial statements:** IDs should be able to confidently review and analyze balance sheets, income statements, cash flow statements, and audit reports to assess the company's financial health.
- **Risk assessment:** They must evaluate financial and operational risks, understand the effectiveness of risk mitigation strategies, and assess the robustness of internal controls.
- **Data-driven decision making:** Leveraging financial and operational data enables IDs to challenge management constructively and contribute to well-informed board deliberations.

The best directors don't echo; they examine.

1.6.3 Strategic Thinking and Business Acumen

- **Big-picture perspective:** IDs must understand the company's industry, competitive landscape, and long-term strategic objectives to provide informed guidance.
- **Scenario planning:** IDs must understand the company's industry, competitive landscape, and long-term strategic objectives to provide informed guidance
- **Value creation:** Their focus should be on sustainable growth, ensuring that management goals are aligned with both shareholder and broader stakeholder interests.

1.6.4 Communication and Interpersonal Skills

- **Effective listening:** IDs should actively listen to management, fellow directors, and stakeholders to fully understand diverse perspectives and concerns.
- **Constructive dialogue:** They must articulate their views clearly, diplomatically challenge ideas when necessary, and facilitate consensus among board members.
- **Networking:** Building strong internal and external relationships allows IDs to gain valuable insights, access expertise, and enhance the board's effectiveness.

1.6.5 Ethical Judgment and Integrity

- **Principled decision-making:** IDs should consistently act with honesty, transparency, and fairness in all board and committee deliberations.
- **Conflict resolution:** They must manage conflicts of interest and sensitive situations professionally, ensuring decisions are impartial and in the best interests of the company and its stakeholders.
- **Building trust:** Establishing credibility with management, fellow

One principled objection is more valuable than unanimous silence.

board members, shareholders, and regulators is essential for maintaining confidence in the board's oversight and governance.

1.6.6 Time Management and Prioritisation

- **Balancing commitments:** IDs must efficiently manage board and committee responsibilities alongside other professional and personal obligations to maintain effectiveness and focus.
- **Focus on impact:** Prioritising critical issues ensures that attention is directed toward matters that significantly affect governance, risk oversight, and overall company performance.
- **Preparation:** Investing sufficient time in pre-meeting review of agendas, reports, and supporting materials enables directors to contribute meaningfully and make informed decisions.

1.6.7 Continuous Learning and Development

- **Training programs:** IDs should participate in director development programs offered by professional bodies such as the Institute of Company Secretaries of India (ICSI), the Institute of Chartered Accountants of India (ICAI), or recognised global governance institutions to enhance their knowledge and skills.
- **Peer learning:** Engaging with experienced IDs and peers provides opportunities to exchange insights, share best practices, and learn from real-world experiences.
- **Feedback and self-assessment:** Regularly evaluating personal performance and seeking feedback helps directors identify areas for improvement and ensures ongoing professional growth.

1.7 Challenges Faced by Independent Directors and How to Overcome Them

IDs play a pivotal role in strengthening corporate governance, yet their responsibilities are often accompanied by significant challenges. These hurdles can range from maintaining genuine independence to navigating complex stakeholder dynamics, balancing committee workloads, and managing regulatory expectations. Understanding these challenges and implementing practical strategies to address them is critical for IDs to perform effectively, uphold their fiduciary duties, and safeguard the company's long-term interests.

1.7.1 Maintaining Independence Amid Pressure

- **Challenge:** IDs may face subtle or overt pressures from promoters, executive management, or dominant shareholders, which can compromise their impartiality and objectivity.
- **How to Overcome:**
    - Uphold a firm commitment to ethical standards and established governance principles.
    - Collaborate with fellow IDs to present a unified and principled stance.
    - Leverage governance frameworks and regulatory provisions that safeguard director independence.
    - Escalate significant concerns to regulators, the audit committee, or other appropriate oversight bodies when necessary.

1.7.2 Limited Access to Information

- **Challenge:** Timely and comprehensive access to relevant company information is critical for effective decision-making. However, IDs may sometimes receive incomplete, delayed, or insufficient data, hampering oversight.
- **How to Overcome:**
    - Proactively request detailed reports, supporting documents, and clarifications from management.
    - Establish clear protocols with management to ensure regular and structured updates.

To challenge a peer is to protect a principle.

- Exercise legal and regulatory rights to obtain necessary disclosures for informed board deliberations.

1.7.3 Balancing Multiple Commitments

- **Challenge:** IDs often serve on multiple boards or have other professional engagements, which can strain their availability, focus, and ability to provide effective oversight.
- **How to Overcome:**
    - Prioritise board and committee responsibilities, managing time rigorously to ensure meaningful participation.
    - Limit the number of directorships to maintain effectiveness and avoid overcommitment.
    - Delegate non-essential tasks where appropriate and concentrate on high-impact contributions that add the most value to the board.

1.7.4 Managing Conflicts of Interest

- **Challenge:** IDs may face actual or perceived conflicts of interest arising from personal relationships, investments, or prior professional roles, which can compromise impartiality.
- **How to Overcome:**
    - Disclose all potential conflicts transparently to the board.
    - Recuse oneself from discussions or decisions where a conflict exists.
    - Adhere strictly to the company's conflict of interest policies and governance guidelines.

1.7.5 Staying Updated in a Rapidly Changing Environment

- **Challenge:** IDs must navigate evolving regulations, emerging risks, and shifting market conditions, which require continuous learning and adaptation.

In governance, the quietest voices often carry the greatest weight.

- **How to Overcome:**
  - Engage in regular training and professional development.
  - Stay informed by subscribing to governance, regulatory and industry updates.
  - Network with governance experts and peers to exchange insights and best practices.

1.7.6 Ensuring Effective Board Dynamics

- **Challenge:** Boardroom dynamics, such as dominance by certain members or insufficient constructive debate, can undermine effective governance and decision-making.
- **How to Overcome:**
  - Foster a culture of open, respectful, and inclusive dialogue among all board members.
  - Employ facilitation techniques to encourage diverse viewpoints and ensure all perspectives are considered.
  - Collaborate with the chairperson to maintain balanced discussions and prevent undue influence by any single member.

1.7.7 Legal and Personal Liability Concerns

- **Challenge:** IDs face potential legal risks arising from board decisions or omissions, which can affect their reputation and, in certain cases, personal assets.
- **How to Overcome:**
  - Clearly understand legal duties and obligations, and secure appropriate indemnity and directors' liability insurance coverage.
  - Document decision-making processes thoroughly to demonstrate due diligence and reasoned judgment.
  - Act diligently, seek expert advice when necessary, and adhere to governance and regulatory standards.

If the committee is the engine, integrity is the fuel.

1.7.8 Navigating Stakeholder Expectations

- **Challenge:** IDs must balance the often-conflicting needs and expectations of shareholders, regulators, employees, customers, and society, which can make decision-making challenging.
- **How to Overcome:**
  - Adopt a stakeholder-centric approach, considering the interests of all relevant parties in board deliberations.
  - Promote transparency through regular, clear, and accurate communication with stakeholders.
  - Align governance practices and strategic decisions with long-term sustainability and ethical standards.

1.8 The Appointment Process and Onboarding of Independent Directors

1.8.1 Introduction

The appointment and onboarding of IDs are crucial for ensuring that the board has the right mix of skills, experience, and independence to govern effectively. A transparent and structured process not only strengthens corporate governance but also lays the foundation for an ID's seamless integration and meaningful contribution to the board.

1.8.2 Identifying the Need for an Independent Director

- **Board skills gap analysis:** The NRC and the board assess the current mix of director skills, independence requirements, and diversity needs to identify gaps and priorities for new appointments.
- **Regulatory requirements:** Ensure compliance with statutory mandates regarding the number, qualifications, and eligibility criteria for IDs.
- **Strategic considerations:** Align the prospective ID's expertise with the company's strategic objectives, sector-specific challenges, and governance priorities to maximise value addition.

A seat at the table means little without a spine in the chair.

1.8.3 Search and Selection Process

- **Candidate sourcing:** Identify potential candidates through professional networks, director databases, executive search firms, and trusted recommendations.
- **Evaluation criteria:** Assess candidates based on qualifications, relevant industry experience, integrity, independence, and any potential conflicts of interest.
- **Due diligence:** Conduct thorough verification of credentials, background checks, and compliance with regulatory requirements.
- **Interviews and board approval:** Engage shortlisted candidates in discussions with the NRC and the full board to evaluate fit, mutual expectations, and alignment with the company's strategic and governance priorities.

1.8.4 Formal Appointment

- **Shareholder approval:** Following the board's recommendation, shareholders approve the appointment at the Annual General Meeting (AGM) or through a postal ballot, in accordance with legal and regulatory requirements.
- **Letter of appointment:** A formal letter is issued to the director, outlining roles, responsibilities, tenure, remuneration, and adherence to the prescribed code of conduct.
- **Disclosure and filings:** Mandatory disclosures are made to stock exchanges and relevant regulatory authorities within the prescribed timelines to ensure transparency and compliance.

1.8.5 Onboarding and Induction

- **Orientation programs:** Introduce the new ID to the company's business model, organisational structure, culture, and key policies to provide a comprehensive understanding of operations.

Between power and principle, the independent must choose the latter.

- **Access to information:** Provide essential documents such as board manuals, past meeting minutes, financial reports, governance charters, and relevant regulatory filings to enable informed decision-making.
- **Meetings with key stakeholders:** Schedule interactions with the Chairperson, Chief Executive Officer (CEO), Chief Financial Officer (CFO), Company Secretary, and other board members to build relationships and understand strategic priorities.
- **Training on legal and regulatory framework:** Conduct sessions covering fiduciary duties, compliance obligations, and corporate governance norms to ensure the ID is fully aware of their responsibilities.
- **Mentorship:** Pair the new ID with a senior ID or the Chairperson to facilitate smooth integration and provide guidance on board dynamics and best practices.

1.8.6 Setting Expectations and Ongoing Support

- **Clarifying role and responsibilities:** Ensure the ID fully understands the scope and limits of their duties, committee assignments, and reporting lines to prevent role ambiguity.
- **Performance evaluation:** Establish clear metrics and processes for regular performance reviews, feedback, and constructive discussions to support continuous improvement.
- **Continuous development:** Encourage participation in director education programs, workshops, and industry forums to enhance skills and stay updated on governance trends.
- **Support infrastructure:** Provide necessary resources such as secretarial assistance, access to expert advisors, and technology solutions for virtual or hybrid meetings to facilitate effective board participation.

Oversight demands scrutiny; leadership demands foresight.

1.8.7 Challenges in Appointment and Onboarding

- **Aligning expectations:** Ensuring a proper match between the board's requirements and the candidate's expertise, availability, and professional interests to maximise effectiveness.
- **Ensuring independence:** Guarding against potential conflicts of interest or relationships that may compromise the director's objectivity and impartiality.
- **Cultural fit:** Integrating new directors smoothly into the board's working style, decision-making processes, and the company's organisational culture.

1.9 Future of Independent Directorship

1.9.1 Recap of the Independent Director's Role

IDs serve as essential pillars of corporate governance, entrusted with protecting shareholders' interests, ensuring transparency, and guiding companies toward sustainable, long-term growth. This section has explored the multifaceted responsibilities of IDs, including their committee obligations, key skills, challenges faced, and appointment and onboarding processes. Far beyond being a statutory requirement, the ID embodies a guardian of integrity, accountability, and enduring value creation, playing a crucial role in fostering trust and effective governance in today's corporate landscape.

1.9.2 Emerging Trends Shaping Independent Directorship

- **Increased focus on environmental, social, and governance:** IDs are increasingly expected to oversee corporate sustainability initiatives, ethical business practices, and social responsibility, ensuring long-term value creation.
- **Technology and digital governance:** Boards face rising cyber risks, data privacy challenges, and digital transformation

Innovation demands vision; governance demands vigilance.

initiatives, requiring IDs to be technologically aware and forward-looking.

- **Diversity and inclusion:** Greater emphasis on gender, cultural, and skill diversity is reshaping board composition, bringing varied perspectives to decision-making and governance.
- **Stakeholder capitalism:** IDs now balance a broader set of stakeholder interests beyond shareholders, including employees, communities, and regulators, promoting holistic and responsible governance.
- **Regulatory evolution:** Laws and governance codes continue to evolve both globally and locally, raising expectations for director accountability, transparency, and proactive oversight.

1.9.3 The Increasing Complexity of the Role

As businesses grow increasingly complex and globalised, IDs must continuously deepen their expertise, adapt to faster decision-making processes, and engage proactively in risk management and strategic planning. At the same time, an evolving regulatory landscape demands heightened diligence and preparedness to navigate legal, financial, and reputational risks effectively.

1.9.4 Opportunities for Aspiring Independent Directors

- **Growing demand:** As corporate governance gains prominence, there is an increasing need for qualified and ethical IDs across industries and sectors.
- **Meaningful impact:** IDs have the opportunity to shape sustainable business practices, enhance transparency, and foster trust in capital markets.
- **Continuous learning:** The role provides rich opportunities for personal and professional growth through exposure to diverse

Complexity demands adaptability; integrity demands consistency.

industries, strategic decision-making, and complex governance challenges.

1.9.5 Preparing for the Future

- **Invest in skill development:** Aspiring IDs should pursue director education, financial literacy, and sector-specific knowledge.
- **Build networks:** Engage with governance forums, mentoring programs, and peer groups to stay connected and informed.
- **Embrace technology:** Familiarise yourself with digital tools and emerging governance technologies.
- **Commit to ethics and independence:** Upholding integrity and objectivity remains the cornerstone of effective directorship.

1.10 Conclusion

The role of the ID is more crucial today than ever before. As guardians of governance, they balance diverse interests, navigate complexity, and provide steady oversight amid change. For beginners embarking on this journey, a blend of dedication, continuous learning, and ethical commitment will be key to making a lasting impact.

By embracing these principles, IDs will continue to be the trusted architects of good governance, contributing to resilient and responsible corporate India.

"An Independent Director wears many hats but must carry one unwavering compass - because true governance lies not in the number of roles they perform, but in the balance, integrity, and judgment they bring to each seat they occupy."

CHAPTER 2

The Owl in the Boardroom: Embodying Wisdom and Watchfulness in Corporate Governance

"The owl sees what others miss; the director acts where others wait."

2.1 Introduction: The Owl as a Governance Metaphor

In the hush of the boardroom, where strategies are charted and risks debated, one figure is expected to bring not only legal acumen but also quiet wisdom and moral clarity: the Independent Director (ID). Amid glossy presentations, complex financial disclosures, and layers of legal compliance, the ID must discern not only what is said, but also what remains unsaid. In an era of mounting stakeholder expectations, Environmental, Social, and Governance (ESG) imperatives, and reputational landmines, the ID must not only see, but see through.

The metaphor of the Owl captures this role with remarkable precision. Across cultures and civilisations, the Owl has symbolised wisdom, vigilance, independence, and the ability to navigate darkness. The Owl does

The wisest director sees what others ignore; and asks why.

not roar or command by force. Its strength lies in silent observation, nocturnal clarity, and the ability to notice what others overlook. Patient in its watch, decisive in action, the Owl embodies the very essence of the ID.

In many ways, IDs are the Owls of the corporate world. They are expected to be strategically informed, morally anchored, and courageously objective. Unlike executive directors or promoter stakeholders, they do not wield positional power. Their influence stems not from hierarchy, but from integrity, insight, and judgment. This makes their contribution both subtle and profound, often undervalued, yet critical in moments of corporate reckoning.

India's corporate history is punctuated by such moments. Scandals like Satyam, governance collapses such as IL&FS, and high-profile boardroom battles like Tata–Mistry have illuminated not only the failures of oversight but also the silence or powerlessness of independent voices within the boardroom. Yet, these episodes have also driven reform. Today, the ID is no longer a ceremonial appointee but a statutory guardian, with duties clearly defined by the Companies Act, SEBI regulations, and global governance norms.

But law alone cannot create true independence. Nor can mere box-ticking replace conscience, character, or courage. The question facing corporate India today is not merely how many IDs sit on a board, but how they think, act, dissent, and lead. This is where the Owl returns – not as a decorative metaphor, but as an archetype of ethical leadership in a time of ambiguity.

This section proposes a reimagining of the ID's role through the lens of the Owl. It blends symbolism with statute, myth with mandate, to explore what it truly means to be an ID in 21st-century India. Drawing from case studies, regulatory frameworks, behavioural science, and boardroom psychology, it outlines a model of independent oversight rooted not only in governance codes but also in wisdom, vigilance, and moral resilience.

For those who serve as Independent Directors – or aspire to – the Owl offers a compelling leadership archetype: one who sees in darkness, speaks

True wisdom is not in knowing all answers, but in asking better questions.

with purpose, and acts with courage when others hesitate. The boardroom does not need more ceremonial owls carved into wood; it needs real ones – wise, watchful, and willing to protect what matters most.

2.2 The Owl as a Symbol: Mythology, Metaphor, and Meaning

Across human civilisations, animals have served as symbolic mirrors for human traits-courage, cunning, strength, and wisdom. Among them, the Owl holds a uniquely paradoxical place. Neither revered for its power nor feared for its aggression, the owl instead earns its distinction through silence, keen perception, and insight. Its symbolic resonance, both ancient and modern, provides a compelling metaphor for the type of oversight, vigilance, and moral vision expected of IDs in today's boardrooms.

2.2.1. Ancient Civilisations and the Owl's Wisdom

In Greek mythology, the Owl is famously associated with **Athena**, the goddess of wisdom, strategy, and just warfare. The *Glaucus* Owl, a small, sharp-eyed nocturnal creature, perched on Athena's shoulder as a symbol of her divine judgment. This owl did not represent passive knowledge, but rather discernment in ambiguity, a critical skill in war, governance, and justice. The Athenians believed that the Owl's ability to see in the dark mirrored Athena's gift to perceive truths hidden from ordinary eyes.

This resonates powerfully with the role of IDs: operating in the shadows of management presentations and filtered reports, they are called upon to *see the full picture,* to read between lines, understand hidden risks, and protect against ethical missteps.

In Roman traditions, too, the Owl was a harbinger not of doom, as sometimes misread, but of omens and foresight. When an Owl was seen in the forum, it meant something was about to change. This echoes the ID's task to signal discomfort, alert the board to upcoming disruption, or issue a quiet warning before a governance breakdown.

An owl watches in silence but never sleeps.

In Indian symbology, the Owl is associated with Lakshmi, the goddess of wealth and prosperity. Here, the Owl signifies not only material abundance but also disciplined stewardship a reminder that prosperity must be guarded through foresight and ethical wisdom. In some regional traditions, the Owl represents the protector of wealth, an alert guardian ensuring wealth creation is not corrupted by greed or short-termism. For IDs in Indian companies, this symbolism is profound: they are, after all, custodians of shareholder wealth and defenders against value erosion, whether due to fraud, opacity, or recklessness.

2.2.2. The Owl as a Metaphor for Corporate Oversight

Beyond ancient lore, the Owl has permeated modern imagination as a metaphor for clarity in complexity. Owls are not merely nocturnal – they are *exceptionally adapted* to function in darkness. Their large, forward-facing eyes provide binocular vision, and their silent wings allow them to glide undetected. Their heads swivel nearly 270 degrees, granting them a panoramic view of their environment. These biological traits, when interpreted metaphorically, mirror the core capabilities required of an ID:

- **Silent observation**: IDs often withhold judgment while others speak, listening carefully before intervening. Like the Owl, they act not with noise, but with careful timing and precision.
- **Panoramic perception**: Effective oversight requires not only vertical expertise – such as finance or law – but also horizontal awareness, understanding culture, ethics, stakeholder pressures, and market trends.
- **Decisive action**: The Owl rarely strikes, but when it does, it is swift, precise, and final. Similarly, IDs must know when to escalate concerns, register dissent, or, in extreme cases, resign in protest.

Moreover, the Owl's nocturnal vision serves as a compelling allegory for perceiving what others cannot: the undercurrents of organisational dysfunction, early warning signs of financial misreporting, or erosion of psychological safety in the boardroom.

Boardroom wisdom begins when ego exits.

2.2.3. Owls and the Psychological Archetype of Wisdom

Viewed through a Jungian lens, the Owl symbolises the "Wise Elder" archetype – an inner guide that balances knowledge with humility. In corporate governance, this archetype is essential. Boardrooms, particularly in promoter-driven companies or high-stakes environments, can become echo chambers dominated by groupthink or charismatic leadership. The ID, like the wise elder, provides a counterpoint of reflection – a pause in a room obsessed with speed.

Wisdom, after all, is not merely about knowing more; it is about understanding what not to ignore. It encompasses the courage to ask naïve questions, challenge the consensus, and voice uncomfortable truths.

In essence, the Owl is far more than a decorative symbol in corporate brochures or awards – It is a profound metaphor for the qualities that render IDs indispensable.

"The courage to see in darkness, the humility to speak rarely but wisely, and the clarity to act without fear."

2.3 The Independent Director: Origins and Evolution

The concept of the ID has evolved over decades in response to corporate scandals, governance failures, and the growing complexity of modern business. While independent oversight may seem a natural feature of today's boards, its emergence was neither automatic nor universally embraced. The role was shaped through crisis, reform, and the recognition that unchecked managerial power poses systemic risks to companies, markets, and society. This section traces the origins of the ID both globally and in India, and examines how the position has matured from a largely symbolic presence to a statutory cornerstone of contemporary corporate governance.

2.3.1. Global Origins: From Advisory Boards to Fiduciary Guardians

In the early 20th century, corporate boards in the United States (US) and the United Kingdom (UK) were largely composed of insiders

– founders, executives, major shareholders, or their allies. Directors were expected to advise and support management rather than challenge it. The concept that board members should act independently of company promoters or executives was virtually non-existent.

By the 1970s, corporate failures and rising shareholder activism began to challenge this paradigm. High-profile bankruptcies such as Penn Central (1970) and the Watergate scandal in the US sparked calls for greater accountability and transparency in corporate governance. This prompted a shift toward more balanced boards and the gradual inclusion of non-executive directors – the precursors to today's independent directors.

The Cadbury Report (UK, 1992) marked a significant milestone in formalising the role of the ID. It recommended that boards include a sufficient number of non-executive directors who are "independent of management and free from any business or other relationships which could materially interfere with the exercise of their independent judgment." This standard became a global governance benchmark, later reinforced by the OECD Principles of Corporate Governance (1999, 2004, and 2015) and incorporated into corporate laws and listing requirements worldwide.

In the US, the Sarbanes-Oxley Act of 2002, enacted in the aftermath of the Enron and WorldCom scandals, further strengthened the role of IDs, particularly in audit committees, by imposing stringent requirements on financial literacy, conflict-of-interest avoidance, and whistleblower protections.

Key Principles Globally Established

- **Structural independence** from management and significant shareholders.
- **Functional independence** in thought and action.
- **Board-level oversight** of audit, risk, remuneration, and governance.
- **Protection of minority shareholders** and long-term value creation.

The vigilant eye sees trouble long before the alarm.

2.3.2. The Indian Journey: From Clause 49 to the Companies Act, 2013

India's journey toward embedding IDs in corporate governance has been shaped by global influences, domestic crises, and regulatory activism. Prior to the 2000s, Indian boards were often dominated by promoters, families, or state appointees. Independent oversight was limited, and board deliberations frequently lacked challenge or diversity of thought.

The introduction of Clause 49 of the SEBI Listing Agreement in 2000 marked a turning point. Drawing from the Cadbury and Sarbanes-Oxley frameworks, Clause 49 mandated that:

- At least 50% of the board is composed of non-executive directors.
- In the case of an executive chairperson, at least 50% of the board must be independent.
- Audit Committees must have a majority of IDs.

These measures established the first structural framework for board independence in India. However, implementation was often weak, and companies frequently appointed "friendly" or "nominal" IDs, resulting in tokenism.

The Companies Act, 2013, brought the next major shift by codifying the role of ID under Section 149. The Act:

- Defined independence and eligibility criteria.
- Introduced a formal Code of Conduct (Schedule IV).
- Prescribed minimum tenure, rotation limits, and mechanisms for performance evaluation.

This legislation transformed Independent Directorship from a nominal role to a statutory cornerstone of Indian corporate governance.

It's not enough to attend meetings; one must observe the silences.

Key features included:

- At least one-third of the board in listed companies must be IDs.
- IDs must not have pecuniary relationships with the company or its key personnel.
- IDs must play key roles in Audit, Nomination, and Risk Committees.
- Mandatory training and performance evaluations.

The Act also emphasised the duty of professional scepticism, expecting IDs to question, challenge, and uphold the interests of shareholders, especially non-controlling ones.

2.3.3. From Decorative Appointments to Governance Anchors

Despite structural reforms, the practical evolution of IDs in India has been uneven. For many years, appointments were often based on social proximity rather than strategic fit. Boards were populated with retired bureaucrats, family friends, or industry allies who lacked either the incentive or the courage to challenge management.

This began to change following a series of governance crises:

- **Satyam (2009):** The collapse of a major IT company due to accounting fraud exposed failures in independent oversight. Several IDs resigned in the aftermath, and public trust in corporate boards was severely shaken.
- **IL&FS (2018):** Massive defaults by a systemically important NBFC highlighted serious lapses in risk oversight by the board and its committees.
- **Tata–Mistry Conflict (2016):** The abrupt removal of a CEO and the ensuing fallout revealed tensions between promoter dominance and board autonomy, placing ID at the centre of public attention.

A director who stays alert sees risk before it becomes reality.

In each case, scrutiny fell on IDs not merely for being absent or uninformed, but for remaining silent in the face of obvious risk.

2.4 Wisdom: Strategic Judgment in Uncertain Environments

In times of turbulence, boards are not judged by their prior credentials, but by the quality of their decisions under pressure. The ability to make wise, timely, and well-informed decisions in complex and uncertain environments is the defining trait of effective IDs. More than technical knowledge or regulatory familiarity, it is this strategic wisdom grounded in experience, humility, and critical reasoning that elevates boardroom oversight from mechanical compliance to principled leadership.

2.4.1. The Nature of Boardroom Uncertainty

Uncertainty in the boardroom does not stem merely from a lack of data, but from the incompleteness of meaning. Markets shift rapidly. Regulatory frameworks evolve. Stakeholder expectations fluctuate. Strategic decisions like entering a new market, acquiring a distressed asset, or handling a cybersecurity breach rarely come with black-and-white answers. They require judgment under ambiguity, often with incomplete information, short timeframes, and high reputational or financial stakes.

IDs are not expected to predict the future. But they are expected to evaluate the credibility of projections, the resilience of strategy, and the ethical contours of decision-making. Wisdom, in this context, is about asking the right questions when the path is unclear.

2.4.2. Components of Strategic Wisdom

Unlike technical intelligence, which emphasises depth within a domain (e.g., accounting, law, operations), strategic wisdom is integrative and cross-functional. It draws upon a combination of cognitive, emotional, and moral faculties. Key components include:

- **Discernment:** The ability to separate signal from noise and distinguish what truly matters from distractions. In boardrooms flooded with data, discernment helps IDs focus on core risks and long-term implications.

- **Perspective-taking:** Wisdom involves viewing issues through multiple lenses -shareholders, employees, customers, regulators, and society. These systems thinking enhances the board's capacity to make balanced, informed decisions.
- **Humility and Self-awareness:** Wise directors do not dominate discussions. They are curious, reflective, and willing to acknowledge the limits of their knowledge. They foster dialogue, debate, and constructive dissent.
- **Temporal Orientation:** While management often emphasises short-term outcomes, wise IDs extend the board's focus to long-term horizons, highlighting sustainability, succession planning, and organisational culture.
- **Moral Anchoring:** Strategic decisions often involve ethical gray zones. Wisdom enables a director to go beyond legal minimums and ask: *Is this right? Is this responsible? Is this consistent with our values and commitments?*

2.4.3. Wisdom in Action: Illustrative Scenarios

Let's explore how wisdom manifests in the practical work of IDs through some real-world-inspired scenarios:

2.4.3.1. Evaluating a High-Growth Strategy in a Risky Market

A company proposes an aggressive expansion into an emerging market with uncertain political stability and limited legal recourse. Management projects exponential growth, and investor enthusiasm is high.

A wise ID might:

- Probe the assumptions behind financial models.
- Question currency, legal, and compliance risks.

A sleeping board breeds a waking scandal.

- Recommend scenario planning and downside protection mechanisms.
- Encourage a staged entry or strategic partnership rather than a full acquisition.

Here, wisdom lies in tempering ambition with prudence and ensuring a risk-adjusted strategy is pursued rather than blind optimism.

2.4.3.2. Navigating an ESG Crisis

A viral video emerges showing environmental damage caused by a company's supply chain partner. Public outrage intensifies, and the board must act swiftly.

A wise ID might:

- Insist on verifying facts before public statements.
- Prioritise transparency and accountability over Public Relations spin.
- Question how governance processes allowed the lapse to occur.
- Advocate for structural change, not cosmetic fixes (e.g., supplier audits, sustainability KPIs).

Wisdom here involves balancing speed with integrity and ensuring short-term communications do not obscure long-term accountability.

2.4.3.3. Responding to a Whistleblower Allegation Against the CEO

An anonymous whistleblower raises allegations of harassment and financial impropriety against the CEO. The chair hesitates, citing the CEO's importance to the firm's valuation.

A wise ID:

- Asserts the non-negotiable importance of process integrity.
- Pushes for an independent investigation, ensuring neutrality.

Discernment is knowing the difference between what is legal and what is right.

- Guards against retaliation and preserves whistleblower anonymity.
- Recognises that credibility and culture are long-term assets, not to be sacrificed for short-term optics.

Wisdom here lies in ethical clarity under institutional pressure.

2.4.4. Boardroom Structures That Enable Wisdom

Individual wisdom is not enough. Boards must create conditions that allow wisdom to surface and be heard. This includes:

- **Psychological safety:** Ensuring that dissenting voices, especially from IDs, are not penalised or sidelined.
- **Diverse composition:** Wisdom thrives in cognitively diverse environments where different life experiences and professional lenses come together.
- **Adequate preparation time:** Wisdom requires context. IDs need access to timely, relevant information, not voluminous data dumps.
- **Chairmanship that values reflection:** Board chairs play a crucial role in shaping the tempo of meetings. Wise decision-making needs space for thought, not just motion.

2.5 Watchfulness: Vigilance, Red Flags, and the Art of Oversight

If wisdom enables IDs to make sound decisions amid complexity, watchfulness allows them to detect danger before it escalates into disaster. In the boardroom, watchfulness is not passive observation; it is active, disciplined attentiveness to signs of misalignment, misconduct, or strategic drift. Like an Owl silently scanning its environment before striking, the ID must cultivate a trained instinct to sense what doesn't feel right and act before the damage becomes irreparable.

In today's corporate landscape marked by volatility, opaque reporting, and heightened stakeholder scrutiny, vigilance is not optional. It is a core duty.

Not every decision is difficult; but every decision deserves depth.

2.5.1. The Anatomy of Boardroom Watchfulness

Corporate governance failures rarely occur overnight. They often begin as subtle breaches, missed disclosures, rushed decisions, unexplained resignations, or overconfident projections. Yet too often, directors overlook these "small signals," either due to unfamiliarity, excessive trust, or hesitation to probe. This is where the watchfulness of the ID becomes critical.

Watchfulness encompasses both strategic and ethical dimensions:

- **Strategic vigilance** ensures the company's direction remains aligned with its long-term interests and risk appetite.
- **Ethical vigilance** ensures the company's conduct aligns with laws, values, and stakeholder trust.

Effective watchfulness requires a threefold perspective: looking back (compliance), looking around (monitoring), and looking ahead (anticipation).

2.5.2. Domains Where Vigilance is Crucial

IDs must sharpen their oversight across several high-risk areas:

2.5.2.1. Financial Reporting and Disclosure

This remains the classic and most critical domain of watchfulness. Effective IDs should:

- Review not only the financial statements but also the narratives behind the numbers.
- Scrutinise accounting judgments, revenue recognition policies, and off-balance-sheet liabilities.
- Ensure the Audit Committee receives candid, unfiltered insights from both internal and external auditors.
- Test for consistency between boardroom optimism and financial reality.

A wise board never confuses growth with greed.

Warning signs may **include** frequent auditor changes, last-minute financial disclosures, or unexplained delays in publishing results, all of which warrant closer examination.

2.5.2.2. Related Party Transactions

While legal, Related Part Transactions (RPTs) remain one of the most common avenues for governance abuse. Vigilant IDs should:

- Probe whether the transaction genuinely serves the company's interest or primarily benefits insiders.
- Demand valuation fairness, competitive benchmarking, and transparent disclosure.
- Monitor for patterns, not just isolated events, for example, repeated high-margin contracts with the same promoter-linked entity.

2.5.2.3. Culture and Human Capital

Watchfulness extends beyond numbers to the human fabric of the organisation. IDs should remain alert to:

- High attrition among senior management.
- Patterns in whistleblower complaints or internal grievances.
- Signals of toxic leadership, ethical erosion, or gender- and diversity-blind spots.

Culture is often "felt but not seen." Wise IDs listen between the lines, draw insights from independent HR audits, and seek direct (even informal) interaction with employees beyond the C-suite.

2.5.2.4. Risk Management and Strategy Drift

Strategic watchfulness requires IDs to actively monitor the alignment between risk and strategy:

- Scrutinise the assumptions underpinning strategic initiatives.

Sound judgement requires quiet reflection, not loud consensus.

- Evaluate whether the company's risk appetite is being exceeded without sufficient mitigation or contingency measures.
- Review preparedness for cybersecurity threats, climate risks, regulatory changes, and exposure to emerging markets.

Red flags may include abrupt pivots in the business model, excessive leverage, or a promoter-driven obsession with diversification that compromises disciplined strategy execution.

2.5.3. Red Flags: What the Vigilant Director Watches For?

IDs should cultivate pattern recognition, a key trait of seasoned watchdogs. While no single red flag is definitive, recurring patterns can indicate deeper governance or strategic concerns and warrant structured inquiry:

Red Flags	**What It May Indicate**
Frequent changes in CFO or Compliance Officer positions	Governance discomfort; pressure on ethics or compliance
The CEO is dominating all board discussions	Weak board culture; lack of counterbalance or independent challenge
Important matters tabled without sufficient notice	Management opacity; attempts to avoid scrutiny
Unusually optimistic forecasts without a basis	Strategic myopia; potential window-dressing of results
Closed-loop related party transactions	Promoter self-dealing; governance failure
Whistleblower complaints are not reaching the board	Poor escalation mechanisms; lack of accountability
Lack of post-mortems after failed projects	Learning failure; board passivity

The owl does not rush to speak; but always speaks last and well.

No single red flag is definitive. However, recurring patterns of concern should trigger a thorough, structured inquiry by the ID.

2.5.4. Tools That Enable Vigilance

Watchfulness strengthens when IDs are supported by structured mechanisms. Effective boards should insist on:

- **Board dossiers:** Comprehensive briefing packs that go beyond operational KPIs to include risk updates, litigation summaries, ESG metrics, and whistleblower data.
- **Deep dives:** Regular in-camera sessions with auditors, risk officers, and compliance heads without management present to surface unfiltered insights.
- **Committee functioning:** Empowered Audit, Risk, and NRC Committees that enable IDs to probe deeply rather than merely review.
- **External expertise:** Periodic engagement with legal, strategy, or ESG experts to test assumptions and bring independent perspectives.

2.5.5. The Psychology of Watchfulness

True vigilance is not fuelled by suspicion, but by alertness without paranoia. It requires:

- **Cognitive independence:** Maintaining distance from the pull of executive optimism.
- **Fearless inquiry:** Asking "naïve" questions without hesitation or fear of embarrassment.
- **Composure under pressure:** Staying calm when management pushes back, especially in high-stakes discussions.

As with the owl, stillness should never be mistaken for passivity. The vigilant ID observes with patience, but acts with precision when intervention is necessary.

A wise director knows when to listen, and when to lead.

In governance, wisdom without watchfulness is blind; watchfulness without wisdom is reactive. The truly effective ID blends both. They are not watchdogs barking at every movement, but guardians who detect patterns, sense risk, and choose their interventions deliberately.

Like the owl perched above the forest, they may not sound the alarm at every rustle, but when silence must be broken, they are ready. In the next section, we explore how these twin traits, wisdom and watchfulness, translate into meaningful independent oversight within key board committees.

2.6 Independent Directors in Key Board Committees: The Nerve Centres of Oversight

While the full board bears ultimate responsibility for corporate governance, it is within board committees that the detailed mechanics of scrutiny, accountability, and strategic guidance come to life. IDs, particularly under India's regulatory framework, are not merely participants in these committees; they often form the cornerstone of their integrity and effectiveness.

2.6.1. The Legal and Regulatory Mandate

Under Indian corporate law, the Companies Act, 2013, and SEBI (Listing Obligations and Disclosure Requirements) Regulations prescribe that IDs serve as members or often chairs of the board's most critical committees:

- Audit Committee
- Nomination and Remuneration Committee (NRC)
- Stakeholders' Relationship Committee

In listed companies, the Audit and NRC are required to have a majority of IDs, with the chair usually being an ID. Beyond statutory compliance, the rationale is profound: these committees oversee the most sensitive areas of governance, financial reporting and audit integrity, executive remuneration and succession planning, and shareholder grievance resolution, where conflicts of interest are most likely to arise. IDs bring impartiality, diligence, and judgment, ensuring these functions are carried out with transparency and accountability.

2.6.2. The Audit Committee: The Owl's Keenest Vision

The Audit Committee serves as the sentinel of financial integrity within the boardroom. It oversees financial statements, audit reports, internal controls, fraud risks, and whistleblower mechanisms.

IDs serving on this committee must:

- **Engage deeply with auditors:** Treat audit reports as more than technical checkboxes, probing assumptions, judgments, and conclusions.
- **Identify inconsistencies:** Compare management narratives with financial realities to detect potential misstatements or omissions.
- **Safeguard auditor independence:** Ensure internal and external auditors operate without undue influence.
- **Recommend corrective actions:** Intervene promptly when internal controls fail or fraud risks emerge.

Here, the combination of wisdom and watchfulness is critical. Understanding complex accounting structures is not enough; the ID must question unexplained fluctuations, unusual transactions, or opaque disclosures. History has shown that inattentive or compromised Audit Committees can facilitate window-dressing, off-book transactions, or even corporate fraud, underscoring the vital role of vigilant ID.

2.6.3. The Nomination and Remuneration Committee: Governance of Leadership and Pay

The NRC is the guardian of board composition, CEO succession, and executive compensation, arguably the most politically sensitive domain of governance.

The owl speaks when it must; not when it is convenient.

Independent Directors serving on the NRC must:

- **Link pay to long-term value**: Ensure executive remuneration rewards sustainable performance, not short-term optics or transient market reactions.
- **Scrutinise non-financial metrics**: Integrate ESG and other qualitative indicators into incentive plans to promote holistic performance.
- **Assess board competencies and succession**: Evaluate skills, experience, and diversity to guide effective succession planning.
- **Uphold fairness and meritocracy**: Resist groupthink, promoter dominance, or favouritism in board appointments and talent management.

Here, watchfulness involves resisting opaque variable pay structures or compensation inflation. Wisdom requires balancing talent retention with alignment to shareholder and stakeholder interests. The NRC should act not as a rubber stamp, but as a strategic talent and governance committee, shaping leadership in the service of long-term corporate resilience.

2.6.4. Stakeholders' Relationship Committee: Voice of the Minority

The Stakeholders' Relationship Committee (SRC) serves as the guardian of shareholder rights, particularly those of minority investors. In India, where promoter shareholding often dominates, this committee ensures that non-controlling shareholders are treated fairly and transparently.

ID is in the SRC must:

- **Monitor grievance redressal**: Ensure timely, effective resolution of shareholder complaints and high-quality engagement.

Your voice may be a minority; but it may carry the majority's conscience.

- **Oversee fair treatment in corporate actions**: Scrutinise processes for buybacks, mergers, delisting, or other structural changes affecting shareholder value.
- **Detect patterns of concern**: Identify recurring issues or dissatisfaction that may indicate deeper governance risks.

In this domain, vigilance safeguards voice. Even seemingly routine complaints can signal systemic issues such as misreporting, insider dealings, or opacity in governance. The SRC empowers IDs to act as the ethical conscience and voice of minority stakeholders within the boardroom.

2.6.5. Other Committees: Expanding the Arena

As corporate complexity increases, companies are forming additional specialised committees where IDs play critical oversight roles:

- **Risk Management Committee**: Identifies and monitors emerging risks, including cybersecurity threats, climate-related exposures, and geopolitical shocks.
- **CSR Committee**: Ensures that corporate social responsibility initiatives are genuine, impactful, and aligned with company values rather than being purely cosmetic.
- **ESG Committees**: Integrates environmental, social, and governance considerations into the company's core strategy, moving beyond compliance to value creation.

These committees require IDs to combine domain expertise, governance judgment, and long-term strategic thinking, reinforcing their role as guardians of both risk and ethical oversight across the organisation.

2.6.6. Pitfalls: When Committees Fail

Committee effectiveness is compromised when:

- **Perfunctory meetings**: Sessions are superficial, dominated by management-prepared slides, with little critical discussion.

A strategic mind without ethical clarity is a boardroom liability.

- **Passive oversight:** IDs hesitates to challenge executives or ask probing questions.
- **Limited access to information or expertise:** Committees lack independent data, analysis, or expert input.
- **Restricted debate:** Chairpersons discourage robust discussion or curtail time for alternative viewpoints.

Such dysfunction transforms committees from active oversight bodies into ceremonial formalities, even if they appear compliant on paper, undermining the board's governance purpose.

2.6.7. The Chair's Role in Empowering Independent Directors

A strong committee chair, often an experienced ID, sets the tone for rigor, neutrality, and engagement. Effective chairs:

- Ensure every member is heard.
- Bring in external perspectives when needed.
- Insist on structured minutes, clear action plans, and follow-through.

Where leadership is weak or overly aligned with management, committees risk becoming ornamental rather than operational.

Within the committee room, IDs do more than fulfil a duty; they shape the company's future. Here, they exercise not just authority, but judgment, balance, and courage. The Owl metaphor is apt: not an idle observer, but a working sentinel, especially in these critical governance nerve centres. Committees are where the silent, systemic strength of independence manifests most sharply, influencing performance, risk oversight, and corporate reputation.

The long-term is the only term the owl cares about.

2.7 Challenges and Pressures Facing Independent Directors

Independent Directors (IDs) occupy a unique and demanding position at the heart of corporate governance. Entrusted with safeguarding integrity, protecting stakeholder interests, and ensuring accountability, they operate in boardrooms that are rarely neutral. Independence on paper often collides with complex realities - social expectations, economic dependencies, political influences, and organizational hierarchies -requiring IDs to exercise both courage and discernment.

The pressures they face are subtle yet pervasive, from psychological biases and relational dynamics to structural limitations within governance frameworks. This chapter delves into the multifaceted challenges confronting IDs, the risks of compromise, and the strategies that distinguish resilient directors who navigate these pressures while upholding their ethical mandate and strengthening the foundations of good governance.

2.7.1. The Spectrum of Pressure: From Subtle to Structural

IDs face pressures not only from promoters or management, but also from peers, institutional investors, and regulators. These pressures range from nuanced social cues to systemic structural constraints:

Type of Pressure	Manifestation
Social	Fear of isolation, peer conformity, or reluctance to disrupt collegial harmony.
Economic	Dependence on board fees, anxiety over reappointment, or exclusion from future opportunities.
Political	Pushback from influential promoters; entanglement with political or business affiliations.
Informational	Restricted access to data; selective or delayed disclosures from management.
Reputational	Risk of personal credibility damage if governance failures occur under their watch.

In every policy lies a principle waiting to be upheld.

In India, where promoter control remains entrenched, these pressures are often magnified. IDs may appear formally autonomous but are informally constrained by networks of loyalty, indebtedness, or subtle coercion. The result: a delicate balance between maintaining independence and navigating influence in the boardroom.

2.7.2. Capture and Compromise: The Erosion of Effective Independence

Boardroom "capture" is often subtle rather than overt. It occurs when:

- IDs become overly familiar with management, eroding critical distance.
- Dissenting views are discouraged or subtly penalised.
- The chairperson or Lead ID fails to protect space for independent perspectives.
- IDs are appointed for appearance rather than substance – retired bureaucrats, compliant professionals, or "celebrity" names who avoid scrutiny.

When such conditions persist, independence becomes largely symbolic. Boards may meet regulatory checklists, yet true oversight and accountability remain hollow, undermining governance and stakeholder trust.

2.7.3. Psychological Barriers to Independence

Even when external conditions are supportive, internal barriers can compromise an ID's effectiveness. Common psychological challenges include:

- **Deference to authority:** Deferring to the CEO's "vision" or the promoter's stature rather than critically evaluating decisions.
- **Fear of embarrassment:** Hesitating to ask "naïve" questions or challenge assumptions for fear of appearing uninformed.
- **Overconfidence:** Relying solely on personal instincts without engaging in rigorous analysis or inquiry.

Wisdom that forgets ethics becomes arrogance.

- **Desire for collegiality:** Prioritising harmony over truth-seeking, open debate, or constructive dissent.

In such instances, the issue is not ethical failing but cognitive passivity, a reluctance or inability to exercise the independence that the role inherently demands.

2.7.4. Structural Weaknesses That Undermine Independence

Certain governance structures can limit the functional effectiveness of IDs:

- **Insufficient onboarding:** New IDs may receive minimal context, company background, or clarity on expectations.
- **Time constraints:** Directors serving on multiple boards may struggle to dedicate sufficient attention to each company.
- **Opaque information flows:** Management often controls what information is shared, when, and in what form, restricting independent assessment.
- **Lack of succession planning:** Long-serving IDs may become entrenched, reducing objectivity and fresh perspectives.
- **Weak performance evaluation:** Boards often fail to conduct meaningful peer reviews or self-assessments, limiting feedback and growth.

Without robust infrastructure and processes, even well-intentioned IDs can be under-informed, under-prepared, and overpowered, reducing the board's overall effectiveness.

2.7.5. How Effective Independent Directors Navigate the Minefield

Resilient IDs develop strategies to maintain independence while constructively engaging with stakeholders:

- **Assertive diplomacy:** Speak up with data, tact, and persistence. Challenge ideas without being confrontational and never compromise on core principles.

The owl does not seek the spotlight; but guards it from burning the forest.

- **Boardroom alliances:** Form informal coalitions with fellow IDs or committee chairs to collectively raise concerns and strengthen oversight.
- **Clarifying boundaries:** Respect management's operational domain while insisting on transparency and accountability in governance matters.
- **Continuing education:** Stay abreast of evolving regulations, governance trends, and sector-specific developments to make informed decisions.
- **Personal exit policy:** Be prepared to resign when governance violations cross ethical red lines, safeguarding personal integrity and signalling seriousness to the board.

By combining principled assertiveness, collaboration, and vigilance, effective IDs navigate complex board dynamics without compromising their mandate.

2.7.6. Whistleblower Allegations and the Independent Director's Dilemma

Whistleblower complaints, especially those implicating senior management or promoters, often present the most challenging scenarios for IDs.

Challenges include:

- **Pressure to suppress or manage internally:** A tendency to avoid formal processes in order to protect reputation or relationships.
- **Loyalty conflicts:** Balancing the company's public image with the ethical imperative to investigate the truth.
- **Legal and personal risks:** Potential liability arising from inaction or perceived complicity.

Strong IDs respond with procedural rigor:

- **Insist on independent investigations:** Engage external experts to ensure impartiality.

Leadership is quiet influence, not loud authority.

- **Protect the whistleblower:** Safeguard anonymity and prevent retaliation.
- **Document dissent:** Record objections or recommendations formally if the board fails to act.

This is the crucible where the ethics of independence are most visible.

2.8. From Oversight to Impact: Building Long-Term Stakeholder Trust

IDs are often perceived narrowly as compliance watchdogs, guardians of legality and procedural integrity. Yet in today's environment of stakeholder capitalism, ESG imperatives, and reputation-driven markets, oversight alone is no longer enough. True impact emerges where oversight ends: in cultivating long-term, trust-based relationships with all stakeholders.

The wise Owl does not merely watch; it discerns patterns, anticipates consequences, and safeguards the forest, not just a single tree. Likewise, impactful IDs elevate their role from monitor to mentor, catalyst, and conscience, shaping organisational resilience, ethical behaviour, and sustainable value creation.

2.8.1. The Trust Deficit in Corporate India

Trust is both fragile and foundational. In India, several high-profile governance failures – IL&FS, Yes Bank, DHFL, Satyam have eroded public faith in boards. These events revealed:

- Weak challenge to executive decisions.
- Passive complicity or silence from IDs.
- Inadequate risk awareness and lack of crisis foresight.

Restoring trust requires visible, verifiable action - not just statements of independence, but tangible demonstrations of integrity. IDs are uniquely

In the architecture of governance, wisdom is the cornerstone.

positioned to lead this cultural shift and rebuild confidence in corporate governance.

2.8.2. Redefining Independence: Beyond the Letter of Law

Impactful IDs do not define independence merely as the absence of affiliation. They embody:

- **Moral Independence**: The ability to think and act according to principle, rather than personal preference.
- **Intellectual Independence**: The courage to ask naïve questions, challenge assumptions, and engage critically with experts.
- **Systemic Independence**: Awareness of how decisions impact not just shareholders, but the broader ecosystem – including employees, suppliers, regulators, and communities.

This deeper model of independence fosters public confidence that board decisions are made in service of long-term value, not short-term gain.

2.8.3. Stakeholder-Centric Governance: The New Paradigm

Impactful IDs actively consider how board decisions affect a broad spectrum of stakeholders:

Stakeholder	Independent Director's Role
Shareholders	Ensure capital is protected and stewarded for long-term growth.
Employees	Oversee fair labour practices, diversity, and workplace safety.
Customers	Monitor product safety, pricing ethics, and service quality.
Communities	Align corporate social responsibility (CSR) initiatives to genuine societal needs.
Environment	Advocate for sustainability integration in strategy and transparent reporting.

A wise director listens twice, speaks once, and acts with foresight.

This stakeholder lens expands the Director's field of view. As the owl sees beyond the immediate prey, the ID must see beyond the quarterly results.

2.8.4. Transparency and Communication: Earning Rather Than Demanding Trust

Boards have historically operated in relative opacity, but transparency is the foundation of credibility. Impactful IDs foster trust by:

- Encouraging clear, plain-language disclosures and reports.
- Supporting open investor engagement and responsiveness to inquiries.
- Advocating for ESG reporting that reflects reality, not just public relations messaging.
- Ensuring the voices of employees and customers reach the boardroom through surveys, townhalls, or dashboards.

Trust is earned not through perfection, but through accountable imperfection – acknowledging failures, explaining decisions, and demonstrating a commitment to continuous learning.

2.8.5. Anticipatory Governance: The Future-Facing Board

Trust is not merely reactive – it is anticipatory. Great IDs enable the board to:

- **Detect early signals:** Identify technological disruptions, social unrest, and climate-related volatility.
- **Build resilience:** Implement scenario planning, enhance digital preparedness, and strengthen succession depth.
- **Challenge orthodoxy:** Reconsider business models before markets, competitors, or regulators force change.

Transparency demands openness; trust demands consistency.

Impactful IDs asks the probing questions that challenge comfort zones:

- What could disrupt our business in the next 5 years?
- Whose trust are we risking, and why?
- Are we obscuring critical risks behind metrics or reports?

2.8.6. Examples of Impact in Practice

- **Environmental oversight:** An ID at a manufacturing firm identified unsafe waste disposal practices, prompting a comprehensive ESG strategy overhaul that enhanced both compliance and corporate reputation.
- **Human capital protection:** At a fast-growing tech startup, an ID intervened to pause aggressive hiring incentives that were causing employee burnout, safeguarding workforce wellbeing and brand integrity.
- **Financial transparency:** A financial-sector ID advocated greater disclosure of related-party transactions, resulting in improved investor confidence and trust.

In each instance, the ID moved beyond being a silent observer to a strategic actor, shaping outcomes that extend beyond compliance to meaningful, long-term impact.

2.9. The Way Forward: A Vision for Independent Directorship in 21st Century India

As India's corporate ecosystem matures, IDs must evolve from symbolic stewards to strategic sentinels of integrity, innovation, and inclusion. The next decade will demand far more than compliance checklists and formal charters; it will require boardroom visionaries – leaders who wield wisdom not as ornament, but as a guiding principle in every decision.

Board transparency demands vigilance; stakeholder trust demands authenticity.

The Owl, long revered for its silent strength and far-seeing eyes, remains an apt metaphor for the future of Independent Directorship: a role defined by measured courage, anticipatory insight, and enduring relevance in safeguarding the interests of shareholders, stakeholders, and society at large.

2.9.1. Reimagining the Role: From Regulatory Appendage to Strategic Asset

Today's IDs are too often seen as necessary formalities mandated by law but marginal in practice. The future must recast them as:

- Custodians of ethical culture, not merely approvers of audits.
- Scouts for strategic risk and opportunity, not just compliance monitors.
- Curators of board effectiveness, not passive meeting attendees.

To achieve this transformation, IDs must be selected for strength of character, diversity of thought, and capacity for stewardship – not solely for past prestige or a passive reputation.

2.9.2. The Five Pillars of the 21st Century Independent Director

To truly embody wisdom and watchfulness, tomorrow's IDs must anchor themselves in five foundational qualities:

- **Moral courage:** The fortitude to speak truth to power, even at personal or professional risk.
- **Systems thinking:** The ability to understand how decisions ripple across stakeholders, markets, and time.
- **Deep engagement:** Commitment to preparation, active participation, and post-meeting reflection, not mere presence.

Governance innovation demands creativity; ethical stewardship demands integrity.

- **Technological literacy:** A working understanding of Artificial Intelligence (AI), cybersecurity, data privacy, and digital transformation.
- **Stakeholder empathy:** The capacity to balance the interests of investors, employees, customers, and society without compromising responsibility.

These are not merely "soft skills"; they are essential survival tools in a complex, fast-evolving corporate landscape.

2.9.3. Governance for the Future: Trends That Will Shape the Independent Director's Role

Several emerging forces are set to transform boardroom governance and redefine the ID's role:

- **Climate risk as fiduciary risk:** Boards will need IDs who understand ESG science, sustainability frameworks, and the financial implications of environmental decisions.
- **AI and automation:** Directors must balance technological efficiency with ethical considerations, human impact, and regulatory compliance.
- **Geopolitical flux:** IDs will play a crucial role in navigating compliance, reputation, and supply-chain risks amid global instability.
- **Social license to operate:** Public expectations of corporate conduct increasingly influence trust, valuation, and talent retention.

The ID of the future will no longer merely observe these shifts – they must act as translator, moderator, and navigator, ensuring that strategy, ethics, and risk management remain aligned in an evolving corporate landscape.

Digital governance demands knowledge; policy alignment demands clarity.

2.9.4. Building the Next Generation of Independent Directors

For the evolution of Independent Directorship to succeed, three systemic shifts are essential:

A. Board Composition

- Diversity must extend beyond gender to encompass age, geography, sectoral experience, and neurodiversity.
- Rotation of IDs should preserve continuity in institutional memory, ensuring a long-term perspective is not lost.

B. Independent Director Training and Evaluation

- Ongoing learning in digital transformation, ESG, ethical dilemmas, and crisis leadership should be mandatory.
- Peer evaluation and structured feedback should guide decisions on ID renewal or replacement.

C. Empowered Governance Culture

- Chairs and CEOs must cultivate an environment where IDs can challenge constructively and question fearlessly.
- Agendas should emphasise forward-looking, value-creating discussions, not merely retrospective reviews.

With these foundations, boardrooms can evolve into spaces where intelligent dissent is valued, strategic oversight is rigorous, and IDs truly serve as catalysts of integrity and long-term value creation.

2.9.5. The Final Imperative: Wisdom That Walks, Not Watches

The Owl's power lies not only in what it observes, but in how it acts on that vision. Likewise, the legacy of the ID will not be defined by mere

ESG integration demands commitment; stakeholder engagement demands inclusivity.

observation, but by interventions that are principled, timely, and transformative.

The future of governance in India and globally will hinge on leaders who combine technical fluency with ethical clarity, independence with insight, and oversight with ownership. IDs must evolve from being a structural formality to a living embodiment of corporate conscience.

Epilogue: The Owl in the Boardroom – A Final Reflection

When the boardroom is clouded by complexity or compromise, it is the Owl, the ID, who must see through illusion, detect quiet danger, and guide the collective toward wiser, long-term decisions. The Owl does not simply watch; it acts with foresight, courage, and unwavering responsibility.

To sit in silence is easy.
To speak with wisdom is rare.

To act with integrity, foresight, and courage that is the calling of the true Independent Director.

"Like the owl, the Independent Director must perceive what others overlook and speak only when it matters most -for in their wisdom and watchfulness lies the quiet strength that upholds the boardroom to its highest standards."

CHAPTER 3

Satyam, Shivam, Sundaram: A Moral Framework for Independent Directors in India

"Truth guides, Goodness governs, Beauty inspires – the independent director's compass in India."

3.1 Introduction

In an era of profound transformation in India's corporate landscape, the role of the Independent Director (ID) has never been more critical – or more scrutinised. Amid scandals, regulatory pressures, and complex boardroom dynamics, a fundamental question arises: **What moral compass guides the ID?**

This section proposes a distinctive philosophical framework – **Satyam (Truth), Shivam (Goodness), Sundaram (Beauty)** – rooted in India's civilisational ethos, as a contemporary guide for IDs. It contends that beyond legal statutes and corporate codes, it is adherence to enduring values that will ensure the dignity, effectiveness, and moral authority of the ID.

A director's first loyalty is to truth; not to titles.

3.2. Satyam: The Pursuit of Truth in Governance

3.2.1 Truth as Transparency

For the ID, **truth begins with transparency**. Practically, this entails:

- **Demanding full access to information**, not merely what is selectively provided in board packs.
- **Questioning assumptions** behind financial statements, valuations, forecasts and projections.
- **Disclosing dissent**, when necessary, both in writing and in public records.

Satyam is not merely about detecting fraud; it is about **fostering an environment where concealment** becomes impossible. In today's world of complex accounting, layered subsidiaries, and sophisticated financial instruments, truth is often the first casualty and, simultaneously, the foremost obligation. History provides stark lessons: corporate collapses from **Satyam to Infrastructure Leasing & Financial Services (IL&FS)** demonstrate that when truth is absent, governance systems crumble, stakeholder trust erodes, and systemic risk proliferates.

3.2.2 Courageous Integrity

Truth requires courage. IDs must:

- Speak the inconvenient truth, even if it risks unpopularity with promoters, management, or fellow board members.
- Step down when governance failures become normalised and compromise the company's ethical foundation.
- Resist pressure, inducements, and subtle silencing tactics, ensuring independence is not merely formal but fictional.

"Integrity is the seatbelt of governance; the independent director fastens it"

Every ethical stand is an offering to the institution's soul.

Many directors rationalise silence as prudence. Yet prudence without principle is cowardice. Satyam, in essence, is a call to be the moral whistle within the boardroom, raising alarms long before external crises force attention. It is the courage to uphold truth as both shield and compass, guiding not just compliance, but conscience.

3.2.3 Truth and Fiduciary Literacy

Modern boards navigate a labyrinth of complex challenges, including cybersecurity, Environmental, Social, and Governance (ESG), Artificial Intelligence (AI), and global capital markets. Upholding truth in this context requires:

- Constant upskilling or staying abreast of evolving risks and governance standards.
- Understanding financial engineering to discern substance from window-dressing.
- Recognising ethical implications of emerging technologies and strategic decisions.

Truth is not merely honesty; it is epistemological responsibility – knowing what you need to know and asking what you do not.

"To guard the truth is not merely to speak it, but to demand its presence in every document, every disclosure, and every decision."

3.3. Shivam: The Pursuit of Goodness in Decision-Making

3.3.1 Goodness Beyond Compliance

Compliance ensures legality; goodness ensures morality. Laws and regulations form the baseline of corporate governance, but Shivam challenges IDs to operate above this floor – to embed ethics, empathy, and social responsibility into decision-making.

The boardroom is a battlefield; dharma is your only weapon.

IDs guided by Shivam:

- **Evaluate ethical consequences:** Decisions on downsizing, mergers, or cost-cutting are analysed not just for regulatory adherence but for human impact on employees, communities, and future generations.
- **Prioritise long-term value over short-term gains:** A profitable strategy that undermines trust, environmental sustainability, or social cohesion may meet legal standards but fails the test of goodness.
- **Champion fair processes:** From remuneration and succession planning to board nominations, Shivam ensures decisions are transparent, equitable, and just, countering favouritism or bias.

Goodness brings **humanity into governance**. An ID practising Shivam asks: *"Even if this is legal, is it right? Even if it is profitable, is it fair?"* The principle turns abstract ethics into actionable oversight.

3.3.2 Stewardship for All Stakeholders

While the Companies Act, 2013, and Securities Exchange Board of India (Listing Obligations and Disclosure Requirements) introduce stakeholder language, Shivam elevates it from regulatory rhetoric to a living principle. Under this paradigm, the ID becomes a trustee for multiple constituencies, ensuring that corporate decisions generate inclusive benefits rather than concentrated gains.

"Where the CEO dreams, the independent director wakes."

3.3.3 Key constituencies include:

- **Minority shareholders:** Safeguarding their voice and protecting against promoter overreach.
- **Workers and employees:** Promoting fair treatment, safe work environments, and growth opportunities.

Integrity is the compass in the maze of decisions.

- **Customers:** Ensuring quality, transparency, and ethical marketing.
- **Society and environment:** Championing sustainability, fair practices, and community engagement.

Shivam moves beyond avoiding harm; it calls for proactive goodness. Practical manifestations include:

- **Strategic Corporate Social Responsibility initiatives:** Investing in projects that align with core business objectives and community needs, rather than mere budget compliance.
- **Diversity, equity, and inclusion:** Building policies and practices that encourage representation and eliminate systemic biases.
- **Labour and environmental safeguards:** Ensuring that operational efficiency does not compromise human or ecological well-being.

Through this lens, IDs become architects of responsible corporate power, balancing profit with purpose.

3.3 Ethics in the Age of Disruption

Disruption, whether technological, economic, or social, exacerbates ethical complexity. Shivam equips IDs to **navigate this new frontier with foresight and moral clarity**:

- **Ethical Artificial Intelligence deployment:** Questioning algorithmic bias, privacy risks, and unintended social consequences before adoption.
- **Socio-economic foresight:** Anticipating workforce displacement from automation or digital transformation and recommending reskilling or humane transition policies.
- **Sustainable business models:** Encouraging circular economy initiatives, low-carbon operations, and resilient supply chains that safeguard long-term stakeholder value.

Integrity demands steadfastness; virtue demands courage.

In the 21st century, **Shivam is not sentimentalism; it is strategic morality**. IDs must weigh every decision against the dual axes of legality and goodness, ensuring that corporate actions are **just, sustainable, and socially responsible**.

"The true measure of an independent director's strength lies in their ability to uphold Shivam - choosing integrity over convenience, courage over complacency, and foresight over expedience."

3.4. Sundaram: The Pursuit of Beauty in Conduct

3.4.1 Grace in Governance

Sundaram represents the aspirational dimension of independent directorship – it is the cultivation of elegance, harmony, and moral aesthetics in boardroom conduct. Unlike Satyam (truth) or Shivam (goodness), Sundaram focuses on how governance is enacted, not just what is decided.

An ID guided by Sundaram embodies:

- **Respectful disagreement:** Voicing dissent without personal attack, framing critique constructively.
- **Well-reasoned dissent:** Ensuring challenges are anchored in logic, data, and principle rather than emotion or ego.
- **Dignity in speech, silence, and resignation:** Knowing when to speak, when to listen, and when to leave the board is the most principled option.

"The independent watches the horizon, not just the ledger."

Such directors elevate the tone of board interactions, modelling composure and ethical elegance. They avoid bullying, grandstanding, or performative opposition, demonstrating that the manner in which

Sundaram in governance means decisions that uplift, not just profit.

governance is exercised is as vital as the substance of decisions. Sundaram turns boardrooms into arenas of disciplined discourse, where form and function are in harmony, and ethical action itself becomes aesthetically resonant.

3.5 Legacy Through Leadership

Beauty in governance extends beyond decorum; it is about creating a lasting impact and a culture worth emulating. IDs must constantly reflect:

- What culture am I cultivating? Beyond policies, what norms, habits, and unspoken rules are being reinforced?
- What values am I reinforcing? Are fairness, transparency, and accountability consistently prioritised?
- How will this board be remembered? Will it be as a venue of token compliance, or as a model of principled, visionary stewardship?

Sundaram inspires a higher aesthetic of corporate behaviour, where process and outcome are equally valued. Just as a well-crafted judicial opinion instils confidence in the judiciary, a well-governed company generates societal trust, investor confidence, and enduring stakeholder respect. The ID becomes a curator of corporate culture, shaping the intangible elegance of ethical decision-making.

3.6 Emotional Intelligence and Civility

Sundaram also encompasses emotional intelligence and relational wisdom. A director who embodies beauty in governance demonstrates:

- **Active and empathetic listening:** Understanding viewpoints fully before responding.
- **Balanced assertiveness:** Maintaining voice without dominating the discussion.
- **Poise under pressure:** Remaining composed during crises, conflict, or high-stakes decisions.

Harmony arises not from silence, but from shared values well-defended.

Civility, in this framework, is not weakness – it is quiet strength that commands respect and fosters trust. IDs who integrate Sundaram into their conduct transform the boardroom into a space of thoughtful engagement rather than transactional debate.

"The strength of an independent director lies in their ability to bring Sundaram to the table, blending wisdom, fairness, and empathy into a governance masterpiece."

Sundaram, therefore, completes the triad of Satyam, Shivam, and Sundaram, reminding IDs that truth, goodness, and beauty are inseparable in the practice of enduring, impactful corporate governance.

3.7. Practical Application: A Code of Satyam, Shivam, Sundaram

To translate philosophy into action, IDs can adopt a living code anchored in the three pillars. Each principle informs specific boardroom practices and prompts reflective questions that guide decisions:

Principle	Boardroom Practice	Guiding Question
Satyam (Truth)	Demand full disclosure, record dissent, probe assumptions, seek facts over narratives	"What is being hidden? What must be revealed?"
Shivam (Goodness)	Prioritise ethics over expediency, protect vulnerable stakeholders, and safeguard long-term value	"Is this good for the many, not just the few?"
Sundaram (Beauty)	Model dignity, encourage deliberation, respect others' perspectives, led by example	"Am I raising or lowering the tone of this boardroom?"

"The chair may steer, but the independent must warn of reefs."

This code transforms abstract values into actionable guidance. Satyam ensures integrity in facts and disclosures; Shivam guides ethical

Satyam, Shivam, Sundaram - truth, goodness, beauty - are the boardroom's true pillars.

judgment and stakeholder stewardship; Sundaram elevates boardroom conduct and culture. Together, they form a triad of practical wisdom, moral courage, and elegant oversight, equipping IDs to navigate complexity, pressure, and ambiguity with principled confidence.

3.8. Cultural and Institutional Relevance

3.8.1 A Dharma-Based Alternative to Agency Theory

While Western governance frameworks often rely on agency theory, which frames directors primarily as monitors of self-interested executives, the Indian context offers a complementary, values-driven lens. Rooted in the civilisational concept of dharma, this approach positions IDs not merely as compliance enforcers, but as stewards of ethical, strategic, and cultural integrity.

The dharma-based model emphasises three interlocking duties:

- **Duty to truth (Satyam):** Ensuring transparency, accuracy, and candour in all board deliberations and disclosures.
- **Duty to the collective good (Shivam):** Prioritising the welfare of all stakeholders – shareholders, employees, communities, and the environment – over narrow self-interest or expediency.
- **Duty to dignified action (Sundaram):** Conducting boardroom interactions with decorum, emotional intelligence, and a commitment to elevating corporate culture.

By aligning governance with these enduring ethical principles, this framework resonates deeply with Indian corporate culture. It transforms board oversight from a purely rules-based exercise into a values-based practice, fostering principled decision-making, long-term trust, and societal legitimacy.

3.8.2 Training and Capacity Building

Embedding the Satyam–Shivam–Sundaram framework into corporate practice requires more than awareness – it demands systematic capacity

When all paths look smooth, the independent checks for hidden dips.

building. IDs must be equipped not only with technical knowledge of laws, regulations, and fiduciary duties, but also with the moral, cognitive, and relational skills that enable principled governance.

Key dimensions of training include:

- **Ethical Reasoning:** Directors should be able to:
  - Analyse dilemmas beyond legal compliance, considering long-term societal and stakeholder impact.
  - Balance competing interests, e.g., profitability vs. employee welfare or ESG priorities vs shareholder returns.
  - Recognise ethical grey zones, where the "right" choice is not immediately obvious and apply structured moral frameworks to guide action.
- **Value-Sensitive Decision-Making:** Boardroom decisions should be assessed through the lens of dharma principles:
  - **Satyam:** Is the decision transparent, truthful, and based on sound evidence?
  - **Shivam:** Does it promote collective good, safeguarding vulnerable stakeholders?
  - **Sundaram:** Does it uphold dignity, civility, and constructive board culture?

Training modules can incorporate scenario-based exercises, using historical governance failures or contemporary dilemmas to build pattern recognition, foresight, and judgment.

- **Narrative Competence:** Beyond numbers and rules, governance is about stories of risks, opportunities, and human impact. IDs must:
  - Develop the ability to listen attentively to management narratives, whistleblower accounts, and stakeholder feedback.
  - Interpret subtleties in language, tone, and framing that may indicate deeper issues.

Ethical stewardship demands integrity; fiduciary duty demands diligence.

- Communicate concerns or dissent persuasively, ethically, and strategically to the board.

- **Board Evaluations with Moral Metrics:** Traditional board assessments often focus on attendance, preparation, and technical expertise. To truly embed Satyam–Shivam–Sundaram:
  - Evaluation criteria should include ethical foresight, courage to dissent, and contributions to stakeholder-centric outcomes.
  - Peer feedback and 360-degree assessments can identify directors' effectiveness in applying moral and strategic judgment, not just procedural compliance.

- **Mentoring and Continuous Learning:** New and aspiring IDs benefit from mentorship by experienced directors who embody wisdom and watchfulness. Programs should:
  - Pair seasoned directors with newcomers for guided exposure to real board scenarios.
  - Offer workshops on emerging challenges like Artificial Intelligence ethics, climate risk, ESG compliance, and socio-economic impact.
  - Encourage reflection sessions where directors discuss ethical dilemmas faced during meetings and their decision-making rationale.

By integrating these elements into training, evaluation, and mentorship, boards can translate abstract principles into actionable governance behaviours, creating directors who are not only legally compliant but ethically resilient, strategically insightful, and culturally attuned.

Conclusion: The Triadic Compass for 21st Century Independent Directors

India's IDs stand at a pivotal crossroads. On one path lies proceduralism, box-ticking, and risk avoidance – a safe but ultimately hollow approach to governance. On the other hand lies purpose-driven, ethically courageous, and morally grounded leadership – a path demanding vigilance, discernment, and integrity. The framework of Satyam, Shivam, Sundaram provides a compass for this transformative journey.

In practice, this triadic framework means:

- **Satyam (Truth):** Anchoring board decisions in transparency, facts, and courageous disclosure. Truth is not merely a compliance requirement; it is the lifeblood of trust and accountability.
- **Shivam (Goodness):** Ensuring that governance decisions protect the many, not just the few. Ethical foresight becomes a strategic imperative, guiding boards to consider the welfare of employees, communities, and the environment alongside shareholders.
- **Sundaram (Beauty):** Elevating the conduct of governance itself. Civility, dignity, and deliberative rigour transform the boardroom into a space where process and substance are equally valued, leaving a legacy of principled leadership.

For India's corporate ecosystem – here, promoter influence remains strong, stakeholder expectations are rising, and complex global risks abound – this framework does more than inspire. It operationalises character as capability. The strength of an ID lies not in their designation or tenure, but in their courage to speak, discernment to act, and wisdom to balance competing interests.

"True leadership in governance arises when Satyam, Shivam, and Sundaram come together -where truth fuels transparency, integrity shapes decisions, and harmony builds lasting stakeholder confidence."

The ID who embodies this triad does more than oversee; they anchor the board, safeguard stakeholders, and elevate corporate India to its highest ideals. In a world of complexity and uncertainty, they are the Owl in the boardroom – a sentinel, a guide, and a custodian of enduring trust.

CHAPTER 4

Independent Directors' Role in Crisis Management, Corporate Scandals, and Risk Management in India

"Guardians in the Storm: How Independent Directors Navigate Risk, Scandal, and Uncertainty."

4.1 Introduction

Independent directors (IDs) have emerged as central pillars of corporate governance, particularly in the Indian context, where promoter-driven boards often concentrate authority and obscure accountability. Their mandate extends beyond statutory compliance; they are expected to act as ethical sentinels, strategic advisors, and risk stewards, ensuring that board decisions align with long-term value creation and stakeholder trust.

The importance of IDs becomes especially pronounced during corporate crises, financial scandals, or governance failures, when executive oversight may be compromised, information asymmetry is high, and reputational stakes are enormous. Historical episodes such as the Satyam scandal (2009), the Infrastructure Leasing & Financial Services

In a scandal, the truth leaks long before the headlines hit, if only someone is listening.

(IL&FS) liquidity crisis (2018), and the Yes Bank distress (2020) underscore both the vulnerabilities of Indian corporate boards and the vital role IDs can play in restoring confidence and guiding strategic remediation. In these moments, IDs are tasked not only with reactive oversight but also with anticipatory governance – identifying warning signals, challenging management assumptions, and ensuring ethical and transparent decision-making.

A critical yet often under-explored dimension of their function is enterprise risk management (ERM). Risk governance today is far more than a checklist; it is a strategic enabler that safeguards a company's resilience against operational, financial, regulatory, technological, and Environmental, Social, and Governance (ESG)-related disruptions. Indian corporations are increasingly exposed to globalised economic shocks, cybersecurity threats, climate-related risks, and evolving regulatory expectations. In this complex risk environment, IDs play a dual role: monitoring risk exposure and guiding strategic risk appetite, ensuring that organisations are not only compliant but also agile, sustainable, and future-ready.

This section examines the multifaceted responsibilities of IDs in crisis management, corporate scandals, and risk governance. It highlights their contributions to decision-making under pressure, ethical stewardship, and risk-informed strategy, illustrating how effective IDs can transform governance from a reactive function to a proactive, value-creating capability.

4.2 Risk Management Oversight

4.2.1 Regulatory Foundation for Risk Management Oversight

The responsibilities of IDs in risk management are not left to interpretation – they are clearly embedded within India's regulatory framework. The Companies Act, 2013, along with the Securities Exchange Board of India (SEBI) (Listing Obligations and Disclosure Requirements)

When crisis knocks, the boardroom's weakest question becomes its strongest regret.

Regulations, 2015 (LODR), provide explicit mandates that empower and obligate IDs to take an active role in risk governance. Together, these statutes ensure that risk management oversight is not optional but integral to corporate governance in India.

- **Risk Management Committee (RMC)**: For the top 1,000 listed entities (by market capitalisation), this committee must include a majority of board members, with at least one ID. Their role includes defining risk management policies, overseeing the risk management framework to ensure risks are identified, assessed, and mitigated systematically, and monitoring key risk indicators.

  Here, IDs act as guardians of balance, ensuring that the company's pursuit of growth does not compromise its resilience. Their presence on the RMC adds an external, objective perspective that prevents promoter or management bias from underestimating or ignoring risk exposures.

- **Audit Committee**: Another board committee with a majority of IDs serves as a critical checkpoint for financial risk management. Its responsibilities include reviewing internal controls & financial reporting systems, scrutinising audit reports & statutory compliance and detecting financial irregularities, related-party transactions, and fraud risks.

  Because most corporate scandals in India (Satyam, IL&FS, DHFL) have been rooted in financial misstatements or inadequate disclosures, the Audit Committee is often the first line of defence. IDs in this space must not only rely on audit reports but also exercise professional scepticism, asking hard questions and probing areas where numbers may mask deeper issues.

- **Corporate Governance Responsibilities**: The spirit of Indian governance codes, including the erstwhile Clause 49 of the SEBI Listing Agreement (now subsumed under LODR), emphasises that boards must cultivate a risk-conscious culture. IDs are expected to: familiarise themselves with risk-related matters across the business, ensure that risk appetite is clearly articulated and aligned with corporate strategy and encourage management to embed risk awareness into decision-making at all levels, not just at the top.

This elevates risk governance from a committee-level exercise to a boardroom philosophy – with IDs serving as both custodians of compliance and champions of resilience.

Why This Matters

Together, these regulatory foundations reflect a shift in governance expectations: risk management is no longer a reactive safeguard but a strategic responsibility. IDs, by virtue of their statutory role, are uniquely positioned to ensure that risk oversight is integrated, forward-looking, and values-driven, rather than a mere tick-box exercise.

4.3 Key Areas of Risk Management Oversight by Independent Directors

IDs are not passive observers – they are the board's critical guardians of resilience and foresight. Their oversight spans multiple dimensions of corporate risk:

- **Strategic risk assessment:** IDs must view every strategic decision – be it mergers and acquisitions, capital expenditures, international expansions, or digital transformations – through a risk-conscious lens. They should challenge assumptions, probe into expected return on investment, and demand robust contingency planning to ensure that ambition does not outpace prudence.
- **Operational and financial risk review:** Through careful scrutiny of internal audit reports, MIS dashboards, and business continuity plans, independent directors should identify operational bottlenecks, cost overruns, fraud vulnerabilities, and supply chain risks. On the financial side, they must rigorously review liquidity positions, debt structures, and market exposures, ensuring that financial health remains strong even in volatile conditions.

Scandals do not start with fraud; they start with tolerance.

- **Regulatory and compliance risk:** India's regulatory landscape – from FEMA and FCRA to SEBI norms and environmental laws – demands vigilance. IDs must ensure compliance is not episodic but embedded, recognising that lapses can carry heavy legal, financial, and reputational consequences.
- **Cybersecurity and technology risk:** In a digitised world, cyber resilience is corporate resilience. IDs should insist on periodic assessments of IT systems, cyber-defence strategies, data protection policies, and incident response protocols. A single breach can destroy trust built over decades; oversight in this domain is non-negotiable.
- **Environmental, Social, and Governance and reputational risk:** ESG considerations are no longer optional – they are central to investor sentiment and regulatory scrutiny. IDs must champion sustainability strategy, benchmark practices against global standards, and ensure transparent sustainability risk reporting. Reputation, once lost, is seldom regained.
- **Risk Culture and internal controls:** Finally, IDs shape the tone from the top. They must foster a risk-aware culture where ethical conduct, transparent reporting, and accountability are non-negotiable. This includes ensuring effective whistleblower mechanisms and conducting periodic reviews of internal controls to guard against complacency.

"The true power of an independent director lies not in reacting to crises, but in anticipating risks and embedding resilience into the DNA of the organisation."

4.4. Best Practices in Risk Governance by Independent Directors

IDs add real value when they go beyond oversight to embed proactive risk governance into the DNA of the board. Some best practices include:

In a storm, the guardian's role is not to hide; it is to hold.

- **Early warning systems**: Advocate for real-time dashboards and monitoring mechanisms that flag red signals – declining Key performance indicators, audit anomalies, whistleblower complaints – before they escalate into crises.
- **Risk appetite statements**: Work with management to clearly articulate the company's risk appetite and tolerance thresholds, ensuring they align with long-term strategy and are reviewed periodically as market realities shift.
- **Scenario planning and stress testing**: Encourage management to conduct best-case, worst-case, and black swan simulations, testing resilience under diverse scenarios such as market shocks, supply chain breakdowns, or reputational crises.
- **Integrated risk reporting**: Insist on consolidated reports that connect risk metrics to business performance, enabling boards to see risk not as an abstract metric, but as a direct driver of value creation and protection.
- **Board-level risk champions**: Lead or actively participate in board taskforces on emerging risks – Artificial intelligence ethics, climate transition, cybersecurity, or geopolitical disruptions – ensuring the board is not blindsided by fast-moving external forces.

"Best-in-class boards are those where independent directors don't just monitor risks -they translate them into foresight, resilience, and strategic advantage."

4.5 Global Standards and Learnings for the Indian Context

Indian boards can draw from international governance models such as:

- **United Kingdom Corporate Governance Code**: Places strong emphasis on the board's responsibility for defining risk appetite and ensuring the presence of a robust, transparent risk management system. The principle reinforces that oversight is not passive it requires active calibration of how much risk an organisation is willing and able to bear.

- **COSO ERM Framework**: Promotes the integration of risk into business strategy and performance, rather than treating it as a compliance add-on. For IDs, this underscores the need to ensure that strategic choices are evaluated through a structured risk lens, enabling resilience and opportunity capture.
- **Organisation for Economic Co-operation and Development Principles**: Highlight board diversity, accountability, and risk oversight as central to sustainable governance. The principles remind Indian boards that effective risk management is inseparable from inclusivity, transparency, and fairness in decision-making.

4.6 Real-World Illustrations of Risk Management Failures

Aspect	Infrastructure Leasing & Financial Services	Yes Bank	Jet Airways	Cognizant India
Industry	Infrastructure Financing	Banking and Financial Services	Aviation	IT / Professional Services
Year of Major Crisis	2018	2020	2019	2016–2019 (FCPA probe)
Type of Risk Failure	Credit, Liquidity, Strategic	Credit Concentration, Governance	Operational, Strategic, Financial	Compliance, Reputational
Root Cause	Reckless lending, misreporting, shadow guarantees	Risky lending, inflated books, promoter interference	Unsustainable pricing, poor capital management	Bribery for regulatory approvals

Crisis demands clarity; response demands decisiveness.

Early Warning Signals Ignored	High leverage, ratings downgrade, cash crunch	NPA surge, whistleblower complaints, promoter borrowing	Mounting losses, delayed salaries, cash burn	Internal compliance alerts, legal red flags
Role of Board/ IDs	Passive, failed to question management	Suppressed dissent; IDs failed to act on red flags	Unqualified Board, weak governance	Lacked oversight over India operations
Risk Management Committee	Ineffective, did not assess intercompany guarantees	Present but weak; internal models ignored	Largely absent; not proactive	Inadequate ethical compliance audits
Audit Committee Action	Rubber stamp; failed to detect financial manipulation	Ineffective; allowed NPAs to be under-reported	Not equipped to oversee financial distress	Limited insight into vendor dealings
Whistleblower Protection	Virtually non-existent	Internal complaints suppressed	Not known	Weak at India level; retaliation feared
Regulatory Oversight	RBI, NCLT, Ministry of Corporate Affairs, SFIO, CAG	RBI, SEBI, ED, CBI	DGCA, IBC process attempted	US DOJ, SEC under FCPA
Immediate Consequences	Default, public panic, liquidity crunch in the Non-Banking Financial Company (NBFC) sector	Moratorium, restructuring, SBI-led rescue	Suspension of operations, Insolvency and Bankruptcy Code, insolvency process	$25 million in fines, top executive exit
Stakeholder Impact	Investors, lenders, employees, NBFC sector	Depositors, investors, employees, entire BFSI sector	Employees, passengers, lessors, vendors	Shareholders, employees, regulatory reputation

Risk assessment demands vigilance; mitigation demands action.

Long-Term Fallout	Massive regulatory overhaul in NBFCs	Bank under reconstruction and public Sector Undertaking (PSU) control	Still awaiting full resolution; brand collapse	Enhanced global compliance protocols
Systemic Impact	Triggered the NBFC crisis; shook investor confidence	Loss of trust in private banking; PSU burden	Reduced investor appetite in aviation	Reputational risk for the Indian IT sector
Internal Controls	Weak, opaque intercompany dealings	Ignored credit norms, internal limits	Non-existent stress testing	Lax ethical due diligence and third-party control
ESG & Compliance Culture	Ignored ESG norms; no transparency	Poor governance and compliance	Environmental and labour issues are neglected	Ethical guidelines are not enforced uniformly
Role of Regulators	Reactive; later intervention and forensic audits	Active intervention by RBI with a reconstruction plan	Minimal proactive action until bankruptcy	United States (US) enforcement agencies took the lead
Recovery Plan	Government takeover; new board; asset monetisation	Capital infusion by SBI & consortium; management overhaul	Insolvency process under NCLT	Internal investigation; leadership and compliance revamp
Lessons Learned	Need for strong ID vigilance & credit risk checks	Avoid promoter overreach; empower risk function	Require industry expertise on board; operational risk plan	Compliance culture must go beyond paperwork

Board oversight demands scrutiny; executive accountability demands enforcement.

4.7 Enhancing Independent Directors' Role in Risk Management

To elevate their contribution beyond compliance, IDs can adopt proactive strategies that embed risk awareness and resilience throughout the organisation:

- **Specialised induction and continuing education**: Regulators and industry bodies should mandate risk-focused training for IDs, incorporating domain-specific case studies, crisis simulations, and regulatory updates. Continuous learning ensures directors remain equipped to anticipate and mitigate emerging threats.
- **Use of risk dashboards and Artificial Intelligence tools**: Boards can adopt digital dashboards and Artificial Intelligence analytics to monitor key risk indicators in real time, visualise risk heatmaps, and detect early warning signals, enabling informed and timely decision-making.
- **Third-party risk audits**: Championing independent external assessments allows IDs to receive unbiased evaluations of operational, financial, and strategic risks, strengthening governance objectivity.
- **Multi-stakeholder dialogue**: Engaging with auditors, rating agencies, proxy advisors, and major shareholders provides IDs with diverse perspectives on emerging risks, enhancing the board's situational awareness.
- **Linking remuneration to risk outcomes**: Ensure that executive incentives are tied not only to financial performance but also to risk management success, aligning leadership behaviour with sustainable, long-term value creation.

"By combining specialised knowledge, technology, external insights, and incentive alignment, independent directors transform risk governance from a regulatory checkbox into a strategic lever for resilience and long-term value."

Crisis leadership demands resilience; corporate ethics demands consistency.

Conclusion

As India's corporate landscape evolves from predominantly promoter-led enterprises to professionally managed organisations, the role of IDs in shaping risk governance has never been more critical. The resilience, sustainability, and credibility of businesses increasingly hinge on boards that do more than approve policies – they anticipate threats, challenge assumptions, and embed a culture of vigilance across the organisation.

Risk management is no longer confined to spreadsheets, compliance checklists, or internal audits. It is a board-level, strategic imperative. IDs must combine technical literacy, regulatory insight, and ethical judgment to interpret complex risk landscapes – be it financial volatility, cybersecurity threats, climate transition challenges, or ESG-driven stakeholder pressures.

Effective IDs are proactive risk stewards. They go beyond monitoring and reporting to:

- Shape a risk-aware culture, where employees are empowered to surface concerns without fear.
- Insist on robust scenario planning and stress testing, anticipating disruptions before they materialise.
- Ensure risk-adjusted strategic decisions, balancing ambition with prudence and long-term sustainability.
- Serve as ethical anchors, challenging management when incentives, strategies, or operations stray from legal, moral, or reputational standards.

In essence, the modern ID transforms from a compliance overseer into a guardian of organisational integrity and resilience. Their active engagement not only protects the company from foreseeable and unforeseen risks but also builds trust with investors, employees, regulators, and society at large. As India steps onto the global stage, boards with visionary, courageous, and informed IDs will not merely survive

Risk appetite demands definition; risk culture demands reinforcement.

turbulence - they will set the benchmark for governance excellence. The next decade of corporate success will be defined not by rules alone, but by the foresight, judgment, and ethical backbone of those who sit at the boardroom table.

"In times of crisis, the Independent Director becomes the board's backbone - standing firm when others falter, asking the hard questions when silence is easy, and steering the company not just out of scandal, but toward redemption and resilience."

CHAPTER 5

The Invisible Backbone: Are Independent Directors Truly Independent in India?

"Guardians by Title, Watchers by Choice: Unveiling the Reality of Boardroom Independence in India."

5.1 Introduction

In the intricate ecosystem of corporate governance, IDs are widely regarded as the sentinels of integrity, fairness, and accountability. They are expected to act as impartial guardians, ensuring that boards make decisions in the best interest of shareholders, employees, and other stakeholders, rather than serving the narrow interests of promoters or management. In India, where promoter-led companies remain prevalent and ownership structures are often concentrated, the role of independent directors is especially critical. Legislators, regulators, investors, and civil society alike place immense trust in these directors to provide objective oversight, challenge executive decisions when necessary, and safeguard the long-term health of organisations.

The invisible backbone breaks first when governance is tested.

Yet, beneath the formal structures and regulatory mandates lies a pressing question: *Are ID in India truly independent, or does their autonomy exist more on paper than in practice?* Do they exercise real authority, or are they constrained subtly or structurally by financial incentives, cultural hierarchies, informational asymmetries, and boardroom dynamics?

This section explores the evolution of independent directorship in India, the expectations placed on these directors, the practical and systemic challenges they face, and the reforms needed to strengthen their role. By examining both successes and failures, it seeks to illuminate the paradox of independence, its promise, its limitations, and the critical steps required to ensure that IDs become not just formal placeholders, but genuine stewards of corporate governance.

5.2 Evolution of Independent Directorship in India

The concept of IDs is not new, but its prominence has grown in response to global and domestic corporate crises. Internationally, scandals such as Enron and WorldCom in the early 2000s highlighted the need for impartial oversight at the highest levels of corporate governance. In India, the journey began with the Securities Exchange Board of India's (SEBI) Clause 49 of the Listing Agreement in 2000, which mandated the inclusion of independent directors on the boards of listed companies. This framework was later strengthened and codified under the Companies Act, 2013, which formally defined the role, qualifications, and fiduciary duties of IDs.

India's transition from a predominantly promoter-centric model to a more stakeholder-inclusive governance ecosystem has been gradual, marked by incremental reforms and evolving expectations. Yet, the true measure of independent directorship lies not in the mere presence of these directors on boards, but in their ability to exercise genuine independence, question assumptions, and influence decisions with courage, insight, and integrity.

A silent Independent Director is neither independent nor a director.

5.3 Legal Framework and Mandate

The Companies Act, 2013 and SEBI's Listing Obligations and Disclosure Requirements (LODR) Regulations lay down detailed criteria for the appointment and functioning of IDs:

- Must not be a promoter or related to the promoter/directors.
- No material pecuniary relationship with the company, other than sitting fees.
- Must possess integrity, relevant expertise, and experience.
- Appointed for a term up to five years, eligible for reappointment for another term, with a cooling-off period after two terms.

In addition to structural independence, IDs are expected to:

- Participate in board and committee meetings.
- Oversee financial reporting and audit processes.
- Ensure proper risk management and internal control systems.
- Uphold ethical standards and legal compliance.

Despite this strong legal framework, multiple systemic and cultural factors erode the independence in practice.

"An independent director is not a watchdog - but must bark when needed and bite when necessary."

5.4 Challenges to Independence

5.4.1 Promoter Influence and Boardroom Dynamics

A significant proportion of Indian companies are promoter-driven, with promoters often controlling board appointments. This creates a structural conflict: "independent" directors may have personal or professional ties to promoters, undermining their autonomy. Many directors

The cost of true independence is discomfort; the cost of its absence is collapse.

hesitate to challenge promoters' decisions due to the risk of being sidelined, replaced, or marginalised, which compromises the spirit of independent oversight.

5.4.2 Lack of Information and Access

IDs frequently operate in an information-constrained environment. They rely heavily on management-prepared reports, presentations, and data packs, which may omit critical details, selectively present information, or mask underlying risks. Limited access to independent verification or external audits further restricts their ability to exercise meaningful oversight.

5.4.3 Tokenism and Cosmetic Compliance

In some organisations, the presence of IDs serves primarily to fulfil regulatory mandates rather than to strengthen governance. Board meetings often become procedural formalities, where IDs are neither encouraged nor empowered to voice dissent, ask probing questions, or critically evaluate decisions. This symbolic participation undermines the very purpose of independent directorship.

5.4.4. Reappointment and Remuneration Dependencies

Reappointment of IDs typically requires approval from the board and shareholders, often influenced by promoters. While their remuneration may not match executive pay, it can still be substantial for retired bureaucrats, ex-bankers, or professionals. Coupled with the prospect of lucrative post-board opportunities, this creates subtle pressures to conform rather than challenge management decisions.

5.4.5. Legal and Reputational Risks

IDs are increasingly held liable for corporate misconduct, sometimes even when they had minimal involvement or awareness. The fear of litigation, regulatory scrutiny, or reputational damage discourages many

Independence without courage is merely decoration.

capable individuals from accepting board positions or from exercising assertive oversight once appointed.

Collectively, these challenges create an environment where formal independence may exist on paper, but practical autonomy is frequently compromised. IDs must navigate a delicate balance between compliance, courage, and strategic influence to fulfil their fiduciary mandate effectively.

5.5 Case Studies of Governance Failures

5.5.1 Infrastructure Leasing & Financial Services: The Towering Collapse of Oversight

The 2018 implosion of Infrastructure Leasing & Financial Services (IL&FS) remains a stark reminder of how governance lapses can threaten the financial system. The company, with a labyrinthine structure of over 300 subsidiaries, accumulated debt exceeding Rs. 90,000 crores. Despite a board populated with experienced professionals and eminent independent directors, critical warning signs went unheeded. Audit reports, internal risk assessments, and external credit downgrades were either inadequately scrutinised or insufficiently challenged. The crisis revealed systemic issues: over-reliance on management-provided information, limited engagement of IDs in risk evaluation, and groupthink that discouraged dissent. When regulators intervened, many directors resigned in quick succession, claiming surprise at the scale of the collapse, underscoring the gap between formal independence and effective oversight.

5.5.2 Satyam Computers: Deception Behind the Numbers

The Satyam scandal of 2009 exposed the vulnerability of IDs to sophisticated financial manipulation. Over several years, the board failed to detect inflated revenues, fictitious cash balances, and unreported liabilities, despite repeated audit reviews and risk reports. A dubious acquisition deal further highlighted the board's lack of critical evaluation. The

An Independent Director must answer not just to the boardroom, but to the public trust.

scandal demonstrated that legal compliance and procedural presence are insufficient; IDs must exercise proactive inquiry, cross-verification, and continuous scepticism to uphold the integrity of financial disclosures.

5.5.3 NSE Co-Location Scam: Subtle Lapses, Massive Consequences

In 2018, the National Stock Exchange (NSE) faced allegations of preferential access to trading infrastructure for select market participants. Investigations revealed lapses in governance oversight at multiple levels, implicating board members, including IDs, in failing to question and monitor critical operational processes. The case highlighted that independence is not merely about sitting on the board; it requires vigilance, proactive questioning, and the courage to investigate anomalies. It also emphasised the importance of understanding technological and operational risk, beyond financial statements, in modern corporate governance.

5.5.4 Yes Bank: The Perils of Passive Oversight

The downfall of Yes Bank in 2020 illustrated the consequences of a reactive board culture. Founder Rana Kapoor's aggressive lending and concentrated exposures were insufficiently challenged by the board, including IDs. Related-party transactions, high-risk loans, and capital adequacy issues were either overlooked or inadequately debated. Regulatory intervention came too late, after the crisis had metastasised. The Yes Bank saga underscored the need for IDs to exercise continuous scrutiny, demand detailed risk analyses, and actively shape organisational risk culture rather than merely rubber-stamp management proposals.

5.5.5 Dewan Housing Finance Limited (DHFL): Silent Compliance and Systemic Risk

Dewan Housing Finance Limited serves as another cautionary tale. Promoters allegedly siphoned off thousands of crores through shell entities, yet the board, including independent directors, failed to detect these patterns of financial misconduct. Risk reporting and internal controls were either insufficient or inadequately questioned. This failure highlights how boards can become ceremonial, with IDs constrained by social, economic, and reputational pressures, reducing their role to procedural compliance rather than strategic oversight.

Key Takeaways Across Cases:

- Formal presence does not equal functional independence.
- Over-reliance on management information is a persistent vulnerability.
- IDs often face subtle pressures – social, economic, or reputational – that discourage dissent.
- Effective oversight requires proactive questioning, external verification, technological literacy, and courage to act.
- Transparent and structured board processes, coupled with a culture that values dissent, are critical to preventing systemic governance failures.

These cases collectively illustrate a fundamental truth: independent directors are the linchpins of corporate governance, but their effectiveness depends on active engagement, moral courage, and systemic support, not just on regulatory compliance or boardroom presence.

5.6 Reforms and Regulatory Measures

5.6.1 SEBI Initiatives

SEBI has introduced several reforms aimed at strengthening the role of IDs:

- Enhanced disclosure requirements for appointment, resignation, and performance.
- Mandatory disclosure of the skills and expertise matrix of the board.

Independence hidden behind walls is freedom half-lived.

- Separation of the Chief Executive Officer and Chairperson roles.
- A database of eligible professionals to serve as IDs.

5.6.2 Corporate Governance Committees

The Kotak Committee Report (2017) made several recommendations to bolster board independence, many of which have been accepted by SEBI. These include improved disclosure, increased role of audit committees, and enhanced scrutiny of related-party transactions.

5.6.3 Board Evaluation Mechanisms

Annual board evaluations, including peer review of IDs, are now mandatory. However, their implementation often lacks rigour and objectivity.

5.6.4 Comparative Global Practices

Countries like the United Kingdom (UK) and the United States (US) have more evolved board cultures where independent directors play a critical role in governance. In the UK, the Corporate Governance Code emphasises board diversity, tenure limits, and robust appointment processes. In the US, shareholder activism and class-action lawsuits create natural deterrents for board complacency.

India can learn from these jurisdictions by encouraging more diverse and empowered boards, instituting genuine independence, and increasing accountability.

5.7. Way Forward

5.7.1. Independent Appointment Process

A truly ID can only emerge from a transparent and autonomous selection mechanism. Companies should adopt nomination processes that minimise promoter influence, incorporating external search committees or oversight by regulatory bodies. Open, merit-based selection ensures that directors are chosen for competence, ethical integrity, and ability to challenge management, rather than personal or social connections. Such a process can break the cycle of "compliance capital" and foster boards capable of robust oversight.

5.7.2. Improved Training and Certification

IDs operate in an increasingly complex corporate landscape, encompassing Artificial Intelligence, cybersecurity, Environmental, Social, and Governance (ESG), and global financial markets. Mandatory certification programs, such as those offered by the Indian Institute of Corporate Affairs (IICA), coupled with continuous education modules, can equip directors with the necessary skills and knowledge. Periodic simulations, case studies of governance failures, and workshops on ethical decision-making can transform directors from formal attendees into strategic contributors and risk stewards.

5.7.3. Strengthening Whistleblower Mechanisms

IDs must serve as the first line of defence for whistleblowers. Companies should establish fully anonymised and protected channels for reporting fraud, unethical practices, or regulatory violations. Directors should proactively monitor these systems, ensure prompt investigation, and escalate critical findings to regulators when required. Strengthened whistleblower mechanisms will not only deter misconduct but also signal that boards take integrity seriously.

5.7.4. Redefining Boardroom Culture

Culture is the bedrock of effective governance. Promoters and chairpersons must actively cultivate an environment where debate, challenge, and dissent are welcomed rather than discouraged. IDs should be empowered to raise difficult questions, critique assumptions, and propose alternative strategies without fear of marginalisation. Formalising mechanisms like "red-flag sessions" or pre-meeting briefings can institutionalise constructive challenge while maintaining collegiality.

5.7.5. Balanced Accountability

While IDs must be accountable for board decisions, regulatory frameworks should differentiate between negligence, wilful complicity, and genuine lack of information. Protections for directors acting in good faith are essential to encourage proactive oversight rather than passive acquiescence. Coupled with regular peer reviews and board evaluations, balanced accountability ensures both responsibility and the courage to act.

5.7.6. Enhancing Transparency and Public Disclosure

Boards should publicly communicate how IDs influence critical decisions, not merely report their presence. Disclosures should include the role of directors in shaping risk policy, approving major investments, overseeing ESG initiatives, and challenging management assumptions. By making the impact of IDs visible, stakeholders gain confidence, the board earns credibility, and independence moves from symbolic to substantive.

5.7.7. Fostering Multi-Stakeholder Engagement

IDs should engage not only with management but also with auditors, rating agencies, regulators, and major shareholders to obtain diverse perspectives. Understanding external expectations and integrating multi-stakeholder insights into decision-making enhances governance quality and reduces blind spots.

5.7.8. Leveraging Technology and Data-Driven Oversight

Modern boards should equip IDs with real-time dashboards, risk heatmaps, and analytical tools to track organisational health. Technology can aid in the early detection of financial, operational, and reputational

Promoter pressures demand resistance; regulatory compliance demands obedience.

risks, enabling directors to act decisively before minor issues escalate into crises.

Conclusion

IDs are meant to be the custodians of stakeholder trust, providing objectivity, balance, and ethical oversight in corporate decision-making. While India has made considerable progress in formalising their roles through legislation, listing regulations, and committee mandates, the practical reality remains fraught with challenges.

Promoter dominance, restricted access to critical information, subtle pressures, and fear of reputational or legal repercussions continue to undermine the effectiveness of IDs. Structural reforms alone cannot suffice; what is equally essential is a cultural transformation within boards, one that values constructive dissent, transparency, and principled engagement.

True independence is not a title or a checkbox; it is a practice. It demands courage to speak uncomfortable truths, conviction to challenge entrenched interests, and responsibility to safeguard long-term value for all stakeholders. Only when independent directors act with genuine autonomy, foresight, and ethical rigour will they evolve from being ceremonial board members to the invisible backbone of resilient, trustworthy, and future-ready Indian corporate governance.

"Independence is not declared by designation but demonstrated in decisions - for the true Independent Director is not the one who merely occupies the seat, but the one who dares to stand alone when duty demands it."

CHAPTER 6

Independent by Title, Dependent by Design: The Illusion of Autonomy in the Indian Boardroom

"Independence is earned in action, not assumed by appointment."

6.1. The Boardroom Mirage: The Discrepancy Between Form and Function

In the architecture of modern corporate governance, independent directors (IDs) are celebrated as sentinels of accountability. Codified in legislation and highlighted in annual reports, they are expected to act as impartial overseers – guarding against managerial overreach, protecting shareholder interests, and ensuring adherence to ethical and regulatory standards. On paper, they occupy a position of esteem within the boardroom hierarchy. In practice, however, many operate in a landscape constrained by subtle dependencies, entrenched hierarchies, and muted influence.

This paradox, the elevation of IDs as pillars of governance, juxtaposed with their frequent marginalisation, is the boardroom mirage of Indian

Wearing a crown does not make one a king, nor does a title make one truly independent.

corporate life. It is not merely a failure of policy; it reflects deeper systemic contradictions embedded in structure, culture, and power dynamics, which often limit the very autonomy these directors are meant to wield.

6.1.1 The Illusion of Presence

To the outside world, the mere presence of IDs on a board signals credibility. Proxy statements highlight their credentials, companies showcase compliance with listing norms, and press releases boast about board committee compositions. Yet, presence alone does not equate to influence or independence.

In many Indian companies, particularly those dominated by promoter families or concentrated shareholding, board meetings often resemble choreographed performances. Agendas are circulated with little room for genuine debate. Financial statements and risk disclosures are approved with a perfunctory discussion. Consensus is cultivated not through rigorous deliberation, but through implicit deference. The outcome is a governance theatre, complete with actors, scripts, and props, where the final decisions are often preordained, and the true power of independent oversight remains largely symbolic.

6.1.2 The Symbolism of Compliance

India's corporate governance reforms, particularly post-2000, have ushered in an era of formal accountability. Regulations now mandate the inclusion of IDs, the formation of audit and nomination committees, and the periodic evaluation of board performance. These frameworks are essential. Yet, over time, the focus has shifted from substance to symbolism – from *independence as oversight to independence as optics.*

The governance checklists are filled. The rules are followed. But the spirit of inquiry, dissent, and vigilance is often absent.

This is particularly evident in companies where IDs owe their appointments to promoters or are reappointed with their tacit approval. In such

A tethered watchdog cannot bite the hand that feeds it.

environments, the capacity for genuinely adversarial questioning or the rejection of management proposals is limited - not by law, but by informal dependencies that are economic, professional, and social in nature.

6.1.3 Dependence Disguised as Discretion

The dependence of so-called "independent" directors manifests in subtle but significant ways:

- **Information asymmetry** means directors must rely on management for key data, limiting their ability to independently verify claims or scrutinise financial assumptions.
- **Reappointment anxiety** influences how directors behave during their tenure, often nudging them toward consensus rather than conflict.
- **Cultural conformity** in hierarchical Indian settings discourages dissent, especially when the board is chaired by a powerful promoter or founder-Chief Executive Officer (CEO).
- **Networked entanglements** where directors serve on multiple boards of allied or interlinked companies create unwritten obligations of reciprocity and silence.

In this sense, independence becomes less a matter of structure and more a matter of will, of professional courage to speak, of moral clarity to act, and of institutional safeguards that enable dissent without penalty.

6.1.4 A Crisis of Authentic Oversight

The consequences of this mirage are not abstract. The absence of authentic oversight by IDs has been a critical enabling factor in some of India's most notorious corporate failures, from Satyam and Infrastructure Leasing & Financial Services Limited (IL&FS) to Dewan Housing Finance Limited (DHFL) and Yes Bank. In each case, boards were formally compliant, committees were constituted, and policies were in

The boardroom curtain may read "independent," but the puppeteer stands behind it.

place. Yet, systemic failures went unchallenged, risks were concealed, and red flags were ignored.

In these instances, the problem was not the absence of independence on paper *but the erosion of independence in practice.*

6.2. Origins of the Illusion: Structural and Cultural Roots

The illusion of boardroom autonomy in India is not a byproduct of individual incompetence or bad faith. Rather, it is the outcome of a complex interplay of structural dependencies and deeply embedded cultural patterns. IDs do not operate in a vacuum they function within a governance ecosystem shaped by concentrated ownership, regulatory inertia, economic incentives, and social norms that subtly discourage dissent.

Understanding this context is essential if one seeks to reform governance not just in letter but in spirit.

6.2.1 Concentrated Promoter Ownership: Control in Disguise

At the heart of Indian corporate governance lies the dominance of promoter-driven firms. Unlike dispersed ownership models seen in many developed markets, a significant portion of Indian listed companies are tightly controlled by founding families or individuals. According to data from the National Stock Exchange, over two-thirds of Nifty 500 companies have a single promoter group controlling more than 50% of equity.

This ownership structure fundamentally alters the board's power dynamic:

- Promoters **select** IDs, often with informal criteria prioritising loyalty or prior relationships.
- Promoters **influence** reappointments and committee memberships, creating implicit expectations of alignment.

Freedom on paper is bondage in practice.

- Promoters **control information flow**, deciding what data is shared with the board and when.

In this context, even a well-meaning ID may find themselves either co-opted or marginalised. Governance becomes less about oversight and more about endorsement a rubber stamp masquerading as a check and balance.

6.2.2 The Flawed Nomination Process: Gatekeepers Without Autonomy

Regulators have attempted to ring-fence board appointments through Nomination and Remuneration Committees (NRCs) composed largely of non-executive and IDs. Yet in promoter-controlled firms, these NRCs often lack genuine autonomy. They may technically vet candidates, but the shortlist is often preordained by those holding controlling stakes.

This creates a self-reinforcing cycle of dependence:

- IDs **owe their seat** to the promoter's support.
- Their reappointment after the first term is contingent on **continued goodwill**.
- Given the prestige and compensation of board positions, few risk open confrontation or voting against management.

Even among well-regarded professionals, there exists an unspoken understanding: defer, or disappear.

6.2.3 Economic Dependency and the Prestige Trap

Serving as an ID on the board of a major listed company carries economic and symbolic weight. Beyond sitting fees and commission, these roles enhance professional visibility and open doors to elite policy, academic, and business circles.

He who sits apart may still dance to the chairman's tune.

For retired bureaucrats, regulators, academics, or former CEOs, board seats offer:

- Financial post-retirement stability.
- Influence and networking opportunities.
- A platform to stay relevant in power circles.

This prestige trap often induces **risk-averse behaviour.** Directors hesitate to probe too deeply or challenge too strongly, fearing removal, reputational damage, or exclusion from future appointments. Unlike public sector boards, where appointments may be politically influenced, but less monetised private board appointments operate in a competitive market where reputational signalling and social networks matter deeply.

6.2.4 Cultural Norms: Harmony Over Dissent

Beneath these structural issues lies a subtler yet equally potent force: the cultural resistance to confrontation.

Indian boardrooms reflect broader societal values, **respect for hierarchy, aversion to conflict, and emphasis on consensus.** Dissent is often seen not as a sign of integrity but as a breach of decorum. IDs may self-censor out of a misplaced sense of collegiality or fear of "disrupting" board unity.

The promoter, especially if they are the founder or patriarch of a family business, often enjoys reverence akin to familial authority. This social capital makes it difficult, even inappropriate in some contexts, for IDs to question decisions, challenge assumptions, or vote against resolutions.

Even the board minutes, meant to be records of debate and decision, are often sanitised, stripping out disagreement and preserving the façade of unanimity.

A nameplate of independence cannot hide the shadow of allegiance.

6.2.5 Tokenism and Regulatory Formalism

Regulatory regimes such as the Securities Exchange Board of India (SEBI) Listing Obligations and Disclosure Requirements (LODR) have laid down clear guidelines on what constitutes an ID. These include:

- No pecuniary relationships.
- No close relatives in executive roles.
- No prior significant employment with the firm.

But these are static criteria, designed to prevent overt conflict of interest – not to ensure active independence in behaviour or judgment.

The reality is more insidious. Directors may be formally independent but remain behaviourally dependent due to:

- Prior indirect associations with promoters.
- Shared networks in industry, bureaucracy, or politics.
- Anticipation of future roles, favours, or patronage.

Thus, regulatory definitions succeed in eliminating only blatant conflicts while ignoring the pervasive soft dependencies that shape actual board conduct.

6.3. Regulatory Ambition vs. Ground Reality

India's corporate governance regime is, on paper, one of the most robust in the developing world. Inspired by global best practices and shaped by crises, scandals, and shareholder activism, the regulatory architecture around independent directorship has evolved significantly in the last two decades. From Clause 49 of the Listing Agreement to the Companies Act, 2013, and SEBI's LODR Regulations, the ambition is clear: to institutionalise accountability through a vigilant and independent board.

However, this ambition often collides with an inconvenient truth: governance, no matter how well-crafted in regulation, falters when divorced from real incentives, culture, and enforcement. The result is a widening chasm between compliance on paper and conduct in practice.

6.3.1 Clause 49 and the Birth of Independent Oversight

The seeds of regulatory intervention were planted in the early 2000s when the Confederation of Indian Industry (CII) recommended a Code of Corporate Governance. This led to the introduction of Clause 49 in the SEBI Listing Agreement in 2000, later revised in 2004 and 2014. Clause 49 mandated:

- A minimum number of IDs based on whether the Chairman is executive or non-executive.
- Formation of key committees (Audit, Nomination, and Remuneration) with a majority of IDs.
- Enhanced disclosures in annual reports regarding related-party transactions, risk management, and board evaluations.

This was a landmark shift, one that signalled India's intent to align with international governance norms. But over time, the spirit of Clause 49 gave way to its ritualisation. IDs were appointed to satisfy numerical thresholds, not to fulfil strategic oversight roles. Governance began to be measured in terms of checkboxes, not courage.

6.3.2 Companies Act, 2013: A Governance Milestone

The Companies Act, 2013, provided legislative teeth to corporate governance. It introduced:

- A formal definition of "ID".
- A mandatory code of conduct for IDs (Schedule IV).
- Rotation of auditors and enhanced board disclosures.
- Mandates on board diversity, director responsibilities, and vigil mechanisms.

Titles can be given; true independence must be earned.

It also required that IDs attend at least one board meeting a year without the presence of executive directors (a move to encourage uninfluenced discussion).

Despite these advances, **the gap between written rules and lived reality** persisted. While boards complied with the letter of the law, its intent was often diluted:

- Many companies rushed to appoint retired bureaucrats or industry veterans with minimal domain expertise but significant political or personal connections.
- Board evaluations, when conducted, often lacked honesty or third-party independence.
- Audit committees, meant to scrutinise internal controls, often rubber-stamped reports tabled by chief financial officers (CFO) with minimal interrogation.

6.3.3 SEBI's LODR and the Evolution of Board Accountability

In 2015, SEBI consolidated and strengthened governance norms through the LODR. The LODR Regulations codified requirements for:

- Disclosure of director relationships and remuneration.
- Enhanced audit committee independence.
- Role clarity for nomination and remuneration committees.
- Mandatory board and committee evaluations.

In 2017, the **Kotak Committee Report on Corporate Governance** further recommended increasing the minimum number of IDs, separating the roles of chairperson and CEO, and introducing stricter rules for related-party transactions.

SEBI adopted several of these recommendations. But again, many boards continued to operate in ways that fulfilled the form but **missed the intent**.

A silent director is often mistaken for a wise one.

6.3.4 The Compliance Conundrum: Performing Governance

Indian boardrooms today are caught in what governance experts call a "performance paradox" they perform governance in visible, reportable ways, while real oversight remains elusive.

- **Board minutes are stylised, not substantive**, often devoid of dissent or complex deliberations.
- **"Independent" audits are not always independent** especially when audit firms rely on long-standing relationships with company management.
- **Whistleblower mechanisms exist**, but few escalate concerns up to IDs due to fears of retaliation or inaction.

This leads to **governance as performance art:** annual reports with glossy governance disclosures, directors attending mandatory training sessions, and ESG frameworks copied from global templates, all while core decisions remain centralised in the hands of a few.

6.3.5 Why Regulation Alone Fails

The Indian regulatory approach, despite its rigor, often fails to consider behavioural incentives and informal power networks that undermine independence:

- Promoters still hold **control over appointments**, limiting director autonomy.
- Regulators are **reactive, not proactive,** intervening after crises rather than shaping conduct in real-time.
- Enforcement is **uneven,** with many companies facing no meaningful consequences for failing the spirit of governance.

Furthermore, the absence of personal liability for many failures of oversight leads to moral hazard. Even when IDs resign citing concerns, they are rarely investigated, debriefed, or held accountable for their tenure.

Independence is tested not in sunshine, but in scandal.

6.4. When Silence Speaks Louder: Passive Oversight in Crisis

In corporate governance, the true test of independence is not during normalcy but in moments of disruption. It is when the company is under pressure financially, legally, or ethically that IDs are expected to rise above affiliations and assert their fiduciary role. Yet, time and again, when India Inc. has faced existential crises, the silence of IDs has been deafening.

This is not just a matter of oversight failure; it reflects a deeper crisis of accountability. In many cases, IDs have either claimed ignorance, resigned quietly, or pointed fingers after the damage was done. The passive oversight during high-profile collapses has exposed the hollowness of the independence claim, raising unsettling questions: Were these directors unaware? Were they incapable? Or were they unwilling?

6.4.1 Satyam: A Wake-Up Call Ignored

The Satyam scandal (2009) remains one of the most iconic failures of boardroom vigilance in India. The company's chairman, Ramalinga Raju, admitted to inflating profits by over INR 7,000 crore. What made the scandal particularly galling was that the company had a **fully staffed, SEBI-compliant board** including prominent IDs, some with stellar academic and public service credentials.

Despite repeated financial irregularities, changes in auditing partners, and questionable related-party transactions (such as the proposed acquisition of Maytas Infra, a company owned by Raju's sons), **no alarm was raised** by the IDs. None publicly questioned the aggressive accounting practices or raised red flags during board meetings. They approved the Maytas deal just days before the fraud unravelled.

The excuse offered later that the promoters misled the board rings hollow. The role of an ID is precisely to question, to verify, and to remain sceptical, especially when red flags are abundant. **The silence of the Satyam board was not a lapse; it was complicity by omission.**

6.4.2 Infrastructure Leasing & Financial Services: The Danger of Deference

In 2018, IL&FS collapsed under a mountain of hidden debt exceeding INR 90,000 crore. The company's layered corporate structure, comprising hundreds of subsidiaries, obscured the true financial risk. Yet the audit committee and board, staffed with experienced professionals, raised no public concerns about the leverage or systemic exposure.

Despite credit downgrades, aggressive borrowing, and ballooning inter-company loans, the IDs did not intervene in a meaningful way. When regulators finally stepped in, many of these directors resigned or expressed "surprise" at the scale of the crisis.

The IL&FS saga revealed how **groupthink and deference to executive power** can paralyse oversight. Directors admitted to being misled by presentations and internal reports – but such reliance on management, without external verification, is precisely what independence is supposed to guard against.

6.4.3 DHFL, Yes Bank, and the Pattern of Passive Directors

The pattern repeats with alarming frequency:

- **DHFL:** Once a high-flying Non-Banking Financial Company, DHFL's promoters were accused of siphoning off thousands of crores through shell companies. IDs either failed to detect these red flags or failed to act upon them.
- **Yes Bank:** As founder Rana Kapoor pursued risky lending practices and concentrated exposures, the board, including IDs, remained largely silent. By the time the Reserve Bank of India intervened, the crisis had metastasised.

From selection to succession, independence is by invitation only.

In each of these cases, IDs were formally present. Board and committee meetings were held, and disclosures were filed. Yet, the actual exercise of governance was absent. Compliance served as a façade, masking a troubling passivity that allowed risk and misconduct to fester.

6.4.4 The Causes of Silence

The question is not merely, "Why did no one speak up?" but rather, "Why was speaking up made so difficult?" Several systemic factors contribute to this silence:

- **Power asymmetry:** In promoter-led companies, directors may feel disempowered, fearing backlash, legal entanglement, or social exclusion.
- **Limited information access:** Directors often rely solely on internal reports and CFO presentations, with little access to independent data or whistleblower channels.
- **Reputation risk:** Raising concerns during a crisis can jeopardise a director's standing, particularly if it results in resignation under duress or exposes them to legal scrutiny.
- **Absence of safe channels:** Unlike Western boards, which have established whistleblower mechanisms and independent investigative processes, Indian directors frequently lack institutional pathways to act autonomously.

Even regulators tend to act retrospectively, holding directors accountable only after a collapse, and rarely supporting dissenting voices in real time. This structural vacuum discourages proactive intervention and reinforces boardroom passivity.

6.4.5 The Ethical Dilemma: Resign or Reform?

When confronted with internal resistance, many IDs choose resignation. While this response is understandable, it is also deeply

A handpicked rebel rarely revolts.

problematic. Resignation may signal a moral stand, but without accompanying public explanation or formal dissent, it risks becoming mere abdication. Rarely do directors issue detailed resignation letters that outline governance concerns. Even less frequently are such concerns escalated to shareholders or regulators. In the absence of whistleblowing or dissenting records, resignation functions as an escape hatch rather than a corrective action.

Worse still, many of these directors continue to serve on other boards, facing little to no accountability for prior oversight failures. This lack of consequence perpetuates a culture of impunity and rotational complacency, undermining the very purpose of independent directorship.

6.5 Economic Dependence: The Golden Handcuffs of Honoraria

Although IDs are not employees, many remain financially tethered to the companies they serve. While their compensation rarely rivals that of executives, it often constitutes a significant portion of their income especially for retired bureaucrats, ex-bankers, academics, and professionals.

Honoraria, sitting fees, and performance-linked bonuses when aggregated across multiple board positions can approach executive-level remuneration. Even more subtly, lucrative post-board opportunities, such as advisory roles, legal retainers, or consulting contracts, frequently arise from companies where directors have cultivated goodwill by remaining "cooperative."

This creates a chilling effect. Directors who fear non-renewal, non-recommendation, or reputational backlash are unlikely to challenge promoters or management. The incentive to retain board positions often overrides the duty to dissent.

Moreover, board selection in India is rarely open or competitive. It is informal, opaque, and often driven by referrals or prior loyalty. This fosters what governance scholar M.K. Sharma terms "compliance

When the nomination is a gift, the conscience becomes a debt.

capital" a director's ability to be minimally disruptive while fulfilling formal obligations.

In such an ecosystem, economic independence is largely illusory. A director may not be on payroll, but they remain very much on a leash.

6.5.1 Informational Dependence: Seeing Through Management's Lens

Boards are expected to function as an oversight body. But in practice, they are often structurally starved of independent information. The flow of data, analysis, and insight comes almost exclusively from management, typically filtered through the CEO and CFO.

This means IDs must make decisions with limited context. Financial reports, internal audit summaries, risk dashboards, and performance metrics are all crafted by those being overseen. Even when external consultants or statutory auditors are involved, their reporting relationships often lie with executive management, not the board.

Several informational disadvantages arise:

- **Time Constraints:** Board meetings are brief and tightly scheduled, with dense agendas. Directors may have a few hours to review hundreds of pages of board papers.
- **Lack of Raw Data:** Directors rarely access the underlying data, relying instead on curated executive summaries.
- **Committee Bottlenecks:** Much of the critical work happens in subcommittees (audit, risk, nomination). But often these committees rely on the same management inputs, reinforcing the echo chamber.

In this environment, the independence of mind is stifled by dependence on the very people being monitored. Without direct access to frontline managers, whistleblowers, or external verifiers, IDs become consumers of a narrative not challengers of it.

A director's true leash lies in the lines of the appointment letter.

6.5.2 Psychological Dependence: Groupthink, Gratitude, and Deference

Beyond money and information lies perhaps the most potent force of all: psychological dependence. Directors are human. They are susceptible to the same biases, insecurities, and social dynamics that operate in any group.

Three key psychological traps erode independence:

- **Groupthink:** Directors may suppress doubts or reservations to maintain harmony. Dissent is uncomfortable, questioning a charismatic CEO or a promoter-founder risks alienation. It is easier to align than to oppose, especially when others remain silent.
- **Social Gratitude:** Many directors are appointed due to personal relationships, mentorships, or reputational goodwill. This fosters a sense of indebtedness or loyalty. In traditional Indian culture, the concept of "karz" (debt of gratitude) runs deep. Challenging someone who "gave you a seat at the table" is emotionally difficult.
- **Status Anxiety:** Board membership in India confers prestige—business-class travel, five-star meetings, and association with powerful names. Losing that position may harm one's self-image or professional stature. Thus, silence is often a self-preservation mechanism.

These psychological levers make it easy to conform, even for well-meaning directors. They turn boardrooms into places where discomfort is avoided, not confronted.

6.5.3 The Compounding Effect: A Culture of Quiet Compliance

When economic, informational, and psychological dependencies converge, they create a potent system of quiet compliance. Over time, this system normalises passivity, turning once-active professionals into cautious spectators.

If the seat is offered, the voice is borrowed.

A few characteristics of this culture:

- **Polite Abstention:** Directors abstain from controversial decisions rather than vote against them.
- **Coded Language:** Minutes of meetings record "deliberation" but avoid documenting dissent or disagreement.
- **Subtle Self-Censorship:** Directors know what not to ask. Over time, they ask less.

The dependence is not always deliberate. It is systemic, emergent, and self-reinforcing. Even directors who enter the boardroom with good intentions soon learn the unspoken rules of survival: don't challenge too hard, don't embarrass the promoters, and don't become the lone voice.

6.6. The Professionalization and Paradox of Independent Directorship

6.6.1 The Rise of the Professional Independent Director

India's regulatory framework allows an individual to serve as an ID on up to seven listed companies, or three if also serving as a whole-time director. Yet, even within these limits, some directors hold 10 to 15 board positions across listed, unlisted, and private companies.

While on paper this may signal experience and credibility, it often results in:

- **Time dilution:** Real governance requires deep engagement, pre-reading of materials, committee participation, and site visits. Spread thin across multiple entities, many directors rely on secretarial briefings and cursory reviews, limiting their ability to exercise meaningful oversight.
- **Domain disconnect:** A banking veteran may sit on the board of a pharma company. A retired bureaucrat may advise a fintech

startup. With little industry expertise and limited time, these directors are reduced to procedural monitors, unable to offer sectoral insight or challenge assumptions.

- **Tick-box involvement:** Attendance is maintained. Resolutions are approved. Minutes are signed. But the spirit of governance is lost, replaced by the rhythm of repetition.

This industrialisation of board service, turning governance into a portfolio career, has diluted the gravitas of independent directorship. The role has shifted from watchdog to resume-builder, from fiduciary to figurehead.

6.6.2 The Comfort of Familiar Names

Promoters, institutional investors, and search consultants often prefer known names for board appointments. These individuals bring with them a reputation premium trusted by regulators, respected by peers, and unlikely to rock the boat.

However, this leads to "governance homogeneity": the same worldviews, risk appetites, and leadership styles replicated across companies. It is not diversity of thought, but a network of safe bets, bound together by reputation, access, and mutual deference.

As a result:

- Board debates are **predictable** and often superficial.
- Dissent is rare, and **groupthink** becomes the norm.
- **Accountability** diffuses; everyone is responsible, so no one truly is.

This entrenched network model, while stable, is resistant to disruption. New voices struggle to enter. Young professionals, women, technologists, or regional experts are often bypassed in favour of those already "in the circuit."

When tenure depends on favor, truth is spoken in whispers.

6.6.3 The Resignation Cycle: Escape Without Explanation

When a scandal erupts, many IDs resign pre-emptively, citing "personal reasons" or "time constraints." Rarely do they submit detailed resignation letters highlighting governance concerns, even when red flags were evident.

This pattern is problematic:

- **Lack of disclosure:** Shareholders and regulators are left in the dark. Why did the director resign? What concerns were raised? What went unheeded?
- **No legal consequence:** Unless wilful negligence or fraud is proven, most directors escape with no penalty. Their reputations remain largely intact, and they soon reappear elsewhere.
- **Reputation over responsibility:** In India's business culture, association with failure is often seen as more damaging than failing to prevent it. Directors protect their personal brands by distancing themselves regardless of their role in enabling or ignoring the crisis.

This resignation cycle reinforces the absence of accountability. It rewards silence over vigilance and exit over engagement.

6.6.4 Regulatory Blind Spots

While SEBI and the Companies Act have introduced limits and disclosure norms, enforcement remains weak:

- Board evaluations are often self-conducted, templated, and lack transparency.
- Diversity norms have increased token representation, but not cognitive heterogeneity.
- Fit-and-proper criteria are narrowly defined and rarely disqualify serial underperformers.

No director can serve two masters: duty and deference.

Moreover, the absence of a centralised performance record for IDs means that past lapses are not flagged in future appointments. In the absence of a formal reputation system or blacklist, poor oversight is forgotten, not penalised.

6.6.5 Toward a Culture of Stewardship, Not Rotation

Reforming the rotational illusion requires a mindset shift from **"appointment as honour" to "stewardship as duty."** Steps could include:

- **Cap board tenures by sector:** Limit how many boards one can serve within the same industry to avoid echo chambers.
- **Mandatory disclosure of engagement hours:** Directors should disclose how much time they spent on each board meeting, site visits, and committee work.
- **Track record visibility:** Create a publicly accessible, regulator-maintained database of director performance, board meeting attendance, resignations, and company outcomes.
- **Rotational diversity:** Encourage lateral entry academics, entrepreneurs, young professionals, and domain specialists, not just retired bureaucrats or auditors.
- **Exit interviews by regulators:** Mandate regulatory exit interviews or whistleblowing disclosures when IDs resign before term completion.

Ultimately, the illusion of independence cannot be broken by replacing one name with another from the same club. It must be dismantled by reconstructing the role itself, empowering directors with time, tools, and teeth.

6.7. The Regulatory Mirage: SEBI, MCA, and the Limits of Formal Compliance

India's corporate governance landscape appears remarkably well-regulated on paper. The SEBI, Ministry of Corporate Affairs (MCA), and

The anchor of independence cannot hold in a board built on favors.

various provisions under the Companies Act, 2013 have together developed a comprehensive compliance framework. Listed companies are required to constitute mandatory committees, uphold board composition norms, and disclose director appointments, resignations, and evaluations.

However, beneath this structured regime lies a troubling paradox: increased regulation has not resulted in increased independence. Despite frequent circulars, tightening norms, and enhanced reporting, IDs continue to function in dependent, compliant, and frequently compromised ways. **The system obeys the letter of the law while subverting its spirit.**

This is the regulatory mirage, a landscape where governance appears credible from afar but collapses upon closer inspection.

6.7.1 Securities Exchange Board of India's Rulebook: Granular but Gameable

SEBI's LODR regulations mandate that at least 50% of the board in listed companies must be non-executive, and a third must be independent. Additionally, key committees (Audit, Nomination & Remuneration, Stakeholders Relationship, and Risk) must be chaired or substantially comprised of IDs.

These are strong provisions, but three structural flaws undermine their impact:

- **Form over substance:** Directors are "independent" by designation, but their conduct remains subordinate. Compliance is reduced to checklists, committee formation, meeting frequency, disclosures, and not the quality of deliberation or dissent.
- **Low enforcement risk:** SEBI has rarely taken aggressive punitive action against IDs, except in cases of gross negligence or fraud. Directors accused of governance failures often resign and re-emerge elsewhere, untouched by regulatory memory.

Silence is the first betrayal of independence.

- **Boilerplate disclosures:** Corporate governance reports are replete with template language, vague board evaluation statements, and self-congratulatory narratives. Independent assessments are rarely mandated, and peer evaluations are often mutual endorsements.

The result is a compliance culture that is technically sound, but behaviourally hollow.

6.7.2 Ministry of Corporate Affairs' Oversight: Ambitious Mandates, Anaemic Execution

The MCA has made several attempts to enhance boardroom independence through the Companies Act, 2013. These include:

- Fixed terms and cooling-off periods for IDs.
- Mandatory registration of IDs on a database.
- Formal responsibility for directors in cases of fraud or wilful misconduct.

However, practical enforcement remains a challenge:

- **Databank disconnect:** The online repository of eligible IDs has become more of a tick-box portal than a robust governance pipeline. Promoters rarely use it to scout fresh talent, preferring informal networks and referrals.
- **No accountability for appointments:** Board nomination processes are rarely transparent, or merit based. The fit-and-proper criteria are minimal, and disqualification is difficult unless proven wrongdoing occurs.
- **Legal complexity, cultural resistance:** Many directors resist active involvement out of fear of litigation. Ironically, regulation intended to empower directors has also deterred them with many unwilling to accept directorships due to rising legal liabilities without corresponding decision-making authority.

A nod in the boardroom may echo louder than a vote.

6.7.3 The Myth of Transparency

Indian companies have vastly expanded their disclosures, but disclosure is not the same as transparency. The illusion persists because of:

- **Information overload:** Annual reports run into hundreds of pages, filled with repetitive jargon, complex financials, and generic boilerplate. True red flags are often buried under verbose legalese.
- **Sanitised minutes and committee reports:** Board meeting minutes rarely reflect the depth of debate. Dissent, if any, is expunged. Committee reports are structured to highlight compliance, not challenge.
- **Regulatory passivity:** Despite years of high-profile governance failures from Satyam to IL&FS to NSE rarely have IDs been held meaningfully accountable. Penalties are light, and often symbolic.

This gives rise to "compliance theatre" where governance processes are enacted, but their purpose is hollowed out.

6.7.4 Why Regulation Alone Fails

The core issue is that regulation target's structure, not behaviour. It can mandate board composition, meeting frequency, and disclosure templates. But it cannot instil:

Moral Courage to challenge dominant narratives.

- Curiosity to probe deeper into management assumptions.
- Critical Distance from promoter influence.

Furthermore, regulators face political and industrial pressures. Aggressively enforcing director accountability may disincentivise board participation altogether reducing the available talent pool and stalling corporate growth. In this balancing act, regulation is often compromised by pragmatism.

Not questioning is not neutrality, it is complicity.

6.7.5 The Path Forward: Behavioral Governance and Enabling Enforcement

To shift from regulatory mirage to meaningful reform, India needs a multi-pronged approach:

- **Behavioral audits:** Beyond structural audits, conduct behavioural assessments of boards tracking actual dissent, engagement levels, and director effectiveness through anonymised third-party evaluations.
- **Digital governance dashboards:** Mandate companies to publish interactive dashboards showing real-time governance metrics – committee attendance, voting records, director tenure history, and meeting disclosures.
- **Graduated accountability:** Introduce graded penalties for director lapses ranging from mandatory retraining to disbarment linked to frequency and severity of governance breaches.
- **Incentivise disclosure of dissent:** Create safe harbour provisions for directors who raise red flags or submit dissenting notes in board meetings. Protecting such behaviour can normalise vigilance over silence.
- **Public governance scores:** Establish an independent rating agency that evaluates board effectiveness, updated annually, similar to credit ratings, offering stakeholders a clear view of governance quality.

6.8. Inside the Committee Room: The Hollowing Out of Oversight

The board committee system in Indian corporate governance was envisioned as the nerve centre of scrutiny and supervision. Specialised committees, Audit, Nomination & Remuneration, Risk Management, Mandates Corporate Social Responsibility (CSR), and Stakeholders' Grievance were designed to go beyond the broad purview of full board meetings and facilitate granular, critical, and independent evaluations of management decisions.

Conscience that sleeps through meetings wakes in inquiry.

However, the committee room today is not a bastion of oversight; more often, it is a ritualistic chamber, where decisions are ratified rather than debated. IDs who are supposed to lead these committees are frequently reduced to ceremonial participants, constrained by information asymmetry, time scarcity, and a subtle but powerful pressure to conform.

What was intended to be the engine of governance has, in many companies, been hollowed out to a shell of formality.

6.8.1 The Audit Committee: Watchdog or Witness?

The Audit Committee is arguably the most powerful sub-body of a board tasked with overseeing financial reporting, risk exposure, statutory compliance, and interactions with internal and external auditors. SEBI mandates that two-thirds of its members be IDs.

Yet, several structural issues undermine its effectiveness:

- **Dependence on management for information:** Committee members often receive curated financial data, with little ability to cross-verify. Red flags can be masked through technical complexity or sheer volume of paperwork.
- **Superficial engagement with auditors:** Auditors are required to report to the committee, but in practice, they maintain close working ties with company CFOs. IDs may lack the financial depth or courage to challenge audit reports, especially if the tone is muted or caveated.
- **Time-starved agendas:** Meetings are rushed, often bundled with other committee sittings. Key discussions such as related-party transactions or internal audit findings are buried under voluminous agenda books, reducing oversight to optics.

In high-profile failures such as IL&FS or DHFL, audit committees existed, met regularly, and documented their work. Yet, they either missed or ignored the signs calling into question whether structure without substance has any value at all.

The quietest seat is often the most dangerous.

6.8.2 Nomination and Remuneration Committee: The Clubhouse of Continuity

This committee is meant to ensure that board appointments and executive pay align with shareholder interests and corporate performance. But in many Indian companies, the NRC has become the inner circle that perpetuates board homogeneity:

- **Opaque appointment processes:** Nomination decisions are often driven by the chairperson or promoter, rubber-stamped by the committee. Fresh perspectives, sectoral diversity, or cognitive heterodoxy are rarely prioritised.
- **Lax performance evaluations:** Annual assessments of directors are frequently self-filled or peer-reviewed without critical rigor. Underperforming directors are rarely rotated out, and exit interviews are practically non-existent.
- **Compensation disconnect:** Executive pay, especially in promoter-driven firms, remains generous even when company performance falters. The NRC, instead of acting as a gatekeeper, often legitimises excess by benchmarking against handpicked peers.

This leads to a dual erosion of board quality and moral authority.

6.8.3 Risk Committees and CSR Panels: Functionally Fragile, Symbolically Safe

Other statutory committees fare no better.

- Risk Management Committees often suffer from vague mandates, outdated risk registers, and generic discussions. In the age of cyber-attacks, climate volatility, and geopolitical uncertainty, these committees need to be forward-looking and technically competent. Instead, they often default to compliance-mode reviews.
- CSR Committees, especially in large family-controlled firms, become vehicles for philanthropic branding rather than stakeholder

accountability. Decisions on fund allocations are made with limited community feedback or impact metrics.

In both cases, IDs while technically in charge are not equipped with data, expertise, or institutional support to influence outcomes meaningfully.

6.8.4 Committee Fatigue and Informal Workarounds

The burden of committee work is unevenly distributed. A few over-engaged IDs may sit on multiple committees across different firms, leading to what can be called "oversight fatigue."

Symptoms include:

- Attending back-to-back meetings without deep preparation.
- Signing off on minutes without fully understanding their implications.
- Relying on company secretaries or CFO briefings in place of independent judgment.

Compounding this, informal governance structures such as offline discussions, promoter briefings, or WhatsApp-based consensus often pre-empt committee deliberation. What appears in the official minutes is a mere shadow of where the real decisions were made.

6.8.5 Reforming the Committee System: From Ritual to Relevance

Reinvigorating the committee system requires governance by design structural, procedural, and cultural reform:

- **Mandatory disclosures of dissent:** Committee minutes should document key questions raised, not just resolutions passed. Directors who dissent should be named and protected, not neutralised.

A director who watches the storm without warning is part of the wreck.

- **Third-party review of key committees:** Regulatory bodies or shareholder forums should be allowed to commission independent audits of committee performance, especially in critical or distressed companies.
- **Expertise-based committee composition:** Move beyond independence to competence. For instance, risk committees should include experts in cyber, climate, or geopolitical risks not just legacy directors.
- **Time commitments and rotation norms:** Cap the number of committee memberships per director. Encourage fresh appointments every 3–5 years to avoid entrenchment and fatigue.
- **Committee-level key performance indicators:** Tie committee effectiveness to measurable performance indicators, such as action taken on red flags, number of agenda items independently initiated, or stakeholder feedback.

6.9 The Culture of Consensus: Harmony over Honesty

Indian corporate culture often emphasises hierarchy, harmony, and face-saving over confrontation, challenge, and debate. In such a setting:

- **Questioning is viewed as disloyalty.** Directors who raise difficult questions may be perceived as disruptive, "not a team player," or worse, antagonistic to the promoter's vision.
- **Smooth meetings are praised.** Board performance is judged not by the quality of deliberation but by the speed and consensus of decision-making. Disagreements are treated as inefficiencies.
- **The illusion of unanimity is cultivated**. Dissenting voices are subtly ignored, misrepresented in minutes, or discouraged in advance through informal cues.

The illusion of oversight blinds the overseer.

This "groupthink" creates a normative pressure to agree, where directors self-censor to maintain their relevance or avoid isolation.

6.9.1 Social Bonds and the Fear of Isolation

Board members, especially in tightly knit business communities, often operate in circles of interpersonal familiarity and professional reciprocity. Many IDs are former bureaucrats, retired executives, consultants, or legal professionals with overlapping social ties to promoters and management.

This creates powerful psychological anchors:

- **Fear of social ostracism:** Going against the tide can damage future board opportunities, reputational capital, or invitations to elite governance circles.
- **Reciprocal expectations:** When directors are appointed through referrals, the invisible expectation is not to challenge too much. Even when no explicit quid pro quo exists, the perception of "owing" someone clouds judgment.
- **Dependency on goodwill:** Many IDs rely on promoters for reappointment, compensation decisions, or introductions to other boards—making them less likely to rock the boat.

The result is a polite paralysis where directors choose deference over duty and belonging over bravery.

6.9.2 The Professional Cost of Speaking Up

For an ID, dissent carries tangible risks:

- **Non-renewal of tenure**: Many directors who assert independence find themselves quietly dropped at the end of their first term, with vague reasons such as "strategic restructuring" or "board rotation."

To stay seated in silence is to stand against duty.

- **Loss of board opportunities:** The ecosystem is small, and word travels fast. A director labelled as "troublesome" or "activist" may find it hard to secure new appointments, especially in promoter-led firms.
- **Legal and reputational exposure:** Ironically, the more independent a director is raising red flags or documenting dissent the greater their liability becomes when things go wrong. Dissenters can be left holding the bag while the rest of the board claims collective ignorance.

These dynamics create what behavioural economists call "rational passivity": individuals choose inaction not because they are indifferent, but because the costs of action are too high.

6.9.3 The Psychology of Conformity and Silence

Psychological research, from the Asch conformity experiments to the Abilene paradox, has shown that individuals in group settings often:

- Conform to dominant views even when they privately disagree.
- Suppress their concerns if no one else raises them.
- Misinterpret silence as consensus, reinforcing a self-fulfilling cycle.

In the Indian boardroom, this is exacerbated by:

- **Information asymmetry:** IDs often receive filtered data, making it harder to confidently question decisions.
- **Meeting dynamics:** Tight agendas, scripted presentations, and dominant personalities (often promoters or long-serving executives) discourage spontaneous or disruptive inquiry.
- **Lack of peer support:** Few directors will openly back a dissenting colleague, leaving the lone challenger exposed and demoralised.

He who avoids the truth at the table will face it in court.

These factors do not just silence dissent they prevent it from forming in the first place.

6.9.4 Creating a Culture of Constructive Dissent

True independence can only flourish in environments where dissent is not punished but valued where challenge is seen as a sign of commitment, not conflict. This requires:

- **Chairperson-led psychological safety:** Board chairs must explicitly encourage open debate, affirm the legitimacy of differing views, and protect dissenting directors from marginalization.
- **Anonymous feedback loops:** Introduce confidential pre-meeting surveys or digital feedback tools where directors can flag concerns without fear of identification.
- **Red team mechanisms:** Designate a rotating "devil's advocate" role in key discussions to institutionalise contrarian thinking.
- **Dissent documentation protocols:** Mandate that all significant questions, concerns, or dissenting views raised in board meetings be captured in the minutes, along with responses.
- **Training in courageous governance:** Directors should be offered workshops not just in financial or legal acumen but in navigating power, speaking up, and ethical risk-taking.

6.10. Resignations That Speak: When Stepping Down is the Only Voice Left

In a governance culture where meaningful dissent is muted, deliberation is stifled, and oversight is hollowed out, resignation has emerged as the final form of resistance available to an ID.

Over the past decade, India has witnessed a series of high-profile resignations from IDs across listed companies, sometimes under dramatic circumstances, sometimes in quiet protest. These resignations, when accompanied by candid disclosures, offer a rare glimpse into the fractures, frustrations, and failures that simmer beneath the surface of boardroom consensus.

This section explores how resignation has become both an indictment and an appeal, an act that simultaneously signals systemic rot and seeks institutional redemption.

6.10.1 The Resignation as Dissent: A Voice When All Else Fails

While the Companies Act, SEBI's LODR regulations, and governance codes provide mechanisms for board-level escalation, internal pushback is rarely welcomed, especially when it challenges promoter interests or executive decisions.

For many IDs, the only viable way to register serious disagreement is by resigning and making their reasons public.

Some notable examples include:

- 2018: S. Gurumurthy and Ashok Chawla resigned from Yes Bank's board, reportedly due to governance concerns and regulatory friction.
- 2019: Pankaj Vaish and Bharat Doshi quit the IL&FS board, with their departure following exposure of systemic failure and alleged misgovernance.
- 2020–2022: A wave of resignations across firms like Zee, Dish TV, and Future Retail, citing lack of access to information, disagreement with management practices, or serious concerns about financial disclosures.

In many such cases, resignation letters became governance documents in themselves, conveying what minutes did not, and alerting regulators and investors to the dysfunction within.

Forms are filled, boxes are ticked, and governance is mimed.

6.10.2 Systemic Patterns Behind Resignations

A close review of public filings and resignation letters reveals a set of recurring themes:

- **Inadequate access to information:** Directors resign when they feel they are being kept in the dark on financials, related-party transactions, legal risks, or key business decisions.
- **Marginalisation in decision-making:** Some resign because their role has been reduced to ceremonial approval without real deliberation or influence.
- **Disagreements over strategy or ethics:** Others step down when the company pursues aggressive or questionable strategies such as debt-laden acquisitions, regulatory evasion, or misleading disclosures.
- **Lack of response to governance flags**: In several cases, directors cited those repeated concerns raised during meetings were not acted upon leaving them with no option but to exit.

These resignations highlight a painful irony: IDs are asked to take accountability without being given authority.

6.10.3 Regulatory Inertia and the Problem of Disclosure

Although SEBI mandates that listed companies disclose detailed reasons for director resignations, many such filings are deliberately vague. Common phrases include:

- “Personal reasons”
- “Pre-occupation with other commitments”
- “Desire to pursue other interests”

This opacity is often strategic companies seek to avoid triggering investor panic or regulatory scrutiny. But it also robs the market of crucial transparency and diminishes the signalling power of a director’s departure.

An audit trail grows cold under a warm chair.

More troubling is the lack of follow-up by regulatory bodies. Even when IDs cite serious governance concerns, there is no assurance of investigation or redress unless media or public pressure is applied.

6.10.4 The Emotional and Professional Burden of Exit

Resigning is rarely a casual decision. For many IDs, especially those with long-standing ties to the organisation or sector, it is a deeply personal act of protest and self-preservation.

The emotional toll includes:

- Guilt and frustration at being unable to effect change from within.
- Fear of reputational backlash, especially if the resignation is interpreted as weakness or disloyalty.
- Isolation from peers, who may distance themselves to avoid controversy.

Yet, for many, resignation is also a reaffirmation of ethical boundaries and professional integrity. It is the final assertion of independence when silence can no longer be maintained without complicity.

6.10.5 Resignation as Reform Catalyst

Paradoxically, resignations when made thoughtfully and publicly can be catalysts for governance reform:

- They force companies to respond to investor and media queries.
- They alert regulators to systemic issues.
- They embolden other directors to reconsider their roles and responsibilities.
- They raise awareness among institutional investors about risks that are not always visible in financial statements.

Resignations, then, are not mere exits. They are ethical statements—often more powerful than votes cast within the boardroom.

Disclosure is not transparency when light is selectively cast.

6.11. The Legal Labyrinth: Responsibility Without Power

In India's evolving corporate governance regime, IDs are entrusted with a critical fiduciary role. They are expected to uphold the interests of minority shareholders, ensure compliance, guard against misgovernance, and steer corporations toward ethical and sustainable practices.

Yet paradoxically, while the law assigns them vast responsibilities, it often fails to equip them with commensurate powers or protections. This imbalance creates what many practitioners refer to as the "legal labyrinth", a system where IDs can be held accountable for failures over which they had minimal real influence.

This section dissects the legal landscape governing IDs in India, exposing the structural contradictions that make the position both indispensable and untenable.

6.11.1 Expanding Legal Duties: The Burden of Oversight

Over the last two decades, successive reforms from Clause 49 of the Listing Agreement to the Companies Act, 2013, and SEBI's LODR Regulations have significantly expanded the statutory obligations of IDs. These include:

- Ensuring the integrity of financial controls and risk management systems.
- Overseeing related party transactions and scrutinising corporate disclosures.
- Participating in key board committees (Audit, Nomination & Remuneration, Risk).
- Acting as a gatekeeper for corporate ethics and stakeholder fairness.

Section 149(12) of the Companies Act 2013 holds IDs liable for acts of omission or commission committed with their knowledge, consent, or lack of due diligence. This introduces a "vigilant gatekeeper" standard, which effectively demands proactive questioning and continual awareness.

Title demands recognition; autonomy demands courage.

However, the practical authority to enforce or influence many of these areas remains limited, particularly in promoter-dominated or opaque companies.

6.11.2 Asymmetry of Power: Expectations Without Control

Despite being tasked with oversight, IDs:

- Do not appoint the management.
- Lack direct access to internal operational data unless filtered through the executive team.
- Rely on curated agendas, sanitised reports, and time-constrained meetings for forming their views.
- Cannot unilaterally compel investigations or request forensic audits without board consensus.

This creates a dangerous gap: the law assumes control that the boardroom does not confer. When issues like financial fraud, ESG failures, or regulatory non-compliance arise, IDs may be hauled up by enforcement agencies or courts, even when they were systematically kept in the dark.

The risk is not theoretical. In several high-profile corporate collapses (e.g., IL&FS, DHFL, Fortis), IDs faced regulatory action, media scrutiny, and reputational damage, despite not being part of daily decision-making.

6.11.3 Judicial and Regulatory Trends: Strict Scrutiny, Sparse Support

The Indian judiciary and regulators have sent mixed signals regarding the liability of IDs:

- Courts have occasionally quashed charges against IDs when a lack of knowledge or direct involvement could be proven.
- SEBI and SFIO have issued guidance on the exemption for IDs not involved in fraudulent activity.

Fiduciary duty demands adherence; boardroom dynamics demand navigation.

Yet, in practice, enforcement agencies often adopt a "dragnet approach", issuing notices to all directors, regardless of their specific role or level of access. This results in:

- Pre-emptive resignations from boards under stress.
- Legal battles that outlast the director's term or career.
- Deterrence of credible professionals from accepting board positions, particularly in complex or high-risk companies.

6.11.4 The Chilling Effect: Risk Aversion Over Rigour

Faced with growing legal exposure and limited means to shape outcomes, many IDs adopt a strategy of cautious disengagement:

- Avoiding probing questions that may expose them to knowledge-based liability.
- Relying heavily on legal compliance certificates and management assurances.
- Preferring cosmetic diligence checklists and formal approvals over substantive governance.

This chilling effect undermines the very purpose of the ID: instead of acting as a bulwark against misgovernance, they become passive endorsers of executive will, be more focused on self-protection than institutional correction.

6.11.5 Reforming the Liability Framework

If independence is to mean more than ceremonial participation, India's legal regime must be rebalanced to offer clarity, protection, and enabling authority. Potential reforms include:

- **Tiered liability model:** Differentiate responsibility based on level of access, involvement, and committee membership avoiding one-size-fits-all enforcement.

Strategic input demands insight; organizational influence demands independence.

- **Safe harbour provisions:** Extend protection to directors who can demonstrate reasonable reliance on professional advice, or who formally recorded dissent.
- **Pre-litigation consultation mechanism:** Require regulators to consult with IDs before initiating criminal or quasi-criminal action, except in cases of wilful misconduct.
- **Regulatory exoneration window:** Allow ex-directors to proactively seek clearance from SEBI or MCA post-resignation, especially in stressed or controversial companies.
- **Mandatory indemnity and D&O insurance:** Ensure companies provide robust legal indemnity and directors' & officers' liability insurance, with public disclosure of coverage limits.

6.12. Reimagining Independence: Toward a Culture of Courage and Competence

The role of the ID in India today is defined more by aspiration than actualisation. While the law paints them as sentinels of shareholder interest, ethical integrity, and governance excellence, the reality is frequently one of marginalisation, manipulation, and muted influence.

The promise of independence remains largely unfulfilled, not for want of talent, but for lack of systemic enablement.

Yet, to give up on the concept would be to cede the very idea of accountable capitalism. This final section offers a pathway forward, one that reimagines independence not just as a legal designation, but as a culture of courage, clarity, and competence.

6.12.1 From Passive Oversight to Active Engagement

For IDs to become agents of meaningful oversight, their role must shift from ceremonial observers to strategic challengers. This requires:

- Early and substantive engagement in matters of strategy, risk, and capital allocation, not just compliance or crisis response.

Board deliberation demands engagement; stakeholder protection demands independence.

- In-depth understanding of the business model, key performance levers, and stakeholder impact.
- A commitment to asking uncomfortable questions, even at the cost of personal relationships or reputational convenience.

Active engagement does not mean antagonism; it means constructive challenge, informed scepticism, and a willingness to dissent when necessary.

6.12.2 Institutionalising Courage in Governance Culture

Courage cannot be legislated. It must be institutionalised through board culture, selection norms, and incentives.

- Boards must welcome intellectual diversity and contrarian voices, resisting the temptation of groupthink or harmony for its own sake.
- The nomination process for IDs must be re-engineered to prioritise integrity, independence of thought, and public interest credentials over convenience, connections, or tokenism.
- Chairs of the board and key committees should be trained and mandated to create space for dissent, allocate time for strategic dialogue, and protect directors who raise red flags.

As long as independence remains unwelcome in spirit, no statutory definition will make it real.

6.12.3 Competence as the Foundation of Independence

True independence is not just about freedom from conflicts; it is about the capacity to govern with insight and authority.

- Directors must invest in continuous learning across domains like cybersecurity, ESG, forensic accounting, emerging technologies, and regulatory evolution.

Voice in the boardroom demands persistence; true guidance demands authority.

- Board evaluations should assess not just attendance and etiquette, but depth of contribution, analytical rigour, and ethical leadership.
- Mentorship programs for first-time directors, peer reviews, and cross-industry exposure can elevate the collective board IQ.

Competence breeds confidence, and confident directors are more likely to act independently, even in adverse environments.

6.12.4 Enabling Ecosystems: The Role of Regulators and Investors

Transforming boardroom independence requires multi-stakeholder effort.

- Regulators must enforce independence criteria without delay, enhance disclosure norms, and hold chairs accountable for board functioning, not just procedural compliance.
- Institutional investors must actively vote on director appointments, assess board effectiveness, and engage in stewardship dialogues.
- Professional associations (like the Institute of Chartered Accountants of India, Institute of Company Secretaries of India, and ID databanks) must move beyond certification toward capacity building, case-based education, and ethical leadership development.

The system must evolve from one that appoints IDs as a checkbox to one that equips and empowers them as custodians of public trust.

6.12.5 Independence as a Mindset, not a Mandate

Ultimately, independence is not a structural designation, but a personal and professional mindset.

An ID is not defined by who appoints them, but by how they think, speak, and act with integrity, curiosity, and courage.

True independence demands conviction; illusion demands compliance.

They do not merely safeguard balance sheets; they safeguard the soul of the corporation—ensuring that decisions made today stand up to scrutiny tomorrow.

Independence is not easy. It is not always safe. But it is essential for resilient companies, fair markets, and a healthy democracy.

Conclusion: From Illusion to Intention

The time has come to stop mistaking legal compliance for governance excellence, or titles for integrity. The illusion of autonomy must give way to intentional architecture, one where independence is built into the DNA of boards, not stapled on through appointments.

"Independent by Title, Dependent by Design" must cease to be the diagnosis. It must become a cautionary tale that drives reform.

Because in the end, corporate governance is not about ticking boxes. It is about asking the right questions, at the right time, by the right people with the courage to act when the answers fall short.

India's boardrooms do not need more IDs by name.

They need more IDs by nature.

"Titles can be given, but true independence must be earned - and in boardrooms where allegiance outweighs accountability, the illusion of autonomy becomes a silent architect of failure. It is only when Independent Directors summon the courage to act beyond designations that governance is transformed from a facade into a fortress."

CHAPTER 7

Stewards of Sustainability: The Expanding Fiduciary Duty of Independent Directors

"Independent directors are no longer watchdogs; they are guardians of the planet and people."

7.1 Introduction: A Turning Point in Governance

We live at a pivotal moment in corporate **history, a time when the rules of business, governance, and accountability are being rewritten**. Climate change, biodiversity loss, rising inequality, social unrest, cyber-ethics, and governance failures are no longer isolated issues. They are interlinked systemic risks that threaten economic stability, corporate resilience, and societal trust.

What was once considered external to business operations, environmental degradation, social justice, and ethical conduct is now central to how corporations are assessed, valued, and governed. Across sectors and geographies, corporations are facing unprecedented scrutiny from regulators, investors, employees, consumers, media, and even future generations. Stakeholder expectations have evolved, **demanding greater**

The board that ignores the earth soon finds the ground shifting beneath it.

transparency, long-term thinking, and moral leadership from those at the helm of decision-making.

At the heart of this transformation lies the rise of **Environmental, Social, and Governance (ESG)** as a cornerstone of corporate purpose and performance. ESG is no longer a peripheral compliance matter or an investor-driven checkbox exercise. It is a strategic imperative **that influences capital access, customer trust, talent retention, risk management, and brand equity**.

In India, as in other emerging economies, this turning point is even more profound. On the one hand, the country is undergoing rapid economic transformation. On the other hand, it faces acute environmental vulnerabilities, rising social disparities, and complex governance challenges. This makes the role of corporate governance not just relevant but existential. Boards, especially **Independent Directors (IDs)**, are being held to a higher standard not only to oversee financial performance but to safeguard the social and environmental license to operate.

Traditionally, IDs have been viewed as custodians of procedural compliance, neutral actors tasked with ensuring that management adheres to the rules. Their fiduciary responsibilities have been largely defined in legalistic terms: **duty of care, duty of loyalty, and duty of diligence**. These concepts, while foundational, are no longer sufficient in a world where stakeholder capitalism and planetary boundaries redefine the scope of corporate obligations.

The ID of the 21st century must evolve beyond passive compliance and become an **active steward of sustainability**. This role requires a shift in mindset, skillset, and engagement. From sitting quietly in audit committees to probing ESG risks in climate strategy, from signing off on statutory disclosures to scrutinising green claims and human capital metrics, the ID must transform into a vigilant advocate of integrated thinking and long-term value creation.

In this context, **fiduciary duty is undergoing a quiet but significant expansion**. The emphasis is no longer solely on protecting shareholder

Sustainability isn't a footnote it's the foreword to future profits.

wealth but on preserving societal trust and ecological resilience. This is not merely a moral shift; it is a governance imperative. Regulators like Securities Exchange Board of India (SEBI), institutional investors, proxy advisory firms, and rating agencies are converging on a common expectation: that corporate boards will anchor sustainability at the highest level of decision-making, and that IDs will champion this cause with integrity and insight.

This section examines this crucial inflexion point in governance where **ESG principles meet boardroom responsibility**. It seeks to unpack how the role of IDs is being reshaped by ESG dynamics, especially in the Indian regulatory and socio-economic context. Drawing on legal analysis, global benchmarks, policy shifts, and case studies, it offers a roadmap for IDs to rise to this challenge.

It argues that this transformation is not only desirable it is necessary. The survival of corporations, the stability of markets, and the sustainability of our planet may well depend on how IDs interpret and enact their fiduciary duty in the age of ESG.

7.2. Independent Directors and the New Governance Ethic

The traditional view of IDs has centred on procedural oversight ensuring compliance with legal mandates, financial propriety, and protection of minority shareholders. They were expected to act as neutral arbitrators, bringing balance to management decisions and checking potential abuse of power by promoters or executives. However, in the face of today's interconnected risks, this **narrow, compliance-driven model of independence is no longer adequate**.

The **governance ethic** is changing. IDs are being called upon not just to ask whether a decision is legal or profitable, but whether it is **responsible, sustainable, and just**. This shift reflects a broader reimagining of corporate purpose from shareholder primacy to stakeholder capitalism. Under this new paradigm, the boardroom is not merely a space for profit maximisation but a critical arena for negotiating the long-term interests of employees, communities, customers, regulators, and the environment.

This transformation is being driven by several forces:

- **Regulatory pressure**: Indian regulators like SEBI and the Ministry of Corporate Affairs (MCA) are moving rapidly to embed ESG responsibilities into corporate filings, board reports, and disclosure mechanisms. The **Business Responsibility and Sustainability Reporting (BRSR)** framework is a signal that sustainability is no longer optional – it is a matter of law and governance.
- **Investor expectations**: Global institutional investors, sovereign wealth funds, and ESG-focused asset managers are demanding that companies not only disclose ESG data but **demonstrate board-level accountability** for sustainability risks and opportunities.
- **Reputation and trust**: In the digital age, reputation risks can escalate overnight. Board members are increasingly judged by the **ethical tone they set**, and IDs are expected to be the moral compass of the company.
- **Judicial interpretation of director duties**: Courts are beginning to recognise that fiduciary responsibility may extend to **non-financial harm,** including environmental damage or human rights violations. Indian jurisprudence, though still evolving, is likely to reflect global trends toward expanding director liability in ESG matters.

In this new environment, the ID's role is no longer that of a distant reviewer but of an **engaged, informed, and courageous participant** in shaping a company's ESG journey. They must develop the capacity to:

- Understand the **material ESG issues** specific to the company's sector and geography.
- Ask probing questions about ESG **data, strategy, and performance**.
- Ensure that **sustainability is not siloed** in Corporate Social Responsibility (CSR) departments but embedded in core operations.

Independent directors must see beyond the balance sheet to the biosphere.

- Recognise **intergenerational risks** issues like climate change that may not affect this year's bottom line but could determine the firm's long-term viability.

Moreover, the idea of independence itself needs a refresh. It must go beyond the absence of pecuniary ties to include **intellectual independence**, **ethical courage**, and a **systems-thinking mindset**. Truly, IDs are those who can challenge groupthink, raise unpopular concerns, and connect financial performance with broader societal consequences.

As India aspires to become a $5 trillion economy amid climate, demographic, and technological upheavals, the quality of boardroom governance will be pivotal. IDs must embody a **new governance ethic, one that is purpose-driven, risk-aware, and sustainability-oriented**.

7.3. Regulatory Landscape in India

India's corporate governance ecosystem is undergoing a silent revolution, one that is steadily integrating ESG obligations into the very DNA of boardroom responsibilities. At the core of this shift lies a new regulatory paradigm, where **sustainability is no longer a voluntary aspiration but a compliance mandate.** IDs, as key guardians of accountability, are increasingly expected to act as enforcers, interpreters, and stewards of this ESG regulatory wave.

7.3.1 The Emergence of Environmental, Social, and Governance as a Governance Norm

The regulatory conversation around ESG in India has evolved from soft, narrative disclosures in CSR reports to hard, quantifiable, and **auditable sustainability metrics**. This evolution is being spearheaded by multiple government and statutory agencies, including:

- **Securities and Exchange Board of India (SEBI)**
- **Ministry of Corporate Affairs (MCA)**

A company without roots in nature will be blown away by the winds of change.

- **Reserve Bank of India (RBI)** (for ESG-linked credit and green finance)
- **NITI Aayog** (for alignment with United Nation Sustainable Development Goals)

Collectively, these bodies are laying down a **comprehensive architecture** of rules, disclosures, expectations, and incentives to push Indian companies toward responsible capitalism.

7.3.2 Business Responsibility and Sustainability Reporting

Introduced by SEBI as a successor to the Business Responsibility Report, the **BRSR framework** is arguably the single most transformative reform in India's ESG reporting landscape.

- **Mandatory for top 1000 listed companies**: From FY 2022-23 onwards, large cap listed entities are required to file detailed BRSR reports as part of their annual disclosures.
- **Quantitative and qualitative metrics**: The BRSR requires disclosure across nine ESG principles, encompassing greenhouse gas emissions, gender diversity, human rights, community engagement, product responsibility, and ethical conduct.
- **BRSR core (2023-24 update)**: A subset of the BRSR, the BRSR Core introduces **assurance requirements** for a standardised set of ESG metrics. It marks a significant move toward third-party verification and global comparability.

Implication for Independent Directors: IDs are now expected to:

- Review and understand ESG metrics as part of board disclosures.
- Ensure the accuracy, completeness, and reliability of data presented in the BRSR and BRSR Core.
- Ask questions about underlying ESG strategies and how they are being operationalised.

A company without roots in nature will be blown away by the winds of change.

7.3.3 Companies Act, 2013 and Environmental, Social, and Governance Aligned Duties

While the Companies Act, 2013, does not use the term "ESG" explicitly, it embeds many of its principles into director obligations:

- **Section 166(2)**: Directors must act in good faith for the benefit of the company, its employees, the community, and for the protection of the environment.
- **Section 135**: Mandates CSR for companies meeting certain thresholds, requiring board-level oversight of social development spending and impact.
- **Board's Report (Section 134)**: Requires a detailed statement on risk management, internal controls, and performance – all of which increasingly include ESG dimensions.

Implication for Independent Directors:

- Legal duty of care now extends to **non-financial harms** (e.g., environmental pollution, labour exploitation).
- CSR obligations require monitoring and strategic alignment with the company's ESG vision.
- Board reports must reflect ESG risks in a **comprehensive, not perfunctory,** manner.

7.3.4 Securities Exchange Board of India Listing Obligations and Disclosure Requirements Regulations and Environmental, Social, and Governance

The **Listing Obligations and Disclosure Requirements (LODR)** Regulations have been progressively amended to include several ESG-related mandates:

- **Board composition**: LODR now requires enhanced diversity and the presence of at least one woman ID on the board of the top 1000 companies.

Environmental risk ignored is a lawsuit in waiting.

- **Risk management**: Companies must form Risk Management Committees (RMCs), which are now expected to consider **climate, reputational, and sustainability risks**.
- **Disclosure enhancements**: Companies must disclose ESG-related risks and opportunities, especially in their Management Discussion and Analysis section.

Implication for Independent Directors:

- IDs serving on Audit or RMCs must ensure that ESG risks are properly identified, monitored, and reported.
- They must verify the link between disclosed ESG risks and actual **enterprise risk management (ERM)** processes.

7.3.5 Environmental, Social, and Governance and Board Evaluation Norms

SEBI has also nudged companies toward ESG-integrated governance by strengthening **board evaluation norms**:

- Board evaluations now include assessments of how well the board addresses sustainability issues.
- ESG competence and awareness are increasingly becoming key parameters in **director effectiveness reviews**.

Implication for Independent Directors:

- IDs must engage in **self-assessment** and peer review based on ESG competence.
- Lack of awareness or negligence in ESG matters may impact reappointment or tenure extensions.

7.3.6 Judicial and Quasi-Judicial Trends

Although Indian courts have not yet ruled extensively on ESG-specific director liability, there are early signals from the **National Company**

Law Tribunal and **Securities Appellate Tribunal** that directors may be held accountable for:

- Greenwashing and misleading sustainability claims.
- Failure to prevent or respond to environmental or labour violations.
- Gross negligence in identifying reputational or systemic ESG risks.

The legal precedent is evolving, and IDs would be wise to proactively build ESG diligence into their decision-making.

7.3.7 Regulatory Trends to Watch

Several upcoming or potential reforms will further reshape ESG governance:

- **Taxonomies for green and transition finance**
- **Mandatory climate stress testing** for financial institutions (in line with RBI's evolving ESG agenda)
- **Unified ESG rating frameworks** (to address credibility issues with third-party ESG scores)
- **Director ESG training requirements**, possibly mandated by ICSI or SEBI

7.4. Global Environmental, Social, and Governance Frameworks and Comparative Insights

As India accelerates its ESG journey, it is both necessary and instructive to study how global regulatory regimes, capital markets, and boardroom practices are responding to the rise of sustainability governance. IDs in India, especially those on boards of internationally exposed companies, must be aware of these developments not only to ensure alignment but also to anticipate evolving stakeholder expectations and legal obligations.

The sustainable boardroom reads both the carbon ledger and the financial ledger.

7.4.1 Environmental, Social, and Governance Goes Mainstream: From Voluntary to Mandatory

Across the globe, ESG disclosures are transitioning from voluntary principles to **mandatory frameworks backed by enforcement**. While the definitions and emphases vary by jurisdiction, the overarching trend is clear: sustainability performance is increasingly seen as material to financial risk and fiduciary responsibility.

7.4.2 United States: Securities and Exchange Commission's Proposed Climate Risk Disclosures

The United States (US) Securities and Exchange Commission has proposed new rules requiring listed companies to disclose:

- Material climate-related risks and governance.
- Scope 1 and 2 emissions, and Scope 3 (if material).
- Climate-related targets, scenario analysis, and transition plans.

Boards are now being held accountable for climate risk oversight, and IDs are expected to possess sufficient **climate literacy** to interrogate such disclosures. Failure to do so may result in shareholder litigation or regulatory enforcement.

7.4.3 European Union: Corporate Sustainability Reporting Directive and Taxonomy Regulation

Europe is leading the charge with an integrated, rigorous ESG framework:

- **Corporate Sustainability Reporting Directive (CSRD)** mandates double materiality reporting, financial and impact-based.
- **European Union Taxonomy Regulation** provides a classification system for environmentally sustainable activities.

A business that breaks society's trust bankrupts its soul.

- Boards must ensure that disclosures are **audit-ready**, **assured**, and **aligned with science-based targets**.

IDs on European boards are expected to steer ESG strategy, not just review it. Many boards have dedicated **sustainability committees**, with IDs as active members or chairs.

7.4.4 United Kingdom: Task Force on Climate-related Financial Disclosures & Stewardship Code

In the United Kingdom (UK), Task Force on Climate-related Financial Disclosures (TCFD) compliance is now mandatory for large companies. The **UK Corporate Governance Code** and **FRC Stewardship Code** emphasise long-term value, ethical behaviour, and stakeholder engagement—all requiring active board oversight.

IDs in the UK are encouraged to engage with stakeholders, participate in ESG strategy formulation, and challenge greenwashing.

7.4.5 Global Environmental, Social, and Governance Reporting Standards: A Convergence of Frameworks

The alphabet soup of ESG standards, Global Reporting Initiative (GRI), Sustainability Accounting Standards Board (SASB), TCFD, CDP, and others, is finally giving way to convergence:

- The **International Sustainability Standards Board (ISSB)** under the IFRS Foundation is developing unified global ESG disclosure standards.
- The **European Sustainability Reporting Standards** under CSRD are set to become a benchmark for high-quality sustainability reporting.

Indian companies with global investors, suppliers, or operations will increasingly be asked to comply with these frameworks, and boards must ensure that their governance and risk systems are equipped to meet them.

Treating people right isn't philanthropy, it's risk management.

Implication for Independent Directors:

- Understand the ESG frameworks applicable to the company's sector and geography.
- Ensure that reporting teams have access to capacity-building and assurance tools.
- Prevent misleading disclosures by reviewing materiality assessments and ESG KPIs with rigour.

7.4.6 Environmental, Social, and Governance Ratings and Investor Activism

Global ESG rating agencies like **MSCI, Sustainalytics, Refinitiv**, and **ISS** influence investment flows and corporate reputations. However, there is growing concern about inconsistent methodologies, lack of transparency, and divergence in ratings. Despite this, **investor activism driven by ESG metrics is rising globally**:

- Shareholder proposals on climate action, diversity, and human rights are surging.
- Proxy advisors are recommending votes against directors on ESG grounds.
- Major funds like **BlackRock, Vanguard, and Norges Bank** have published ESG voting guidelines targeting boards.

IDs are now directly in the line of sight. Reputational or ESG performance failures can result in:

- Negative votes at AGMs.
- Public activist campaigns.
- Exclusion from ESG investment portfolios.
- Pressure to resign or be replaced.

Social silence on the board speaks volumes outside it.

7.4.7 Comparative Board Practices: What Global Boards Are Doing Differently

Boards in ESG-mature jurisdictions are implementing structural changes to embed sustainability into board functioning:

- **Board-level ESG Committees**: Dedicated committees overseeing sustainability strategy, risks, and disclosures.
- **Director ESG training**: Many listed companies mandate formal ESG training or onboarding for new IDs.
- **Sustainability Key Performance Indicators (KPIs) in CEO compensation**: ESG-linked metrics are increasingly part of executive incentive schemes, overseen by Remuneration Committees.
- **Stakeholder engagement sessions**: Boards hold dialogues with investors, non-governmental organisations (NGOs), or employees on ESG topics, an area still underdeveloped in Indian governance practice.

7.4.8 Lessons for Indian Independent Directors

India is at an early, but accelerating, stage of ESG integration. IDs must view global practices as a **strategic benchmark** and **regulatory trajectory**:

- **Don't wait for domestic mandates.** Proactively adopt global best practices on ESG oversight, committee structuring, and training.
- **Anticipate global investor expectations.** Especially for companies listed overseas or with FPI exposure, international ESG compliance is non-negotiable.
- **Ask hard questions about readiness**: Do we have the right ESG skills at the board level? Are we aligned with TCFD,

ISSB, or CSRD? Are ESG risks part of our ERM and audit scopes?

7.5. Reimagining Fiduciary Duty in the Environmental, Social, and Governance Era

At the heart of boardroom governance lies the concept of fiduciary duty, a sacred obligation of trust, care, and loyalty that directors owe to the corporation. Traditionally, fiduciary duty in India has been interpreted through the lens of shareholder protection, financial prudence, and legal compliance. However, the growing dominance of ESG as a governance standard necessitates a **fundamental rethinking of what fiduciary duty entails** in the 21st century.

This section unpacks how fiduciary duty is evolving globally and in India and what this means for IDs tasked with steering companies through ESG transformation.

7.5.1 The Traditional Triad: Duty of Care, Loyalty, and Prudence

Under Indian company law, particularly sections 166 and 149 of the Companies Act, 2013, directors, including IDs, are bound by three core fiduciary duties:

- **Duty of care**: To act with informed judgment and due diligence.
- **Duty of loyalty**: To prioritise the interests of the company over personal gain.
- **Duty of prudence**: To act in good faith, with skill and competence, as any reasonable person would.

These duties were traditionally exercised within a **shareholder-centric model**, focused on profitability, disclosure, and risk avoidance. ESG, however, introduces **new forms of materiality,** environmental, social, and reputational, that demand broader interpretations.

A company blind to inequality is blind to instability.

7.5.2 Expanding the Circle: From Shareholders to Stakeholders

One of the most transformative shifts in corporate governance is the movement from **shareholder primacy to stakeholder capitalism**. IDs now operate in a context where:

- **Employees**, **communities**, **future generations**, and **the environment** are considered legitimate constituencies.
- Risks are not confined to financial loss but include **climate disruption**, **biodiversity collapse**, **social unrest**, and **human rights violations**.
- The failure to act on ESG issues can cause systemic harm both to the company and to society at large.

Thus, fiduciary duty is no longer simply about protecting investors. It is about **preserving long-term enterprise value**, **ensuring ethical conduct**, and **preventing harm** to people and the planet.

For IDs, this means:

- Evaluating not just the legality but the **morality** of decisions.
- Asking: "What are the second- and third-order effects of this decision on non-shareholding stakeholders?"
- Balancing competing interests with a clear commitment to **sustainability and justice**.

7.5.3 The Emergence of Environmental, Social, and Governance Fiduciary Duty Globally

Courts, regulators, and academic bodies across the globe are beginning to treat ESG as **core to fiduciary duty**, not peripheral to it:

- **Delaware Courts (USA)**: Recent rulings hold that boards must oversee "mission-critical" risks, including ESG risks, under the Caremark doctrine.

Inclusion is not a slogan; it's a safeguard.

- **UK Companies Act, Section 172**: Requires directors to consider the long-term consequences of decisions, employee interests, supplier relationships, and environmental impact.
- **EU Corporate Sustainability Due Diligence Directive**: Imposes legal liability on directors for failing to prevent environmental or human rights abuses in their supply chains.

These trends point to a growing convergence: **if directors ignore ESG risks, they may be deemed to have breached their fiduciary duties.**

7.5.4 Environmental, Social, and Governance Materiality and the Duty of Care

One of the most powerful arguments for an expanded fiduciary duty comes from the concept of **ESG materiality**:

- Climate risk, for instance, is now viewed by many investors (e.g., BlackRock) as a **material financial risk**.
- Governance failures such as fraud, gender discrimination, or opaque related-party transactions can destroy brand value overnight.
- Social unrest caused by labour exploitation or environmental injustice can result in regulatory penalties and shareholder lawsuits.

IDs, therefore, must:

- Regularly **review ESG risk registers** and verify integration into ERM.
- Ensure that climate, diversity, and social risks are part of strategic decisions, not mere compliance checklists.
- Bring **external ESG expertise** into boardrooms when needed.

Failure to exercise this care could amount to **gross negligence** in the modern legal and investor environment.

Independent directors must ask: "Who benefits, and who bears the burden?"

7.5.5 The Duty of Loyalty: Guarding Purpose, Not Just Profits

Traditionally, loyalty was understood as allegiance to the corporation and its financial interests. But in the ESG era, **corporate purpose** is being redefined not merely to generate returns, but to create value responsibly.

Boards and IDs are being judged on whether:

- They are **greenwashing** or genuinely embedding ESG into the company's purpose and operations.
- They align executive compensation and incentives with **sustainability performance**.
- They resist **short-termism** and act to preserve **intergenerational equity**.

A truly loyal director is not one who prioritizes profit at all costs, but one who protects the company's reputation, legitimacy, and social license to operate.**4.6 Intergenerational Responsibility and Future-Oriented Fiduciary Duty**

One of the most profound contributions of ESG is the idea that companies must be accountable not just to current stakeholders but to **future generations**. Climate change, ecological degradation, and inequality are long-term risks that cannot be managed with short-term thinking.

IDs must now:

- Understand and oversee **transition strategies** (e.g., decarbonisation, circular economy, fair labour).
- Insist on **science-based targets** and long-term scenario planning.
- Ensure that **capital allocation decisions** consider sustainability impact over multiple decades.

This is a **fiduciary duty in the age of planetary limits,** and it demands courage, foresight, and humility.

The boardroom is no sanctuary from social reckoning.

7.5.6 Legal and Ethical Imperatives in India

India is at a critical juncture. While statutory interpretations of fiduciary duty in ESG contexts are still evolving, the groundwork has been laid:

- **Section 166(2)** of the Companies Act, 2013 mandates that directors act in the interest of employees, the community, and the environment.
- The **Kailash Satyarthi Child Labour case** and **Sterlite Copper judgment** illustrate that courts are willing to question corporate governance through a human rights and environmental lens.
- With the rise of climate litigation, ESG misstatements, and whistleblower cases, **director liability is no longer unthinkable**.

7.6 Boardroom Culture: From Compliance to Stewardship

Board dynamics set the tone for an organisation's governance. ESG cannot be an afterthought or a standalone item on the board agenda. It must become a **core philosophy**, reflected in how the board:

- Frames strategy.
- Assesses performance.
- Evaluates risk.
- Defines purpose.

IDs are uniquely positioned to **challenge inertia**, **question greenwashing**, and **push for a genuine sustainability culture**. They must:

- Lead by example in discussions around climate, diversity, and ethics.
- Encourage cross-functional engagement between ESG teams, internal audit, and the board.
- Promote long-termism over quarterly obsession.

Stakeholders remember how you made them feel, not just what you earned.

7.6.1 Culture-building questions IDs should raise:

- Are we embedding ESG into board deliberations or delegating it to a single department?
- Is ESG treated as integral to value creation or a PR exercise?
- Do we model integrity, inclusivity, and courage in the boardroom?

7.6.2 Environmental, Social, and Governance Committees and Oversight Architecture

As ESG oversight becomes more complex, many boards are reconfiguring their committee structures to address it:

- **Dedicated Environmental, Social, and Governance or Sustainability Committee**
    - Focuses on ESG strategy, disclosures, targets, and stakeholder engagement.
    - Often chaired or strongly represented by IDs.
    - Oversees progress on climate commitments, Diversity, Equity & Inclusion (DEI), and sustainable supply chains.
- **Expanded Mandate for Risk and Audit Committees**
    - Risk committees now cover climate, cyber, and social risks.
    - Audit committees increasingly verify ESG reporting accuracy.
    - IDs must ensure robust ESG internal controls and assurance frameworks.
- **Nomination and Remuneration Committee**
    - Links ESG performance to executive KPIs and incentives.
    - Promotes board-level diversity and succession planning aligned with ESG goals.

Reputations are lost faster than markets crash.

IDs must **evaluate whether committee charters reflect ESG duties** and whether oversight mechanisms are effective, inclusive, and transparent.

7.6.3 Environmental, Social, and Governance Strategy: Asking the Right Questions

IDs should not be passive recipients of ESG presentations. They must **ask probing, strategic questions**:

- Is our ESG strategy aligned with national/international benchmarks (e.g., SDGs, TCFD, BRSR)?
- How are ESG risks integrated into ERM?
- Are we transitioning fast enough toward net-zero or inclusive practices?
- What are the reputational risks if ESG goals are missed?
- How are stakeholder concerns addressed and measured?

Such questions force the management to think beyond cosmetic metrics and toward **transformational outcomes**.

7.6.4 Environmental, Social, and Governance Literacy and Capacity Building

Boardrooms are only as effective as their knowledge base. Given the technical and evolving nature of ESG, IDs must:

- Undergo **formal ESG education** (e.g., courses by GRI, SASB, CFA Institute, or national academies).
- Demand regular **ESG briefings** from management and external experts.
- Encourage **scenario workshops**, stress tests, and ESG horizon scanning sessions.

Social license is the currency of corporate longevity.

Boards without ESG literacy risk groupthink, greenwashing, and governance failure. IDs must lead the charge in ensuring their boards are equipped for ESG oversight.

7.6.5 Data, Disclosure, and Materiality

One of the most tangible ESG responsibilities in the boardroom is overseeing **data integrity and transparency**:

- Review the **materiality assessment** process: Are the ESG issues prioritised by stakeholders and sectoral relevance?
- Scrutinise **BRSR and international ESG filings**: Are they consistent, accurate, and independently assured?
- Monitor **progress on ESG KPIs**: emissions, diversity, board composition, energy intensity, etc.

IDs should insist on:

- Third-party ESG audits or assurance.
- Clear policies for ESG data governance.
- A direct line of sight between ESG data, strategy, and disclosure.

7.6.6 Executive Performance and Environmental, Social, and Governance Incentivisation

Boards are increasingly tying ESG outcomes to executive pay. This is where IDs, especially those on NRCs, can exert a powerful influence.

Examples of ESG-linked incentives:

- CEO bonuses tied to emission reductions.
- Senior management KPIs linked to employee well-being and diversity.
- Penalties for regulatory violations or ESG target failures.

Good governance starts where shortcuts end.

IDs must ensure that:

- ESG-linked incentives are **material, measurable, and transparent.**
- Remuneration reflects **both financial and ethical performance**.
- The system does not reward short-term green optics over long-term impact.

7.6.7 Whistleblower Protection and Ethical Oversight

Robust ESG governance also demands a strong **ethical infrastructure**:

- A credible and anonymous **whistleblower system** for ESG-related misconduct.
- Oversight of **supply chain ethics**, human rights, and anti-bribery protocols.
- Transparent mechanisms for conflict-of-interest declarations.

IDs play a critical role in upholding these norms. When whistleblower concerns emerge, they must ensure swift, fair, and independent inquiry – even if it implicates senior management.

7.6.8 Stakeholder Engagement and Board Dialogue

Boards must move from unidirectional disclosures to **active stakeholder engagement**. This includes:

- Hosting ESG stakeholder dialogues.
- Participating in investor ESG briefings.
- Inviting ESG experts, civil society, or regulators to board meetings.
- Understanding how the company is perceived by **external ESG rating agencies**.

IDs must **bridge the gap between boardroom and society,** reflecting external voices in internal governance decisions.

Ethics delayed is risk delivered.

7.6.9 Environmental, Social, and Governance in Crisis Management and Resilience Planning

ESG blind spots can turn into crises oil spills, strikes, data breaches, and climate disasters. Boards must incorporate ESG into:

- Business continuity planning (BCP).
- Crisis communication protocols.
- Post-crisis remediation oversight.

IDs should stress-test the company's **resilience to ESG shocks** and ask: Are we crisis-ready from a sustainability and reputation standpoint?

7.7 Risks, Liabilities, and Legal Safeguards for Independent Directors in the Environmental, Social, and Governance Era

As ESG expectations rise, so too do the **risks and liabilities** faced by the board members, especially IDs. The role that was once perceived as a gatekeeper for compliance is now under growing scrutiny for ESG oversight. Failing to adequately address climate change, social inequity, or governance lapses may no longer just be an ethical failure; it can also be a legal one.

This section delves into the **legal landscape**, reputational risks, and protective mechanisms available to IDs in India as they confront the growing responsibilities and exposures in the ESG era.

7.7.1 The Expanding Spectrum of Liability

The traditional scope of director liability fraud, misreporting, and insider trading has widened to encompass ESG-related risks. Today's liabilities include:

- **Greenwashing**: Misrepresentation of ESG performance or sustainability claims in public filings or advertisements.

The boardroom mirror must reflect integrity, not illusion.

- **Inadequate oversight of material ESG risks**: Especially climate risk, Diversity, Equity, and Inclusion (DEI) issues, or human rights violations in the supply chain.
- **Negligence in BRSR disclosures**: Inaccurate or misleading ESG data under SEBI's mandatory Business Responsibility and Sustainability Reporting regime.
- **Failure of duty of care**: Ignoring or minimising ESG warnings, whistleblower complaints, or red flags raised by assurance providers or internal audits.

Example: If a company is sued for environmental damage caused by operations, and the board failed to act on internal ESG risk reports, IDs may be held accountable for breach of fiduciary oversight.

7.7.2 Key Legal and Regulatory Triggers in India

The Indian legal framework is evolving to catch up with global ESG enforcement trends. Relevant triggers for ESG-related director liability include:

- **Companies Act, 2013**:
    - **Section 149(12):** IDs are liable only for acts of omission/commission that occurred with their knowledge, consent, or lack of diligence.
    - **Section 166:** Directors must act in good faith and in the best interest of the company, employees, community, and environment.
- **SEBI's LODR Regulations**: Require ESG disclosures (BRSR) and may invoke penal action for misstatements or omission of material ESG data.
- **Environmental and Labour Laws**: Board members may be questioned in cases of pollution, biodiversity loss, or labour rights violations.
- **Public Interest Litigations (PILs)**: Growing use of PILs in India on environmental and social issues may name boards as co-respondents.

Independence without vigilance is indifference.

- **Whistleblower protection framework**: Mishandling of complaints or retaliatory actions can expose IDs to liability.

7.7.3 Emerging Litigation Trends

Globally, ESG-related litigation is on the rise and may influence Indian legal strategy:

- **Climate litigation**: Directors sued for failing to mitigate or disclose climate risks (e.g., Australia's REST Super case).
- **Diversity lawsuits**: Boards challenged for lack of gender or racial diversity disclosures (e.g., US-based class actions).
- **Human rights abuses**: Directors held liable for failing to prevent labour exploitation or unsafe working conditions.
- **Breach of duty claims**: Shareholders initiating suits for non-disclosure or inadequate management of ESG material risks.

These precedents serve as warnings: **IDs cannot plead ignorance in ESG blind spots.**

7.7.4 Reputational and Career Risks

Beyond legal exposure, ESG failures can inflict **irreparable reputational harm** on IDs:

- Loss of **credibility and board seats.**
- Blacklisting by institutional investors and governance watchdogs.
- Media backlash, especially in high-profile controversies.
- Negative ESG ratings that taint the director's professional profile.

Given the increased transparency and public scrutiny around ESG, the **cost of inaction is rising.** IDs must act as responsible fiduciaries, not passive advisors.

Transparency is not optional it's armor.

7.7.5 Mitigating Risk: Proactive Steps for Independent Directors

To protect themselves while fulfilling their ESG oversight role, IDs can adopt a multi-pronged approach:

- **Documented Diligence**
  - Ensure that board minutes reflect ESG discussions and concerns.
  - Ask for ESG risk reports and document follow-ups on red flags.
- **ESG Committees and Advisors**
  - Recommend the creation of board-level ESG committees.
  - Advocate for external ESG experts or assurance providers to be brought into strategic discussions.
- **Robust Whistleblower Handling**
  - Ensure strong grievance redressal systems.
  - Oversee independent investigation mechanisms.
- **Continuous Training**
  - Enrol in ESG certification programs or board governance courses.
  - Stay informed of changes in ESG laws, frameworks, and investor expectations.
- **Independent Legal Opinion**
  - Where necessary, seek independent legal or sustainability counsel to evaluate potential exposures.

7.7.6 Role of Director and Officer Insurance

Director and Officer (D&O) insurance is a key safety net for IDs. But in the ESG era, its effectiveness depends on:

- **Scope of coverage**: Does the policy cover ESG litigation, regulatory action, and greenwashing claims?

What the board condones, the culture copies.

- **Exclusion clauses**: Are intentional misconduct or ESG-related fines excluded?
- **Policy limits and renewal terms**: Do they reflect the increasing ESG risk landscape?

IDs must proactively review and negotiate D&O insurance policies, not rely on boilerplate corporate coverage.

7.7.7 Safe Harbour Provisions: Limited but Growing

While India lacks explicit ESG safe harbour protections for directors, precedent is being set through:

- Recognition of **good faith action** and **recorded due diligence** as a defence under the Companies Act.
- Increasing alignment with global best practices, such as:
    - Organisation for Economic Co-operation and Development (OECD) Principles of Corporate Governance.
    - IFC's ESG Board Toolkit.
    - G20/OECD Guidelines on Responsible Business Conduct.

Future policy reform in India may expand safe harbour rules, but until then, IDs must proactively build an audit trail of conscientious engagement with ESG matters.

7.7.8 Institutional Backing and Collective Board Responsibility

IDs should not be isolated actors. They must:

- Urge the board to adopt ESG charters, policies, and escalation matrices.
- Encourage institutional collaboration (e.g., ICSI, Chartered Accountants of India (ICAI), NSE) for ESG governance standards.
- Push for **shared board accountability** – ESG oversight is a collective responsibility, not a siloed one.

Whistleblowers are not threats; they're early warning systems.

7.8 Building the Environmental, Social, and Governance-Competent Board: Skills, Composition, and Future Readiness

The ability of a board to drive ESG integration hinges not just on frameworks and oversight but on **human capital,** the directors themselves. Boards that lack the skills, diversity, or foresight to respond to ESG challenges risk becoming irrelevant or even dangerous to corporate survival.

This section examines how IDs can champion a forward-looking board composition, enhance their ESG acumen, and future-proof governance in a rapidly evolving sustainability landscape.

7.8.1 Environmental, Social, and Governance Competence: The New Core Skill

Historically, board members were chosen for their financial, legal, or industry expertise. Today, however, **ESG competence** is no longer optional; it is a strategic imperative. Directors must understand:

- Climate risk and decarbonisation strategies
- Human capital management and diversity imperatives
- Sustainable supply chain practices
- Stakeholder engagement and social license to operate
- ESG standards, ratings, and disclosure regimes

Boards must ask:

Do we have the right mix of ESG-related skills at the table?

IDs, as change agents, should push for board composition reviews that **map existing ESG capabilities and identify gaps**.

An unchecked CEO is a governance time bomb.

7.8.2 Board Diversity: A Strategic Environmental, Social, and Governance Lever

Diversity is not just a social good; it is an ESG imperative and a performance driver. Research has shown that diverse boards:

- Are better at-risk **oversight** and **ethical governance**
- Foster **inclusive decision-making**
- Attract **long-term investors** and **higher ESG ratings**

In India, SEBI mandates at least one woman director, but many boards fall short of meaningful diversity, especially in terms of **caste, region, age, expertise, and stakeholder representation**.

IDs must advocate for:

- **Gender balance** beyond tokenism
- Inclusion of **ESG specialists**, sustainability scientists, or social impact leaders
- Rotation policies that bring in **fresh, purpose-driven perspectives**

7.8.3 Environmental, Social, and Governance-Centric Director Onboarding and Induction

Every new board member must undergo a **comprehensive ESG induction**, including:

- Overview of the company's ESG strategy and material issues
- Review of BRSR and other sustainability disclosures
- Sessions with the Chief Sustainability Officer or ESG teams
- Familiarity with global ESG frameworks: TCFD, GRI, SASB, SDGs

If you're not asking uncomfortable questions, you're not independent.

IDs can design or demand a **standardised ESG onboarding framework** as part of institutional board development.

7.8.4 Continuing Environmental, Social, and Governance Education for Directors

Given the rapidly changing ESG landscape, one-time learning is not enough. Directors must engage in:

- **Annual ESG learning hours**, similar to CPD/CPE credits
- Attending **ESG-focused board conferences**
- Participating in **climate scenario simulations** or workshops on biodiversity, Artificial Intelligence (AI) ethics, or DEI
- Peer learning with other IDs across sectors

India's premier governance bodies (like ICSI, ICAI, CII, and BSE) are beginning to offer ESG certifications. IDs must **champion ESG literacy as a board-wide mandate**.

7.8.5 The Rise of the Environmental, Social, and Governance-Savvy Board Committee

ESG oversight should not be buried in traditional committees without the right competence. Boards are evolving:

- Creating **ESG, Sustainability, or Purpose Committees**
- Appointing ESG leads within each existing committee (e.g., ESG Risk Champion, ESG Audit Liaison)
- Bringing in **external ESG advisors** to sit alongside directors in key deliberations

IDs must **redefine governance architecture** to ensure ESG is structurally prioritised.

Governance gaps are the breeding grounds of scandals.

7.8.6 Chairpersonship and Environmental, Social, and Governance Leadership

The **tone from the top** determines board behaviour. While the chair often sets strategic direction, IDs can ensure:

- The chair is well-versed in ESG matters
- ESG is a standing item in board meetings
- Annual board evaluations include ESG leadership assessments

Where the chair lacks ESG capacity, IDs can serve as **"ESG conscience" figures,** mentoring leadership and amplifying ESG in boardroom debates.

7.8.7 Talent Succession and Environmental, Social, and Governance Futures

Forward-thinking boards must look beyond today's ESG landscape and prepare for the **next wave of sustainability concerns**: AI ethics, intergenerational equity, biodiversity loss, water scarcity, etc.

IDs must work with the **NRC** to:

- Define **ESG leadership profiles** for future appointments
- Ensure **succession plans** include next-generation sustainability leaders
- Embed **ethical foresight** into talent pipelines, not just performance reviews

7.8.8 The Independent Director as Environmental, Social, and Governance Champion

To lead effectively, an ID must themselves evolve:

- From observer to **activist advisor**
- From rule-follower to **principle-led steward**
- From status-quo defender to **transformation driver**

Fiduciary duty is no longer shareholder-exclusive; it's stakeholder-expansive.

This requires courage, insight, and persistence. It also calls for networking beyond the boardroom with regulators, civil society, academic institutions, and ESG think tanks.

Key leadership roles IDs can play include:

- Convening ESG roundtables across sectors
- Writing ESG thought leadership and policy inputs
- Mentoring emerging ESG professionals

7.8.9 Institutionalising Environmental, Social, and Governance Ethos

Ultimately, ESG must move from individual interest to **institutional philosophy**. Boards must:

- Embed ESG into their own **charters and performance evaluations**
- Conduct **annual ESG board self-assessments**
- Publicly commit to **board-level ESG KPIs**

IDs are central to this shift, ensuring that ESG competence is **not an exception but a norm**.

7.9. The Indian Context: Policy, Regulation, and Market Pressure on Environmental, Social, and Governance

India is at a pivotal juncture in the global ESG movement. As one of the fastest-growing major economies, its corporate sector is under dual pressure: to grow inclusively and to do so responsibly. The evolving Indian regulatory ecosystem, coupled with rising expectations from investors and civil society, is turning ESG from a corporate buzzword into a boardroom imperative.

In this section, we examine the unique contours of India's ESG governance landscape, focusing on regulations, market forces, and the critical role IDs must play in navigating these shifts.

Duty of care means asking: What legacy are we leaving?

7.9.1 Regulatory Drivers of Environmental, Social, and Governance in India

India's regulators have taken several progressive steps to institutionalise ESG principles within corporate governance. These include:

A. SEBI's BRSR Framework

- **BRSR** has been made mandatory (from FY 2023–24) for the top 1,000 listed companies by market capitalisation.
- It requires disclosures across **three pillars**:
  - Environmental (energy use, GHG emissions, waste, biodiversity)
  - Social (workforce diversity, human rights, CSR)
  - Governance (board composition, ethics, anti-corruption)
- IDs must ensure:
  - **Authenticity and completeness** of BRSR disclosures.
  - That ESG data reflects actual **management performance**, not just compliance narratives.
  - Cross-verification with internal risk reports, audits, and stakeholder grievances.

B. Companies Act, 2013

- **Section 134(5)**: Directors must ensure the implementation of proper financial controls, which now extend to sustainability-related financial disclosures.
- **Section 166**: Directors are obligated to act in the interest of the environment, employees, and community—not just shareholders.
- **CSR Obligations (Section 135)**: Larger companies must spend 2% of average profits on CSR, requiring board-level scrutiny on impact and alignment with ESG goals.

Compliance is minimum wage for fiduciary duty.

C. Reserve Bank of India's Environmental, Social, and Governance Push

- The **Reserve Bank of India** has introduced ESG guidance for banks and financial institutions, asking them to:
  - o Integrate climate risks into credit decisions.
  - o Disclose ESG metrics aligned with global standards.
- This raises **second-order ESG risk** for companies seeking finance—non-compliance may affect access to capital.

7.9.2 The Policy Shift Toward Stakeholder Capitalism

India's policy stance is slowly shifting toward **stakeholder capitalism**, with government and regulatory actors encouraging long-term, inclusive value creation.

Key policy markers include:

- **National Guidelines on Responsible Business Conduct (NGRBC)**, released by the MCA, which underpin BRSR.
- **SDG-aligned policies** across environmental protection, gender equity, and rural development.
- Proposed **ESG taxonomy and sustainability standards** under development by the ICAI and SEBI.
- Discussions on creating an **India-specific ESG rating framework** to avoid greenwashing and ensure context-relevant assessments.

7.9.3 Market Forces: Investors, Stock Exchanges, and Environmental, Social, and Governance Ratings

IDs must also respond to powerful **market signals** that are reshaping corporate behaviour:

A. Institutional Investors' Expectations

- Asset managers like **Life Insurance Corporation, State Bank of India Mutual Fund**, and global players such as **BlackRock, Norges Bank**, and **UBS** are increasingly factoring ESG into portfolio decisions.
- **Stewardship Codes** and ESG voting policies are encouraging active investor engagement with boards.
- IDs are now expected to **justify ESG strategies and risk responses** to institutional shareholders.

B. Stock Exchange Initiatives

- The **NSE and BSE** have ESG indices (e.g., Nifty100 ESG, S&P BSE ESG100) that reward companies with strong sustainability performance.
- The **Social Stock Exchange (SSE)**, launched in 2023, provides a platform for purpose-driven enterprises and NGOs to access capital.
    - IDs must understand how ESG strategies can create value **beyond profit**, especially for companies exploring blended finance.

C. Environmental, Social, and Governance Ratings and Rankings

- Indian firms are assessed by ESG rating agencies such as **CRISIL, MSCI, Refinitiv**, and **Sustainalytics**.
- Poor ratings can result in:
    - Exclusion from ESG funds.
    - Reputational loss.
    - Negative analyst coverage.

Boards and, by extension, IDs must understand the **methodologies and materiality thresholds** used in these ratings.

7.9.4 Stakeholder Activism and Civil Society Pressure

A distinct trend in India is the rise of **civil society pressure** and **stakeholder litigation** focused on:

- Environmental degradation (e.g., industrial pollution in Tamil Nadu, illegal mining in Goa)
- Labour rights (e.g., gig worker protection, occupational safety)
- Gender equity (e.g., harassment and diversity disclosures)

Social media activism and digital transparency tools mean that **NGOs, activists, and even employees are watching boards**. IDs must:

- Address stakeholder concerns in **real time**.
- Ensure whistleblower protections are upheld.
- Promote boardroom empathy and open engagement, not just regulatory compliance.

7.9.5 The Compliance-Culture Conundrum

One of the biggest challenges in the Indian context is the **tick-box approach to ESG**:

- BRSR becomes a data-filling exercise.
- CSR is treated as philanthropy, not strategy.
- Diversity is symbolic rather than systemic.

IDs must **bridge the gap between form and substance**, ensuring that ESG moves from being a report to being a **reform**.

7.9.6 Independent Directors as Policy Catalysts

IDs can also play a role **beyond the boardroom** in shaping India's ESG discourse by:

- Contributing to **industry consultations** on ESG policy.

The old guard guarded profits; the new guard protects purpose.

- Engaging with think tanks, regulators, and educational bodies to improve ESG capacity.
- Supporting **standard-setting efforts** through their affiliations (e.g., ICAI, ICSI, CII, FICCI).

The **collective voice of experienced IDs** can influence national policy direction on corporate sustainability.

7.10. Tools, Frameworks, and Metrics: An Environmental, Social, and Governance Toolkit for Independent Directors

The journey from ESG awareness to ESG impact is complex, and it requires more than intent; it demands tools, frameworks, and disciplined metrics. IDs, in their evolving fiduciary role, need structured resources to interrogate sustainability strategies, challenge assumptions, measure performance, and steer their companies through the dynamic ESG landscape.

This section offers a practical ESG toolkit tailored to the Indian context, highlighting essential global and local frameworks, boardroom-ready metrics, and decision-support tools to empower IDs as sustainability stewards.

7.10.1 Global Environmental, Social, and Governance Frameworks: A Common Language for Oversight

IDs must familiarise themselves with **widely adopted international ESG frameworks**, which often form the foundation of investor expectations and disclosure practices.

7.10.1 GRI (Global Reporting Initiative)

- Most widely used framework for labour sustainability reporting.
- Emphasises **materiality from a stakeholder perspective**.
- Covers disclosures across energy, emissions, labour, governance, and community impact.

Boardroom conscience is the first line of defense.

7.10.2. SASB (Sustainability Accounting Standards Board)

- Provides **industry-specific ESG standards** relevant to financial performance.
- Ideal for identifying **material ESG issues** by sector.

7.10.3. TCFD (Task Force on Climate-related Financial Disclosures)

- Recommends disclosures on **climate risks**, governance, strategy, metrics, and targets.
- Key to assessing **transition risk and resilience**.

7.10.4. UN SDGs (Sustainable Development Goals)

- A broader development framework of 17 goals.
- Helps align corporate strategy with **national and global priorities**.

7.10.5. IFRS S1 and S2 (via ISSB)

- The ISSB is merging financial and ESG disclosures.
- SEBI has indicated alignment with these global standards.

IDs' role: Ask whether the company has mapped and integrated these frameworks into reporting and risk management. If not, **why not?**

7.11 Indian-Specific Environmental, Social, and Governance Standards and Guidelines

7.11.1. BRSR (Business Responsibility and Sustainability Reporting)

- Mandated by SEBI for the top 1,000 listed companies.
- Covers 9 principles aligned with National Guidelines on Responsible Business Conduct (NGRBC).

The quick gain often hides the long loss.

- Focuses on disclosures across **Environment, Social, and Governance indicators**, including:
- Energy and water consumption
- Workforce diversity
- Training hours
- Supply chain ESG risks
- Anti-corruption practices

IDs' role: Ensure **consistency**, **materiality**, and **actionability** in BRSR disclosures.

7.11.2. NGRBC Principles

- Principle-based framework issued by the Ministry of Corporate Affairs.
- Promotes core responsibilities such as **transparency**, **environmental stewardship**, and **respect for human rights**.
- Acts as a **baseline for board conduct** in ESG decision-making.

7.11.3. CSR Impact Measurement Guidelines

- Ministry of Corporate Affairs issued a framework to move CSR reporting beyond financial inputs to **outcomes and impact**.
- Includes **third-party impact assessment** for projects above INR 1 crore.

7.12 Environmental, Social, and Governance Performance Metrics for Board Monitoring

Effective oversight demands quantifiable indicators. IDs should review ESG KPIs regularly and embed them into the **board's monitoring dashboard**.

Quarterly blindness leads to yearly regret.

7.12.1. Environmental Metrics

- GHG emissions (Scope 1, 2, and 3)
- Energy and water usage
- Renewable energy adoption
- Waste reduction and recycling rate
- Biodiversity footprint

7.12.2. Social Metrics

- Gender and minority representation
- Occupational health and safety incidents
- Employee engagement scores
- Community investment outcomes
- Grievance redressal turnaround time

7.12.3. Governance Metrics

- Board and committee attendance
- Independence and diversity of the board
- Whistleblower complaints and resolution rate
- ESG-linked executive compensation
- Cybersecurity incidents and preparedness

IDs' role: Advocate for **integrated ESG dashboards** that allow **trend analysis** and **comparative benchmarking** over time.

7.13 Environmental, Social, and Governance Risk Mapping and Scenario Analysis Tools

To anticipate and mitigate emerging ESG risks, boards can use:

- **ESG heat maps** to identify and prioritise risks by likelihood and impact.
- **Scenario analysis** (especially for climate risks) using tools like TCFD guidance.
- **Materiality matrices** to reconcile internal and stakeholder perspectives.
- **ESG scorecards** that link risks with controls and KPIs.

IDs' role: Ensure ESG risks are mapped into the company's **ERM** system – not siloed in sustainability reports.

7.14 Environmental, Social, and Governance Score Integration in Decision-Making

Forward-thinking companies embed ESG into:

- **Investment and capex decisions**: e.g., carbon-adjusted ROI.
- **Merger and Acquisitions due diligence**: e.g., human rights or environmental liabilities.
- **Supplier selection**: e.g., ESG rating or audit scores of vendors.

IDs' role: Push for ESG criteria to be integrated into **board approvals, contracts, and procurement policies**.

7.15 Tools for Environmental, Social, and Governance Board Self-Assessment and Accountability

Boards must walk the talk by assessing their own ESG performance through:

- Annual **ESG self-assessment checklists**: Does the board engage meaningfully with ESG?

Sustainability isn't slow; it's strategic.

- External **board evaluation tools**: Focused on ESG orientation, literacy, and leadership.
- Setting ESG-linked KPIs for directors: e.g., ESG training hours, committee leadership, etc.

IDs' role: Recommend ESG-linked director evaluations as part of **board effectiveness reviews**.

7.16 Environmental, Social, and Governance Assurance and Data Integrity

Data credibility is the foundation of ESG trust. Directors must evaluate:

- Internal audit mechanisms for ESG disclosures.
- Use of **third-party ESG assurance providers**.
- Consistency between narrative disclosures and financial reports.

IDs' role: Ensure robust **controls, validations, and audit trails** for all ESG metrics disclosed to the public or investors.

7.17 Capacity Building: Environmental, Social, and Governance Toolkits, Guides, and Platforms

Organisations like **ICSI, CII, NSE, and BSE** are developing ESG toolkits, courses, and platforms that can support directors. Global resources include:

- **World Business Council for Sustainable Development Board ESG Toolkit**
- **National Association of Corporate Directors ESG Oversight Handbook**
- **Harvard Business School ESG Primer for Boards**

IDs' role: Commit to continuous ESG learning and guide **board-wide ESG upskilling**.

Chasing short-term returns can lead to long-term ruin.

7.18. Roadblocks and Remedies: Navigating Practical Challenges in Environmental, Social, and Governance

Even the most committed IDs face an uphill climb when translating ESG ideals into concrete boardroom actions. The Indian corporate environment presents a range of operational, cultural, structural, and psychological barriers that hinder effective ESG oversight. However, with proactive strategies, these barriers can be transformed into pathways for deeper engagement and impact.

This section explores the key challenges IDs encounter and provides practical remedies to overcome them, ensuring ESG is embedded not just in policies, but in practice.

7.18.1 The Compliance Trap: Form Over Substance

The Roadblock:
Many companies treat ESG as a **regulatory checklist** – focusing on disclosures rather than outcomes. BRSR becomes an annual routine, and CSR is often reduced to philanthropic tokenism. Sustainability reports are polished, but the underlying risks and opportunities go unaddressed.

The Remedy:

- IDs must **challenge superficial reporting**. Ask for **impact metrics**, not just input/output indicators.
- Insist on **management presentations** linking ESG disclosures to long-term strategy and risk.
- Set a precedent by **integrating ESG into board discussions beyond compliance,** such as in capital allocation, product innovation, and supply chain governance.

7.18.2 Data Gaps and Measurement Deficits

The Roadblock:
Lack of robust data systems makes it difficult to track ESG KPIs consistently. Many Indian firms lack real-time systems to monitor emissions,

Every ignored ESG red flag is tomorrow's crisis headline.

social metrics, or ethical compliance, especially in multi-tiered supply chains.

The Remedy:

- Recommend investing in **digital ESG reporting infrastructure** (IoT for environmental tracking, HR analytics for social metrics).
- Encourage external ESG audits and **third-party assurance** for credibility.
- Promote alignment with international standards like GRI or SASB to guide consistent and material data collection.

7.18.3 Limited Environmental, Social, and Governance Literacy at the Board Level

The Roadblock:
ESG expertise among board members, particularly IDs, is uneven. Many directors are finance or legal experts but may lack an understanding of climate risk, biodiversity, human rights, or sustainable finance.

The Remedy:

- Advocate for **annual ESG capacity-building workshops** for the board.
- Appoint **ESG-savvy directors** or external advisors with sustainability backgrounds.
- Push for **board composition reform** where ESG proficiency is part of the selection criteria.

7.18.4 Resistance from Promoters and Senior Management

The Roadblock:

In India, promoter-driven companies often have dominant family control. ESG is sometimes seen as a **cost centre or PR tool**, not as a source of long-term value. IDs may face subtle resistance when questioning legacy practices or raising ESG issues.

The Remedy:

- Build ESG narratives around **risk mitigation, investor access, and global competitiveness**.
- Use examples from **peer companies** and **market trends** to make the business case for ESG.
- Document dissent where necessary and ensure board minutes reflect critical ESG discussions.

7.18.5 Fragmented Oversight and Committee Silos

The Roadblock:

ESG-related responsibilities are often split across committees (Audit, CSR, Risk, Nomination & Remuneration), leading to a **fragmented understanding of ESG strategy** and oversight gaps.

The Remedy:

- Propose a **dedicated ESG or Sustainability Committee**, or a cross-functional board task force.
- Encourage periodic **joint sessions between committees** to integrate ESG into risk, remuneration, and audit oversight.
- Advocate for ESG oversight to be made part of **board charters** and committee KPIs.

7.18.6 Lack of Stakeholder Engagement

The Roadblock:

Companies often focus only on shareholders and regulators, ignoring civil society, employees, communities, or environmental stakeholders. This leads to **tone-deaf strategies** and reputational risk.

Profit built on injustice is profit poisoned.

The Remedy:

- Encourage **stakeholder mapping** and **materiality assessments**.
- Propose regular engagement mechanisms such as **town halls, grievance redress platforms,** or **community dialogues**.
- Include **stakeholder feedback summaries** in board packets during strategic discussions.

7.18.7 Greenwashing and Environmental, Social, and Governance Fatigue

The Roadblock:

With ESG gaining attention, there is an increasing tendency to exaggerate efforts, which is commonly termed **greenwashing**. On the other end, prolonged superficial engagement leads to **boardroom ESG fatigue**.

The Remedy:

- Demand **transparency and traceability** for all ESG claims - "show, don't tell."
- Create a culture of **substance over slogans**: focus on specific, measurable, and verifiable ESG outcomes.
- Encourage rotation of ESG themes in board discussions to prevent overload and ensure dynamic engagement.

7.18.8 Short-Termism and Quarterly Pressure

The Roadblock:

Public companies often prioritise short-term results due to **quarterly earnings pressures**. ESG investments (e.g., renewable energy, inclusive hiring, research and development) may not yield immediate returns and are deprioritised.

Independent directors must be moral anchors, not passive observers.

The Remedy:

- Push for **ESG-linked long-term incentive plans (LTIPs)** for executives.
- Encourage **multi-year performance dashboards** that track ESG ROI over time.
- Align ESG performance with strategic narratives during investor calls and analyst briefings.

7.18.9 Jurisdictional and Cultural Diversity in Operations

The Roadblock:

Multinational Indian firms operate across **varying geographies with different ESG standards and cultural sensitivities**. This makes harmonisation difficult and sometimes leads to inconsistent application of policies.

The Remedy:

- Promote **group-wide ESG policies** with localised implementation guidelines.
- Ensure local management teams are trained to align with the group's ESG vision.
- Integrate ESG into **internal audit and cross-border board reviews.**

7.18.10 Weak Environmental, Social, and Governance Benchmarks and Peer Comparisons

The Roadblock:

ESG benchmarking in India is still developing. Without strong industry comparators, companies often assume they are leaders by default.

ESG isn't a trend; it's the soul of modern governance.

The Remedy:

- Use **global benchmarks and sector-specific ESG indices** (e.g., MSCI, Refinitiv, Sustainalytics) to challenge complacency.
- Advocate for **industry-led benchmarking platforms** via associations like CII or FICCI.
- Incorporate **competitive ESG positioning** into strategy sessions and board reviews.

7.19. Vision 2030 – The Future of Environmental, Social, and Governance Leadership and the Independent Director's Legacy

As we look toward 2030, the corporate world stands at a decisive threshold. The integration of ESG priorities into boardroom decision-making is no longer a forward-looking ambition it is a strategic imperative. For IDs, this decade offers both a challenge and an opportunity: to leave behind the archetype of the cautious observer and emerge as architects of sustainability.

This concluding section envisions the future trajectory of ESG governance in India and the transformative role that IDs can and must play to shape resilient, inclusive, and future-ready enterprises.

7.19.1 From Oversight to Insight: The Shift in the Director's Mandate

The ID of 2030 will no longer be defined merely by regulatory compliance or financial acumen. Instead, she or he will be a **strategic navigator**, adept at interpreting climate forecasts, understanding AI ethics, decoding human capital metrics, and influencing corporate culture.

- **Insight over hindsight**: The board will expect IDs to anticipate ESG risks, not just respond after the fact.

Long-term value demands patience; strategic oversight demands insight.

- **Fiduciary duty will be redefined**: IDs will owe loyalty not only to shareholders but also to employees, communities, ecosystems, and future generations.
- **Trust, transparency, and accountability** will be central pillars, not optional values.

7.19.2 The Environmental, Social, and Governance Centric Boardroom: A New Operating Model

Boards in 2030 will not treat ESG as an adjunct; it will be fully embedded in every board function:

- **Strategy**: ESG will be a key pillar of competitive advantage and risk management.
- **Finance**: Capital allocation will be judged through ESG lenses (green bonds, climate-resilient portfolios).
- **Remuneration**: Executive compensation will be tightly linked to ESG KPIs.
- **Risk oversight**: Climate, cyber, social, and reputational risks will dominate board risk registers.
- **Culture**: Diversity, psychological safety, and inclusion will be essential drivers of innovation and resilience.

IDs must **lead this integration** – challenging inertia, setting benchmarks, and asking the right questions.

7.19.3 The Rise of the Environmental, Social, and Governance – Competent Director

By 2030, ESG competence will become a **core eligibility criterion** for IDs.

- **Board nominating committees** will evaluate candidates on sustainability literacy.

Sustainability demands foresight; fiduciary duty demands diligence.

- **Regulators and investors** will scrutinise the ESG credentials of board members.
- **Training and certification** in ESG governance will be standard practice.

Forward-looking IDs will proactively **upskill** through programs offered by ICSI, GRI, TCFD, and leading universities and mentor newer directors to build a pipeline of ESG-ready leaders.

7.19.4 Technology and Environmental, Social, and Governance: New Frontiers of Governance

The intersection of ESG and digital transformation will define the next decade of governance.

- **AI and Big Data** will enable predictive ESG analysis, stakeholder sentiment mapping, and real-time risk detection.
- **Blockchain** will provide traceability in supply chains and ESG disclosures.
- **Internet of Things** will track real-time emissions, water usage, and employee well-being in remote sites.

IDs must embrace these tools to **monitor ESG performance with granularity and credibility**, enhancing board responsiveness and strategic foresight.

7.19.5 The Independent Director as Stakeholder Champion and Ethical Leader

The ID of the future will be **more visible**, **more vocal**, and **more values-driven**:

- Advocating for equitable business practices even when inconvenient.
- Serving as a bridge between the board and broader society.

Environmental responsibility demands action; corporate governance demands vigilance.

- Demanding transparency from the company and practicing it personally.

In a world of rising geopolitical tension, resource scarcity, and social unrest, the ID will be one of the **last lines of defence** against corporate short-termism.

7.19.6 Regulatory Evolution and Environmental, Social, and Governance Convergence

By 2030, Indian ESG regulations will be more harmonised with global standards:

- **BRSR disclosures** will be deeper, more sector-specific, and digitally integrated.
- **ESG assurance** may become mandatory for certain industries.
- **Penalties for greenwashing** and **incentives for ESG innovation** will likely shape board behaviour.
- **SEBI, MCA, and RBI** will coordinate more closely to create an integrated ESG regulatory ecosystem.

IDs will need to **interpret and apply these converging standards** with clarity and agility - guiding the board through a more dynamic legal landscape.

7.19.7 Global Indian Companies: Environmental, Social, and Governance as a Brand Differentiator

As Indian companies expand their global footprint, ESG will be a **reputational asset** and a **strategic moat**:

- Global investors and partners will demand demonstrable ESG maturity.
- ESG-aligned supply chains will unlock new markets.

Resource stewardship demands prudence; operational oversight demands attention.

- Indian companies that lead in ESG will attract top talent, capital, and community goodwill.

IDs will be the **custodians of this global trust** – shaping narratives, setting standards, and aligning corporate ambitions with planetary boundaries.

7.19.8 The Legacy of Environmental, Social, and Governance – Oriented Independent Directors

In 2030 and beyond, the legacy of IDs will not be measured by the number of meetings attended or policies reviewed. It will be defined by:

- The **climate resilience** of the companies they served.
- The **ethical standards** they upheld when no one was watching.
- The **stakeholder value** they enabled through visionary oversight.

In a world increasingly shaped by systemic risks, the ID's moral compass and intellectual courage will determine not just corporate survival but societal well-being.

Conclusion

The road to 2030 is not a straight line; it will be turbulent, nonlinear, and filled with paradoxes. But it also holds the promise of a new corporate epoch: one in which IDs are not merely stewards of capital, but **guardians of the planet, advocates of people, and architects of purpose**.

In embracing this role, IDs will not only redefine corporate governance but also redefine what it means to lead.

7.20. Catalysts in Action – Case Studies of Environmental, Social, and Governance Leadership by Independent Directors in India

While theory guides and vision inspire, it is practice that validates. Across India's corporate landscape, a quiet revolution is underway, led

ESG integration demands commitment; decision integrity demands independence.

by IDs who are moving beyond compliance and into the realm of **true ESG leadership**. This section offers **real-world case-based insights** showcasing how IDs are actively shaping sustainability trajectories within companies, often under complex circumstances and with limited institutional support.

These stories are not just examples; they are **templates for transformation**.

7.20.1 Tata Chemicals – Integrating Climate Risk into Strategy

Context:

Tata Chemicals, a key player in India's green chemistry space, committed early to decarbonisation and circular economy principles. But it was the company's board that gave teeth to its climate agenda.

Role of Independent Directors:

- IDs advocated for incorporating **TCFD-aligned climate risk disclosures** in the annual report well before it became market standard.
- One ID with a background in environmental economics led a special **board workshop** on carbon pricing and future transition risks.
- The board created a **sub-committee on climate resilience**, ensuring cross-functional insights into emissions, water stress, and supply chain adaptation.

Impact:

- Tata Chemicals is now recognised globally for climate governance and ranks highly in ESG indices.
- Its approach inspired ESG governance reforms across Tata Group entities.

Governance frameworks demand compliance; sustainability culture demands reinforcement.

7.20.2 Infosys – Linking Executive Pay to Environmental, Social, and Governance Performance

Context:

Infosys, a global IT major, has been a front-runner in digital sustainability and ethical governance. The board's Remuneration Committee, led by an ESG-savvy ID, played a pivotal role.

Role of Independent Directors:

- IDs pushed for a revamp of the executive compensation framework by introducing **ESG-based scorecards**.
- These KPIs included **gender diversity, energy efficiency, employee wellness, and ethical AI use**.
- Regular ESG performance reviews were institutionalised, with clear thresholds for variable pay triggers.

Impact:

- The move reinforced the board's long-termism and was well received by proxy advisors and institutional investors.
- It positioned Infosys as a model for integrating ESG into human capital governance.

7.20.3 Mahindra & Mahindra – Championing Community-Centric Governance

Context:

With its vast rural footprint, Mahindra & Mahindra faced social scrutiny around local employment and land practices. IDs elevated the issue to a board-level priority.

Role of Independent Directors:

- One ID initiated a **stakeholder mapping exercise** and pushed for including community engagement KPIs in CSR strategies.
- The board insisted on **impact assessments** for major CSR projects, moving from "spending" to "value creation."
- ESG dashboards began capturing **community grievance redressal metrics**, previously overlooked.

Impact:

- Mahindra's CSR now leads in outcome-based reporting and has won accolades for rural empowerment.
- Local community relations improved, reducing project delays and social license risks.

7.20.4 HDFC Ltd – Driving Environmental, Social, and Governance Materiality through Board Committees

Context:

As India's housing finance giant, HDFC faced material ESG risks related to urban infrastructure, affordable housing, and climate exposure in real estate portfolios.

Role of Independent Directors:

- The Audit and Risk Committee, with strong ID participation, **mandated ESG stress testing** as part of its ERM.
- IDs promoted **materiality mapping** that went beyond disclosure compliance to inform strategy.
- Sustainability reports began reporting **ESG-adjusted risk-weighted portfolios**, a rare move in Indian finance.

Leadership accountability demands initiative; corporate conscience demands moral courage.

Impact:

- HDFC became a model for integrating ESG into core lending decisions.
- It led to greater investor confidence, especially from global climate-focused funds.

7.20.5 JSW Steel – Turning Environmental Crisis into Governance Opportunity

Context:

JSW Steel faced heavy criticism regarding emissions, water use, and environmental impact. An ID with a background in regulatory affairs became a catalyst for course correction.

Role of Independent Directors:

- Urged the board to commission an **independent environmental audit** and share findings publicly.
- Led the creation of a **board-level ESG advisory council** with external experts.
- Championed a long-term **ESG reinvestment strategy**, including renewable power sourcing and industrial decarbonisation.

Impact:

- The company witnessed a **shift in investor perception** and was reinstated into multiple ESG indices.
- JSW's ESG disclosures became more credible and specific, improving global ratings.

Innovation for sustainability demands creativity; risk mitigation demands vigilance.

7.20.6 Lessons for the Boardroom

From these case studies, the **common patterns** of ESG leadership by IDs emerge:

Dimension	ESG Leadership Practice
Courage	Challenging management on ESG risks that others overlook
Capacity Building	Initiating board education and stakeholder engagement
Innovation	Suggesting structural reforms like ESG KPIs, dedicated sub-committees.
Long-Termism	Shifting focus from optics to meaningful, measurable change.
Transparency	Insisting on assurance, disclosure, and audit of ESG claims.

These actions illustrate that **IDs can be the fulcrum of ESG transformation**, not just by raising issues, but by enabling systemic responses.

Conclusion

IDs in India are no longer bound by the stereotype of symbolic oversight. Their real power lies in **curiosity, credibility, courage, and continuity**. The case studies presented here prove that when ESG is led from the top with integrity and insight, the results can redefine not just a company's valuation, but its **value to society**.

The journey ahead is long. But the roadmap is clear, and the role of IDs in ESG is now **irreversible, indispensable, and inspirational**.

"In the boardroom of tomorrow, the true mark of an independent director will not be how fiercely they defend profit, but how faithfully they protect the planet, uplift the people, and uphold principles; because stewardship is no longer about guiding a company through quarters, but guiding humanity through crises with conscience, courage, and care."

CHAPTER 8

Women Independent Directors: Champions of ESG and Sustainability

"Women independent directors are not just voices of balance - they are engines of change."

8.1. Introduction

8.1.1 The Emerging Importance of Environmental, Social, and Governance in Corporate Governance

In recent years, the global business landscape has witnessed a profound transformation. Investors, regulators, customers, and civil society now demand that companies go beyond the narrow pursuit of profit to embrace a broader commitment to Environmental, Social, and Governance (ESG) principles. This shift is driven by heightened awareness of climate change, social inequality, human rights concerns, and corporate ethics failures – factors that increasingly influence a company's long-term viability and reputation.

ESG criteria offer a comprehensive framework to evaluate a company's performance across these critical dimensions. Environmental criteria examine how a company manages its impact on natural resources, including carbon emissions, waste management, and energy efficiency. Social criteria assess relationships with employees, customers, suppliers, and communities, focusing on labour standards, diversity, and human rights. Governance criteria relate to leadership structures, ethical conduct, board effectiveness, and shareholder rights.

Incorporating ESG considerations into corporate governance is no longer optional. Regulatory bodies worldwide have introduced mandatory ESG disclosures, and investors integrate ESG metrics into their decision-making. For Indian companies, this global momentum is echoed by initiatives such as SEBI's Business Responsibility and Sustainability Reporting (BRSR), which require listed entities to report transparently on their ESG performance. This growing emphasis on sustainability reflects a fundamental redefinition of corporate purpose, wherein businesses are expected to generate value not only for shareholders but for all stakeholders and society at large.

8.1.2 The Rising Role of Independent Directors

In this evolving governance ecosystem, Independent Directors (IDs) play a pivotal role. Characterised by their detachment from company management and material business relationships, IDs are uniquely positioned to provide unbiased oversight and act as watchdogs for stakeholder interests. Their independence equips them to challenge management decisions that may prioritise short-term gains over sustainable value creation.

The broadening scope of corporate responsibility means IDs are now tasked with overseeing complex ESG-related risks and opportunities. This includes ensuring that companies develop credible sustainability strategies, comply with evolving regulatory requirements, and embed ethical practices across all operations. As stewards of good governance, IDs are expected to champion transparency, accountability, and integrity—core tenets that underpin robust ESG frameworks.

A woman's instinct to nurture extends to nature.

8.1.3 Why Women Independent Directors Matter in Environmental, Social, and Governance Leadership

Within the evolving landscape of corporate governance, women IDs are not just participants; they are catalysts. As businesses grapple with climate change, social inequities, regulatory scrutiny, and the growing demand for corporate purpose, women have emerged as some of the most influential agents of change, particularly in advancing ESG priorities.

Research across global markets has consistently shown that gender-diverse boards, especially those with active participation of women IDs outperform their peers on ESG performance. These boards are more likely to set ambitious sustainability goals, disclose climate-related risks, and adopt policies that reflect a deeper engagement with stakeholder expectations. The reasons for this are both structural and behavioural.

Women bring to the boardroom a diversity of perspectives shaped by multifaceted life experiences, often balancing roles in professional, social, and personal spheres. This breadth of experience translates into a more holistic approach to risk, resilience, and responsibility. Their decision-making tends to be collaborative, inclusive, and long-term oriented, ensuring that ESG issues are not treated as peripheral concerns but as strategic imperatives woven into the core of business models. Moreover, women's IDs frequently embody transformational leadership traits emphasising ethics, transparency, social justice, and sustainability. They are more likely to ask probing questions about environmental impact, insist on stronger disclosure of social risks, and advocate for equitable policies that protect employees, communities, and ecosystems. Their influence is visible in several ways:

- **Environmental stewardship**: Women directors often push companies toward cleaner technologies, responsible sourcing, and proactive climate action.
- **Social responsibility**: They tend to champion initiatives around diversity, equity, inclusion, employee welfare, and community engagement.

Green governance grows stronger under feminine leadership.

- **Governance excellence**: Their presence correlates with improved board oversight, stronger internal controls, and more transparent reporting.

These leadership qualities are not merely anecdotal. Studies have shown that companies with greater female representation on boards demonstrate higher ESG ratings, stronger sustainability reporting practices, and greater investor confidence. This reflects not only the unique lens women bring to board deliberations but also their commitment to embedding sustainability into the company's strategic DNA rather than treating it as a compliance exercise.

Yet, despite their proven value, women IDs remain significantly underrepresented, both globally and in India. Many serve on boards without being given substantive roles in ESG committees or sustainability oversight functions. The barriers they face from entrenched boardroom cultures to implicit biases and lack of succession planning, continue to limit their influence.

The urgency of climate change, the social expectations of a new generation, and the investor community's growing focus on ESG all point to a clear conclusion: the future of sustainable business leadership depends on women being at the centre of boardroom decision-making. Empowering women IDs, expanding their presence in ESG-critical roles, and leveraging their leadership style are not just matters of diversity; they are strategic imperatives for companies seeking resilience and relevance in the 21st century.

8.2. The Growing Importance of Environmental, Social, and Governance and Sustainability in Corporate Governance

8.2.1 Evolution of Corporate Governance Toward Sustainability

Corporate governance has traditionally focused on safeguarding shareholder interests, primarily through financial performance and

Women see sustainability not as strategy, but as survival.

risk management oversight. However, the emergence of global sustainability challenges and stakeholder activism has catalysed a paradigm shift toward a broader governance mandate. The scope of corporate governance now encompasses environmental protection, social justice, and ethical leadership, reflecting the growing consensus that long-term corporate success is inseparable from sustainable business practices.

Sustainability in governance means integrating ESG factors into strategic decision-making, risk assessment, and performance measurement. Companies are expected to manage their environmental footprint, foster positive social impact, and uphold rigorous governance standards to build resilient and future-ready organisations. This evolution underscores the recognition that companies that fail to adapt to sustainability imperatives face not only reputational damage but also financial risks, including regulatory penalties, loss of investor confidence, and operational disruptions.

8.2.2 Global and Indian Regulatory Landscape on Environmental, Social, and Governance

Globally, frameworks such as the United Nations Sustainable Development Goals (UN SDGs), the Task Force on Climate-related Financial Disclosures (TCFD), and the Principles for Responsible Investment (PRI) have set benchmarks for corporate sustainability disclosure and responsibility. These initiatives guide companies on environmental impact reduction, social equity, and governance transparency.

In India, the Securities and Exchange Board of India (SEBI) has played a critical role in institutionalising ESG practices. Securities Exchange Board of India's (SEBI) mandate for BRSR for the top 1,000 listed companies marks a significant step toward mainstreaming ESG disclosures. Additionally, the Companies Act, 2013, introduced Corporate Social Responsibility (CSR) requirements, compelling companies to invest in social development initiatives.

When women lead, the Earth is heard.

These regulations signify a strengthening governance framework that demands higher accountability and transparency on ESG matters. Boards and IDs must now ensure compliance with these evolving standards while integrating ESG into the company's strategic and operational fabric.

8.2.3 The Board's Role in Environmental, Social, and Governance Oversight

Effective ESG governance begins at the boardroom level. Boards have the fiduciary responsibility to oversee how management addresses ESG risks and opportunities. This oversight includes setting the tone at the top, approving ESG strategies, monitoring performance, and ensuring accurate disclosure. IDs have a vital role in this process. Their objectivity enables them to scrutinise management claims, challenge gaps in sustainability efforts, and demand rigorous ESG risk management. Many boards have established dedicated ESG or sustainability committees, often chaired or significantly influenced by IDs, to deepen focus on these areas.

Boards must foster a culture where ESG is not siloed but integrated across all functions and decisions. This holistic approach ensures sustainability becomes a core business value rather than a peripheral compliance exercise.

8.3. The Unique Role of Women Independent Directors in Environmental, Social, and Governance Leadership

8.3.1 Perspectives and Leadership Styles Aligned with Environmental, Social, and Governance

Women's IDs often bring leadership styles that resonate deeply with ESG principles. Research highlights that women leaders tend to emphasise collaboration, inclusiveness, and ethical decision-making qualities essential for navigating complex ESG challenges. Unlike conventional top-down leadership, women directors frequently foster dialogue and seek consensus among diverse stakeholders, ensuring that multiple perspectives inform corporate sustainability strategies.

Women directors carry society's wounds and wisdom to the boardroom.

This leadership approach aligns with the multifaceted nature of ESG issues, which require balancing environmental concerns, social justice, and governance ethics. Women directors' propensity for empathy and long-term thinking supports the integration of sustainability goals into the core business agenda, beyond mere compliance.

8.3.2 Research Insights on Gender Diversity and Environmental, Social, and Governance Outcomes

Quantitative and qualitative studies consistently reveal a positive correlation between gender diversity on boards and improved ESG performance. Companies with women IDs score higher on environmental stewardship, social responsibility, and governance transparency.

For example, a 2022 global survey by MSCI found that firms with at least 30% women on their boards had better carbon emissions management and stronger employee welfare policies. Similarly, in India, data from the Indian Institute of Corporate Affairs showed that boards with women directors were more likely to invest in community development and maintain robust governance practices.

These findings suggest that women's presence on boards is not merely symbolic but substantively contributes to embedding sustainability in business operations.

8.3.3 Enhancing Boardroom Dynamics Through Women's Presence

Women IDs also enhance board dynamics by diversifying thought and reducing the risk of groupthink. Boards dominated by homogeneous perspectives often fail to identify emerging ESG risks or innovative opportunities.

Women bring fresh viewpoints and are often more willing to challenge prevailing assumptions, which leads to more rigorous debates and better decision-making. Their presence encourages accountability and transparency, ensuring that sustainability commitments are not sidelined but actively pursued.

In addition, women directors tend to strengthen board culture by promoting respectful communication and ethical norms, further reinforcing governance integrity.

8.4. Women Independent Directors Driving Environmental Stewardship

8.4.1 Advocacy for Climate Action and Resource Efficiency

Women IDs are increasingly recognised as strong advocates for environmental sustainability within the boardroom. Their commitment to climate action often drives companies to adopt more ambitious targets for reducing carbon emissions, enhancing energy efficiency, and minimising waste. This proactive stance aligns with the urgent global need to combat climate change and transition toward low-carbon economies.

By championing green initiatives, women directors help embed environmental considerations into business strategy rather than treating them as peripheral concerns. Their leadership encourages investment in renewable energy, sustainable supply chains, and circular economy practices, actions that not only benefit the planet but can also improve operational resilience and cost-effectiveness.

8.4.2 Integrating Environmental Risks into Corporate Strategy

Effective management of environmental risks is essential for long-term business sustainability. Women's IDs play a critical role in ensuring that environmental factors such as climate-related risks, water scarcity, biodiversity loss, and pollution are systematically incorporated into corporate risk management frameworks.

They advocate for comprehensive environmental due diligence, rigorous scenario planning, and transparent reporting. This vigilance helps companies anticipate regulatory changes, safeguard their reputations, and

Women's presence makes the boardroom conscience louder.

avoid operational disruptions. By promoting a culture of environmental accountability, women directors contribute to safeguarding shareholder and stakeholder value alike.

8.4.3 Case Examples of Environmental Initiatives Led by Women Directors

Dabur India Limited, one of India's leading FMCG companies, has made notable strides in environmental sustainability. Under the guidance of its board, which includes women IDs, Dabur has implemented various initiatives to reduce its environmental footprint. These efforts encompass waste reduction, energy efficiency, and sustainable sourcing of raw materials. The company's commitment to sustainability is reflected in its comprehensive environmental policies and practices, which align with global standards and contribute to its reputation as a responsible corporate entity.

Globally, women's IDs have been at the forefront of steering companies towards science-based targets for emission reductions, championing investments in green technologies, and encouraging transparent disclosures aligned with frameworks such as the TCFD. Their leadership has been pivotal in integrating environmental considerations into corporate strategies, ensuring that sustainability becomes a core component of business operations.

These real-world examples highlight how women's leadership translates into measurable environmental outcomes that align with corporate sustainability goals.

8.5. Advancing Social Responsibility Through Women Independent Directors

8.5.1 Expanding the Social Dimension of Environmental, Social, and Governance

The social pillar of ESG encompasses a broad array of concerns: labour rights and workplace conditions, diversity and inclusion, community

A woman on the board makes social justice a board agenda.

engagement, human rights, employee welfare, and consumer protection. In an era where social justice and equity issues are at the forefront of public discourse, corporations face mounting pressure to demonstrate their commitment to responsible social practices.

Women IDs have emerged as pivotal figures in advancing social responsibility agendas within companies. Their unique perspectives and leadership styles naturally align with social issues, allowing them to advocate effectively for policies and initiatives that promote fairness, equality, and respect for all stakeholders.

8.5.2 Championing Diversity and Inclusion

One of the most significant social contributions of women IDs is their active championing of workplace diversity and inclusion (D&I). Having personally navigated gender barriers in corporate environments, these directors are acutely aware of the systemic challenges faced by underrepresented groups.

They often push boards and management to establish robust D&I policies, including fair recruitment, retention strategies, and career development programs for women, minorities, and marginalised communities. By doing so, they help cultivate workplaces that are not only more equitable but also more innovative and resilient, as diverse teams have been shown to enhance creativity and problem-solving.

Women IDs also serve as role models, inspiring organisations to embed gender equality into their culture and reporting frameworks, sometimes setting voluntary targets for board and workforce diversity that exceed regulatory requirements.

8.5.3 Enhancing Employee Welfare and Human Rights Oversight

Beyond diversity, women IDs tend to prioritise broader employee welfare issues, such as health and safety, work-life balance, and fair labour

Diverse boards don't just look different; they lead differently.

practices. In a post-pandemic world, where employee well-being has become paramount, their oversight ensures that companies adopt policies that protect and support their workforce effectively.

Moreover, they often push for stringent human rights due diligence, ensuring that the company's operations and supply chains do not contribute to exploitation, forced labour, or unsafe working conditions. This vigilance is especially critical for multinational companies operating in regions with weak regulatory environments or complex social issues.

8.5.4 Fostering Community Engagement and Social Impact

Women directors also elevate the role of CSR by advocating for meaningful community engagement. They emphasise that CSR should transcend compliance and philanthropy to become a strategic lever for positive social change.

Through their influence, companies increasingly invest in education, healthcare, women's empowerment, and environmental justice projects that create shared value for both the company and the communities it serves. Their advocacy often leads to partnerships with NGOs, government agencies, and social enterprises, fostering collaborative approaches to addressing societal challenges.

8.5.5 Case Studies: Social Leadership by Women Independent Directors

Several illustrative examples demonstrate the social impact women's IDs have delivered:

- In a major Indian Information Technology company, a woman ID championed the introduction of mental health support programs and flexible working arrangements, significantly improving employee satisfaction and retention.
- At a global pharmaceutical firm, a woman director played a key role in establishing rigorous supply chain audits that upheld labour

Women are not just stakeholders in society; they are its stewards.

rights and ethical sourcing, enhancing the company's reputation and compliance with international standards.

- Another notable case is a financial institution where a woman ID-led efforts to expand financial inclusion initiatives targeting underserved populations, thereby aligning business goals with social upliftment.

These cases underscore the transformative potential women IDs have in embedding social responsibility as a core governance priority.

8.6. Strengthening Governance Through Women Independent Directors

8.6.1 Governance as the Backbone of Sustainable Corporate Performance

Governance represents the foundation upon which environmental and social initiatives rest. Sound governance ensures that corporate strategies, including ESG efforts, are effectively designed, implemented, monitored, and reported. It embodies principles of accountability, transparency, ethical conduct, and risk management that are essential for the credibility and resilience of any organisation.

IDs, by virtue of their non-executive status and objective outlook, are critical to upholding governance standards. Women IDs, in particular, bring distinctive attributes that enhance board effectiveness and strengthen the overall governance framework.

8.6.2 Promoting Ethical Leadership and Integrity

Women's IDs often emphasise ethical leadership as a non-negotiable board priority. Their approach to governance is frequently grounded in a commitment to integrity, fairness, and ethical conduct that transcends mere legal compliance.

They challenge management decisions that might expose the company to reputational or regulatory risks, advocating for policies that prevent corruption, fraud, and conflicts of interest. By reinforcing a culture of "doing the right thing," women directors help build trust with shareholders, employees, regulators, and other stakeholders.

Their vigilance in this area also involves scrutinising executive remuneration and incentive structures to ensure alignment with long-term sustainability goals rather than short-term financial gains.

8.6.3 Enhancing Board Composition and Effectiveness

Women's IDs contribute significantly to board composition, bringing diversity in thought, experience, and perspective. Their presence counters groupthink – a common governance pitfall where homogeneous boards may overlook risks or innovative solutions.

Research indicates that gender-diverse boards tend to engage in more rigorous oversight and strategic discussions, especially on complex issues such as ESG integration, risk management, and crisis response. Women directors often encourage a culture of open dialogue, respect for dissenting views, and collaborative decision-making, which elevates the board's overall effectiveness.

Furthermore, women ID frequently serve on key board committees such as audit, nomination, remuneration, and ESG committees where they influence critical governance decisions and promote accountability.

8.6.4 Driving Transparency and Disclosure Practices

Transparency is a cornerstone of good governance, essential for maintaining stakeholder confidence and meeting regulatory demands. Women IDs actively champion robust disclosure practices, ensuring that companies provide accurate, timely, and comprehensive information about their financial performance, ESG impacts, and governance structures.

Their advocacy often leads to enhanced sustainability reporting, adoption of global disclosure standards (e.g., GRI, SASB, TCFD), and meaningful stakeholder engagement. Such transparency not only fulfils compliance obligations but also strengthens the company's reputation and investor relations.

8.6.5 Navigating Complex Governance Challenges

The contemporary governance landscape is marked by increasing complexity and volatility from cybersecurity threats and data privacy to geopolitical risks and evolving regulatory frameworks. Women IDs demonstrate adaptability and strategic acumen in navigating these challenges.

Their risk-aware mindset equips boards to anticipate potential disruptions and incorporate resilience-building measures. They often advocate for continuous board education on emerging governance issues and promote the integration of technology and data analytics in board oversight functions.

8.6.6 Case Examples of Governance Leadership by Women Directors

Numerous companies exemplify the governance impact of women IDs:

- A leading Indian conglomerate appointed a woman ID to chair its audit committee, resulting in enhanced internal controls, improved financial disclosures, and stronger regulatory compliance.
- In a global manufacturing firm, a woman ID spearheaded the overhaul of the company's whistleblower policy and ethics hotline, fostering a safer environment for reporting misconduct.
- Another example includes a financial services company where women directors led the board's digital governance initiatives, addressing cybersecurity risks and data privacy concerns proactively.

These examples illustrate how women IDs translate governance principles into practical and impactful actions that safeguard corporate reputation and sustainability.

Where women speak, silence breaks - and scrutiny begins.

8.7. Overcoming Challenges Faced by Women Independent Directors in Environmental, Social, and Governance Leadership

8.7.1 Introduction: The Persistence of Barriers

Despite growing recognition of the value women IDs bring to ESG leadership and corporate governance; they continue to face a range of significant challenges. These obstacles not only hinder their full participation and influence on boards but also impact the pace at which ESG integration is realised. Understanding these challenges is crucial to devising effective solutions that empower women directors and enhance their ability to lead on sustainability issues.

8.7.2 Gender Bias and Stereotypes in the Boardroom

One of the most persistent challenges is the implicit and explicit gender bias entrenched in corporate cultures. Women directors often confront stereotypes questioning their expertise, leadership style, or commitment, especially in traditionally male-dominated industries such as energy, manufacturing, and finance.

Such biases can manifest in subtle ways, such as being excluded from informal networks or decision-making discussions or more overtly, through resistance to their suggestions or undervaluing their contributions. These dynamics can undermine women directors' confidence and diminish their effectiveness in advocating for ESG priorities.

8.7.3 Limited Representation and Tokenism

Although the number of women IDs has increased, their representation on boards often remains low, sometimes falling short of critical mass thresholds needed to influence board culture and decision-making substantively. In many cases, women are appointed as a symbolic gesture toward diversity, a phenomenon known as tokenism, without genuine empowerment or inclusion.

The balance sheet of the earth improves when women balance the boar.

Tokenism limits women directors' ability to steer ESG agendas and may lead to isolation, where their voice is marginalised or treated as representing "women's issues" only. This hampers the broader recognition of ESG as a strategic imperative relevant to the entire board.

8.7.4 Insufficient Environmental, Social, and Governance Expertise and Training Opportunities

While women IDs bring invaluable leadership qualities, some face challenges related to specific technical knowledge of ESG frameworks, metrics, and regulations. The rapidly evolving ESG landscape demands continuous learning and upskilling to stay effective in oversight roles.

Unfortunately, access to tailored ESG training and development programs for women directors can be limited, particularly in emerging markets or smaller companies. This gap constrains their ability to confidently challenge management, evaluate ESG risks, and contribute to strategic decisions.

8.7.5 Work-Life Balance and Time Constraints

Women IDs frequently juggle multiple roles and responsibilities, professional, familial, and social, which can create challenges in managing the time commitments required for active board participation.

The demanding nature of ESG oversight, which often involves attending additional committee meetings, stakeholder engagements, and monitoring complex sustainability initiatives, can exacerbate time pressures. Without organisational support and flexible governance practices, women directors may find it difficult to maintain the sustained focus ESG leadership requires.

8.7.6 Navigating Male-Dominated Networks and Informal Power Structures

Boardrooms are often influenced by informal networks and power structures that have traditionally excluded women. These networks shape access to critical information, mentorship, and influence, which are essential for effective governance and leadership.

Women's IDs may face challenges in penetrating these networks or gaining equal footing in informal discussions. This limits their ability to build alliances, gather support for ESG initiatives, and exercise influence beyond formal meetings.

8.7.7 Strategies to Overcome Challenges

Recognising these challenges, various strategies can be adopted by companies, regulators, and women directors themselves to foster a more inclusive and empowering environment:

- **Strengthening board diversity mandates:** Regulators can enhance requirements for gender diversity and ESG expertise on boards, ensuring minimum representation and balanced skill sets.
- **Comprehensive ESG training:** Boards should provide ongoing, customised ESG training to all directors, with special programs to support women in developing technical proficiency and confidence.
- **Mentorship and sponsorship programs:** Establishing mentorship networks that connect women directors with experienced board members and ESG experts can facilitate knowledge sharing and career development.
- **Promoting Inclusive board cultures:** Boards must foster cultures that value diverse perspectives, encourage open dialogue, and address unconscious bias through awareness and behavioural training.
- **Flexible governance practices:** Adopting flexible meeting schedules, virtual participation options, and reasonable workload expectations helps accommodate diverse life circumstances and sustain women's board engagement.

A woman director may not shout - but she seldom shrinks from truth.

- **Empowering women directors as ESG champions:** Encouraging women directors to take leadership roles in ESG committees and public advocacy strengthens their influence and visibility.

8.7.8 Role of Institutional Investors and Stakeholders

Institutional investors and stakeholders also play a vital role in supporting women IDs by demanding stronger gender diversity and ESG governance from companies. Their voting power, engagement, and stewardship can drive boards to prioritise inclusivity and sustainability.

Active dialogue between investors and companies regarding board composition and ESG performance reinforces accountability and accelerates progress toward more balanced, effective governance.

8.8. Building the Future – Empowering Women Independent Directors as Environmental, Social, and Governance Leaders

8.8.1 The Imperative for Empowerment

As global attention intensifies on ESG integration and sustainable business practices, empowering women IDs to lead in this domain is no longer optional; it is a strategic necessity. Companies with gender-diverse, ESG-savvy boards consistently outperform peers in resilience, innovation, and stakeholder trust.

To build a future where women's IDs are fully recognised as ESG champions, concerted efforts are required across governance structures, talent pipelines, and societal attitudes. Empowerment means equipping women directors with the tools, opportunities, and support systems needed to exercise their influence effectively and sustainably.

8.8.2 Enhancing Recruitment and Selection Processes

Recruitment processes for IDs must be refined to prioritise gender diversity alongside ESG expertise and leadership potential. Search committees and nominating bodies should adopt inclusive practices that actively identify and attract qualified women candidates with strong ESG credentials.

Transparent criteria, unbiased interview processes, and proactive outreach to women leaders across sectors, especially those with sustainability and governance experience, can expand the talent pool. Emphasising diverse perspectives during selection not only enriches boards but also signals a genuine commitment to ESG priorities.

8.8.3 Providing Continuous Education and Capacity Building

Continuous professional development is crucial for women IDs to stay ahead of the evolving ESG landscape. Boards and professional organisations should offer tailored training programs covering emerging sustainability standards, regulatory changes, impact measurement, and stakeholder engagement strategies.

Capacity-building initiatives may include workshops, webinars, peer learning groups, and mentorship opportunities that foster knowledge exchange and confidence-building. By investing in education, companies ensure that women directors can lead ESG conversations with authority and strategic insight.

8.8.4 Creating Supportive Board Cultures and Structures

Empowerment flourishes in board cultures that genuinely value diversity and inclusivity. Boards must cultivate environments where women directors feel heard, respected, and able to contribute fully.

This involves establishing clear governance policies against discrimination and harassment, promoting inclusive meeting practices that encourage participation, and providing platforms for women directors to lead key committees, particularly those focused on ESG, audit, and risk.

When women shape strategy, sustainability follows.

Additionally, governance structures should facilitate effective work-life balance through flexible meeting schedules and remote participation options, enabling sustained engagement.

8.8.5 Leveraging Networks and Alliances

Women IDs can amplify their impact by connecting with networks and alliances dedicated to advancing women in leadership and ESG governance. These platforms offer peer support, advocacy channels, and access to resources that enhance visibility and influence.

Examples include global organisations such as Women Corporate Directors (WCD), 30% club, and regional groups promoting board diversity and sustainability leadership. Participation in such networks enables women directors to share best practices, mentor emerging leaders, and collaborate on systemic change initiatives.

8.8.6 Encouraging Investor and Stakeholder Engagement

Investors and stakeholders increasingly prioritise board diversity and ESG governance as key indicators of corporate health and future readiness. Women IDs' benefit from investor support that reinforces their roles as sustainability stewards.

Active investor engagement through dialogues, proxy voting policies, and public advocacy can motivate boards to prioritise women's leadership in ESG roles. Stakeholders, including employees, customers, and communities, also play a role in holding companies accountable for inclusive governance and sustainability performance.

8.8.7 The Broader Societal Impact of Empowering Women Directors

Empowering women IDs extends beyond individual boards; it contributes to societal progress by challenging gender norms, promoting economic equality, and fostering corporate citizenship.

Women measure success in legacies, not just ledgers.

As visible leaders driving ESG agendas, women directors inspire younger generations, influence policy dialogues, and help create ecosystems where sustainable business practices and gender equity reinforce each other.

Their leadership demonstrates that diverse governance is not only fair but essential for addressing complex global challenges such as climate change, social inequality, and ethical governance.

8.8.8 Conclusion: Toward a Sustainable and Inclusive Boardroom Future

Building the future requires commitment from all corporate ecosystem actors: boards, management, regulators, investors, and civil society. Empowering women IDs as ESG leaders will unlock new pathways for innovation, resilience, and shared value creation.

By embracing diversity as a strategic asset and equipping women directors with the knowledge, authority, and support they deserve, companies will not only improve ESG outcomes but also set new standards for governance excellence.

The future boardroom is one where women IDs lead with confidence, drives sustainability agendas, and embodies the ethical stewardship vital for long-term corporate success.

8.9. Measuring Impact – Evaluating the Contribution of Women Independent Directors to Environmental, Social, and Governance Performance

8.9.1 The Importance of Measurement in Environmental, Social, and Governance Leadership

The role of women IDs in advancing ESG goals is widely acknowledged, but quantifying their actual impact remains a complex challenge. Effective measurement is essential to validate their contributions, identify best practices, and inform future governance strategies.

A woman's judgment demands clarity; her commitment demands perseverance.

Measuring impact also supports transparency and accountability, enabling companies and stakeholders to track progress against sustainability objectives and board diversity commitments.

8.9.2 Defining Key Performance Indicators for Women Directors' Environmental, Social, and Governance Contributions

To assess the influence of women IDs on ESG performance, boards must establish clear and relevant Key Performance Indicators (KPIs). These KPIs should reflect both qualitative and quantitative dimensions of governance and sustainability leadership.

Possible KPIs include:

- **Board diversity metrics:** Percentage of women on boards, proportion of women in key committees (e.g., ESG, audit, nomination).
- **ESG integration in strategy:** Evidence of ESG considerations embedded in board-level decision-making and corporate strategy.
- **Policy adoption:** Number and quality of ESG-related policies initiated or championed by women directors.
- **Sustainability reporting quality:** Improvements in the comprehensiveness and transparency of ESG disclosures attributable to women directors' influence.
- **Stakeholder engagement:** Initiatives led or supported by women directors that enhance engagement with employees, communities, investors, and regulators.
- **Risk management:** Effectiveness of ESG risk identification and mitigation processes where women directors have oversight roles.

She doesn't just join the board; she transforms it for future generations.

8.9.3 Quantitative Approaches to Measuring Impact

Quantitative methods provide measurable data points for tracking women directors' influence, such as:

- Correlating board gender diversity with ESG ratings from third-party agencies (e.g., MSCI, Sustainalytics).
- Analysing financial performance and ESG metrics before and after increasing women's representation.
- Surveying stakeholder perceptions regarding board effectiveness and ESG commitments.
- Monitoring participation rates and leadership roles of women directors in ESG committees.

While quantitative data offers objectivity, it may not capture the full scope of women directors' contributions.

8.9.4 Qualitative Approaches and Case Studies

Qualitative evaluation complements quantitative analysis by exploring the context, behaviours, and influence dynamics of women directors, including:

- Board meeting minutes and interviews revealing advocacy efforts, challenges addressed, and decision-making impact.
- Case studies showcasing successful ESG initiatives driven by women IDs.
- Feedback from peers, executives, and external stakeholders on women directors' leadership style and effectiveness.

Qualitative insights help understand how women directors shape board culture, ethical tone, and strategic priorities around ESG.

8.9.5 Challenges in Measuring Impact

Several obstacles complicate impact measurement:

- **Attribution complexity:** ESG outcomes result from collective board efforts and broader organisational factors, making it difficult to isolate individual contributions.
- **Data availability:** Many companies lack standardised disclosures on board activities linked to ESG or gender diversity.
- **Subjectivity:** Qualitative assessments risk bias and variability in interpretation.
- **Time lag:** ESG initiatives often take years to yield measurable results, requiring long-term evaluation frameworks.

8.9.6 Emerging Tools and Frameworks

Innovations in governance analytics and ESG reporting are improving impact measurement capabilities:

- Integrated reporting frameworks increasingly incorporate governance and diversity metrics.
- Board evaluation tools now include specific modules on diversity and ESG contributions.
- Artificial intelligence and data analytics enable deeper analysis of board behaviours, meeting participation, and sentiment.

These tools offer promising avenues to capture the nuanced impacts of women directors.

8.9.7 Recommendations for Boards and Companies

To strengthen measurement practices, companies should:

- Establish clear objectives and KPIs for women directors' ESG roles during board appointments.

A woman's influence demands assertiveness; her accountability drives social impact.

- Incorporate ESG and diversity criteria into board evaluations and performance reviews.
- Enhance transparency by reporting board composition and ESG oversight activities in annual and sustainability reports.
- Invest in training for board members on data-driven governance assessment.
- Engage external experts for independent evaluations and benchmarking.

8.9.8 The Role of Regulators and Investors

Regulators can mandate more rigorous disclosure requirements relating to board diversity and ESG governance. Investor stewardship groups should integrate these factors into voting guidelines and engagement agendas.

By fostering a regulatory and market environment that values measurable impact, stakeholders can accelerate progress toward more inclusive and sustainable governance.

8.9.9 Conclusion: Towards Evidence-Based Empowerment

Measuring the contribution of women IDs to ESG performance is both a challenge and an opportunity. Robust impact assessment not only highlights their vital role but also informs policies and practices that empower them further.

As companies refine these measurement approaches, they pave the way for greater accountability, continuous improvement, and ultimately, stronger ESG outcomes driven by diverse and effective boards.

8.10. Conclusion and the Road Ahead

8.10.1 Recap of Key Insights

Throughout this section, we have explored the critical and transformative role that women IDs play as champions of ESG and sustainability in today's corporate landscape. From their unique perspectives and leadership styles to their contributions in driving robust governance and ethical practices, women directors have emerged as indispensable actors in steering companies toward sustainable, responsible growth.

We examined the current landscape of women's representation on boards, the multifaceted challenges they face, and practical strategies for empowering them to lead effectively on ESG issues. The discussion also underscored the importance of measuring their impact to validate and amplify their contributions.

8.10.2 The Strategic Imperative of Gender-Diverse Environmental, Social, and Governance Leadership

In an era marked by heightened environmental risks, social inequalities, and governance expectations, companies must embrace board diversity - especially the inclusion of women IDs as a strategic asset. Research and case studies consistently link gender-diverse boards with stronger ESG performance, innovation, and long-term value creation.

Women directors bring distinct competencies such as collaboration, stakeholder sensitivity, and ethical vigilance, which are particularly suited to navigating the complexities of sustainability challenges. Their leadership enriches board deliberations and drives companies toward a triple bottom line: people, planet, and profit.

8.10.3 Challenges as Opportunities for Progress

The barriers women's IDs face, ranging from implicit biases to structural constraints, should be viewed not only as challenges but as catalysts for reform. Addressing these obstacles requires systemic change involving corporate culture shifts, regulatory reforms, and proactive advocacy.

By confronting and dismantling these hurdles, companies unlock the full potential of women directors, fostering more inclusive and resilient governance models that better serve all stakeholders.

A woman's judgment demands clarity; her courage safeguards corporate conscience.

8.10.4 The Role of Ecosystem Actors

The road ahead demands collaboration among all stakeholders in the corporate ecosystem:

- **Boards and companies:** Must commit to transparent, merit-based recruitment; continuous ESG education; and inclusive cultures that empower women directors.
- **Regulators and policymakers:** Should strengthen mandates on gender diversity and ESG governance disclosure to drive consistent standards and accountability.
- **Investors and asset managers:** Need to actively engage with companies on board diversity and sustainability performance, using their influence to promote change.
- **Professional networks and academia:** Play a critical role in nurturing women's leadership pipelines and conducting research to inform best practices.

8.10.5 Emerging Trends and Future Outlook

Looking forward, several trends will shape the evolving role of women IDs in ESG leadership:

- **Technological advancements:** Tools such as AI and data analytics will enhance governance transparency and measurement of women directors' impact.
- **Global policy alignment:** Increasing convergence of sustainability reporting standards will elevate the importance of board diversity disclosures worldwide.
- **Intersectional Approaches:** Greater attention to diversity beyond gender including race, ethnicity, and socio-economic background will broaden perspectives and deepen ESG effectiveness.

Her engagement demands collaboration; her oversight strengthens ESG frameworks.

- **Youth and new voices:** Rising involvement of younger, purpose-driven directors will complement women's leadership to accelerate sustainability agendas.

8.10.6 Call to Action: Toward a Sustainable and Inclusive Corporate Future

Empowering women IDs as ESG leaders is not merely a matter of compliance or optics it is a profound business imperative and ethical obligation. Companies that harness the full potential of diverse boards position themselves to thrive in a world where sustainability, transparency, and social responsibility define success.

The time to act is now. By embracing diversity, fostering empowerment, and rigorously measuring impact, the corporate world can build governance structures that reflect the values and challenges of our times.

8.10.7 Final Thought

The journey toward sustainable and inclusive boardrooms is ongoing, with women IDs at its forefront. Their leadership, resilience, and vision will continue to shape not only the companies they serve but the broader trajectory of global corporate governance.

Together, stakeholders can forge a future where gender-diverse, ESG-driven boards are the norm, and where businesses contribute meaningfully to a better, more equitable world.

"She enters the boardroom not to echo the past, but to shape the future where governance is grounded in integrity, sustainability is second nature, and leadership is as compassionate as it is courageous. In every decision, she proves that when a woman leads, the world is not only better governed it is bettered."

CHAPTER 9

Tone from the Top: Why Boardroom Ethics Begin with Independent Directors

"Independent directors must be more than independent by law; they must be independent by conscience."

9.1 Introduction: The Moral Compass of the Boardroom

In an age where trust is currency and corporate reputations can crumble overnight, ethical leadership has become more than just a lofty ideal – it is a strategic imperative. In boardrooms across India, where decisions shape the destiny of companies, stakeholders, and the broader economy, the question is no longer *whether* ethics matter but *how* they are practiced and reinforced. At the heart of this conversation sits the Independent Director (ID) – a figure expected not merely to oversee, but to guide, to question, and most importantly, to *embody* the ethical standards the board must uphold.

The phrase *"Tone from the Top"* captures the essence of ethical governance. It refers to the values, attitudes, and behaviours demonstrated by

The boardroom sets the tone, and the independent director strikes the first note.

a company's senior leadership, particularly its board of directors, which cascade through the organisation. When the board speaks with integrity, the rest of the company listens. Conversely, when ethical shortcuts are tolerated at the top, misconduct can quickly become systemic.

IDs, by virtue of their autonomy, moral authority, and strategic detachment from management, are uniquely positioned to anchor this tone. But their role is neither simple nor ceremonial. The challenges of boardroom dynamics, the opacity of complex businesses, and the often-subtle pressures of allegiance test the ethical fortitude of even the most seasoned directors. And yet, it is precisely in these conditions that the ID must shine not as a passive observer but as an active moral compass.

This part lays the foundation for understanding boardroom ethics in the Indian corporate context and makes the case for why IDs must be the first responders and final line of defence in upholding integrity at the highest levels of governance.

9.1.1 What is Boardroom Ethics?

Ethics, in the boardroom context, refers to the guiding principles that influence the behaviours and decisions of directors as they fulfil their fiduciary duties. Unlike compliance, which is enforced through rules and penalties, ethics operates in a more nuanced space. It encompasses questions of fairness, transparency, accountability, and the ability to distinguish right from wrong even when the law is silent or ambiguous.

9.1.2 From Compliance to Conscience

Many corporate failures – be it Enron in the United States, Satyam in India, or Wirecard in Germany – did not occur because of a lack of regulation. Each operated under a robust legal framework. Their collapse stemmed from a deficit of ethical governance. Too often, boards were compliant but not courageous; informed but not inquisitive; structured but not principled.

When the top is silent, misconduct echoes loudly below.

Ethical governance, therefore, demands more than ticking regulatory boxes. It calls for conscientious leadership – a culture where directors ask not only, *"Is this allowed?"* but more importantly, *"Is this the right thing to do?"*

9.1.3 Indian Lens: Evolving Expectations

India's corporate ecosystem has seen a rapid evolution in governance norms, particularly post the Satyam scandal of 2009. Securities Exchange Board of India's (SEBI) tightening of Listing Obligations and Disclosure Requirements (LODR), the Companies Act, 2013, and more recent ESG frameworks signal a growing emphasis on ethical stewardship. But cultural and structural challenges remain. In promoter-led companies, boardrooms may still function more as echo chambers than as spaces of independent thought.

Here, the ID plays a critical role not only in speaking truth to power but in reframing the board's very approach to ethical decision-making.

9.1.4 Beyond Laws: The Board as the Ethical Conscience

While laws outline what companies *must* do, ethics shape what they *should* do. This distinction is crucial in the boardroom. Directors are often called upon to navigate grey areas where regulation offers little guidance. Should a company pursue a legally permissible but socially controversial strategy? Should it reward top management with generous bonuses during a year of layoffs and environmental violations?

These are not merely governance questions; they are *ethical* ones.

9.1.5 The Silent Signals of the Boardroom

Ethical leadership is often exercised through subtle cues:

- **Who gets heard in meetings?**
  When IDs raise concerns, are they listened to or sidelined?

Culture doesn't trickle down it cascades from character.

- **What gets minuted and what doesn't?**
  Are ethical disagreements recorded transparently or quietly buried?
- **How does the board react to bad news?**
  Is there defensiveness or a genuine commitment to accountability?

Each of these reflects the "tone" being set from the top, and IDs are instrumental in influencing these signals.

9.1.6 Ethical Risk as Strategic Risk

Finally, companies must recognise that ethical risk is *strategic risk*. A single lapse can wipe out years of brand value, investor trust, and market capital. IDs must therefore treat ethics not as an afterthought but as a core element of risk management.

9.1.7 Reputation: A Non-Renewable Resource

Ethics-related scandals, be they around insider trading, sexual harassment, environmental violations, or misleading disclosures, can inflict irreversible reputational damage. For IDs, safeguarding ethical conduct is not just about fulfilling legal duties; it's about *preserving the soul of the organisation.*

9.2 The Central Role of Independent Directors

9.2.1 Ethics and Independence: A Symbiotic Relationship

The core strength of an ID lies in its detachment from executive management, promoters, or other vested interests. This statutory independence, enshrined in the Companies Act, 2013 and SEBI's LODR Regulations, is meant to cultivate objectivity, judgment, and, crucially, ethical vigilance. Independence is not merely structural or legal; it is *behavioural.* And it is this behavioural independence that determines whether the ID becomes a true ethical gatekeeper or a silent bystander.

The board that permits, promotes the very thing it should prevent.

9.2.2 The Moral Foundation of Independence

An ID's ability to uphold ethics is rooted in several key attributes:

- No financial interest in the company's performance
- No prior relationships with promoters or senior management
- Tenure and remuneration limits that reduce inducement risks
- Legal mandates to act in the best interest of stakeholders

These structural safeguards aim to ensure IDs are not compromised by conflicts of interest. However, independence on paper does not always translate into independence in practice. True ethical leadership stems from courage, being willing to speak up even when it is uncomfortable or unpopular.

9.2.3 Anatomy of Ethical Oversight

IDs sit on various board committees where critical ethical judgments are made. Their responsibilities include questioning, reviewing, approving, and – when necessary – objecting. Here's how they function as ethical anchors within key board functions:

9.2.3.1 Audit Committee

The audit committee is often the most powerful forum for ethical oversight. It handles:

- Review of financial statements and disclosures
- Oversight of internal controls and risk management
- Response to whistleblower complaints
- Interaction with statutory and internal auditors

Here, IDs must be especially alert to signs of:

- Financial misreporting

Tone from the top is the true corporate code of conduct.

- Understated liabilities or aggressive revenue recognition
- Pressure on auditors
- Undisclosed related-party transactions

Ethical Question: Are the books being manipulated to hide poor performance or mislead investors?

9.2.3.2 Nomination and Remuneration Committee

This committee determines board composition and top executive compensation. Ethical red flags here include:

- Excessive executives' pay during periods of underperformance or layoffs
- Manipulated performance metrics to trigger bonuses
- Appointments influenced by loyalty, not merit

Ethical Question: Are we rewarding the right behaviour or entrenching the wrong one?

9.2.3.3 Risk Management Committee

IDs must ensure companies are not only managing financial or operational risks, but also:

- Reputational risks (e.g., from greenwashing or data breaches)
- Legal risks (e.g., from anti-competitive behaviour)
- Ethical risks (e.g., from misleading marketing or unsafe products)

Ethical Question: Are we proactively identifying moral risks or waiting for a crisis?

A whisper from an ethical board can silence a thousand wrongs.

9.2.3.4 Environmental, Social, and Governance and Corporate Social Responsibility Committees

Ethical leadership today includes stewardship over environmental, social, and community impacts. IDs must ensure that:

- ESG reporting is accurate and transparent
- Corporate Social Responsibility (CSR) funds are used ethically and not diverted
- The company's values align with its societal footprint

Ethical Question: Is our ESG strategy genuine or just PR?

9.2.4 Courage in the Face of Consensus

One of the greatest ethical challenges in the boardroom is **groupthink** a tendency to conform to majority opinion even when dissent is warranted. IDs must often stand alone or risk social friction with powerful promoters or long-serving peers.

9.2.5 The Importance of Dissent

Dissent, when exercised responsibly, is a hallmark of ethical oversight. The minutes of Indian board meetings rarely reflect strong disagreement, but silence doesn't always imply consent it may signal suppression. IDs should:

- Record their objections clearly in board minutes
- Insist on deferred voting when decisions are rushed
- Encourage debate, even if uncomfortable

9.2.6 From Watchdog to Steward

IDs are often referred to as "watchdogs," but this label is limiting. Ethics requires not just watching, but *stewarding.* The ID must not only

The board's conscience is its most valuable asset, and its quietest voice.

guard against malfeasance but also *guide* the company toward responsible decision-making.

9.2.6.1 Beyond Policing: Shaping Culture

Ethical leadership is about shaping tone, not just checking controls. The most impactful IDs:

- Ask "why" before "how"
- Seek to understand organisational culture, not just financial metrics
- Foster transparency in informal settings, not just official meetings

9.2.6.2 Building Ethical Muscle

To be ethical stewards, IDs need:

- **Continuous training** in emerging ethical and governance issues
- **Courageous mentorship** partnering with like-minded directors
- **Boardroom allies** fostering a culture of collective conscience

9.3 Instruments of Influence: How Independent Directors Set the Tone

9.3.1 The Ethics Committee and Beyond

Ethical influence is most effective when it is institutionalised. IDs have the formal authority to shape ethical conduct through participation in key committees and board structures. But beyond the formal, they also shape culture through informal engagement, mentorship, and subtle leadership.

While not mandatory under Indian corporate law, many large listed companies have constituted Ethics Committees, particularly in sectors like finance, pharmaceuticals, and IT. These committees are increasingly seen as the *epicentre of integrity* within the board.

9.3.1.1 Ethics Committees: Scope and Composition

Typical responsibilities of an Ethics Committee include:

- Formulating and monitoring the company's code of conduct
- Reviewing whistleblower complaints and fraud reports
- Advising on ethical dilemmas raised by management
- Monitoring third-party ethical compliance (suppliers, partners)
- Leading periodic ethical risk assessments and culture audits

IDs serving on these committees must bring a mix of integrity, experience, and inquisitiveness.

9.3.1.2 Beyond Formal Committees

IDs also influence ethics through:

- Audit Committee oversight of ethics breaches
- Remuneration Committee's linkage of pay to ethical behaviour
- Board-level ESG reviews of human rights, sustainability, and data ethics

They must ask: Are we compensating executives for merely performing, or also for performing *ethically*?

9.3.2 Communication, Culture, and Conduct

The boardroom is more than a forum for decisions it is a microcosm of corporate culture. IDs set the tone through how they communicate, what they prioritise, and how they respond to ethical tension.

The independent director is not just a spectator; they are the ethical compass.

9.3.2.1 Ethical Conversations in the Boardroom

Tone is communicated through:

- The *language* used in board meetings.
- The *issues* that IDs choose to highlight.
- The *examples* they use to frame decisions.

For instance, an ID who consistently asks: "What's the reputational risk here?" embeds caution and foresight into the board's mindset. Directors who inquire about diversity metrics, employee well-being, or ethical sourcing help shift focus from pure financials to holistic value.

9.3.2.2 Challenging Leadership Behaviour

IDs must not shy away from correcting or challenging the Chief Executive Officer (CEO) or Chief Experience Officer's (CXO) behaviour if it conflicts with the company's stated values. This may involve:

- Suggesting a coaching or ethics training intervention
- Encouraging leadership to openly discuss failures, not just successes
- Nudging the CEO to champion ethical issues more visibly

Ethical behaviour becomes part of the culture when leaders are held accountable for their words and actions, not just results.

9.3.2.3 Leading Through Personal Example

Tone from the top starts with the **tone of the top director**. When IDs themselves demonstrate:

- Punctuality, preparation, and humility
- Transparency in declaring conflicts
- Respect for differing opinions

Where independence ends, complicity begins.

They become *living proof* of ethical leadership. Their behaviour ripples across the board, influencing promoters, executives, and even middle management.

9.3.3 Institutionalising Ethics: From Policy to Practice

While policies create structure, culture is built in *practice*. IDs play a central role in bridging this gap.

9.3.3.1 Code of Conduct and Conflict Declarations

Most companies have a board-approved code of conduct. But how seriously is it followed?

- Do IDs *review* the code periodically or just sign it annually?
- Do they insist on *clear examples* of what constitutes a violation?
- Is there a *mechanism* for reporting breaches anonymously?

Ethical practice requires clarity, not just policy.

9.3.3.2 Onboarding and Induction: Setting the Ethical Frame Early

New IDs must be inducted into the **company's ethical expectations**, not just its financials and strategies. IDs should recommend:

- Formal onboarding on corporate values and ethical history.
- Real-life examples of past dilemmas and how they were resolved.
- Early introductions to whistleblower and grievance redressal systems.

This creates alignment from day one.

9.3.3.3 Culture Audits and Pulse Checks

Proactive boards conduct **ethical culture assessments** through surveys, interviews, or external audits. IDs should ask:

- Do employees feel safe to speak up?
- Is there trust in the internal grievance system?
- Are values like fairness and transparency visible at lower levels?

Where these are lacking, IDs must push for structured interventions.

9.3.4 The Informal Power of Boardroom Allies

Ethical influence also flows through *relationships*. An ID need not always act alone. Often, informal alliances with like-minded directors or senior executives can help push back against unethical tendencies.

9.3.4.1 Informal Pre-meeting Discussions

Many board decisions are influenced before the formal meeting begins. IDs should use pre-meeting briefings to:

- Surface potential ethical concerns in advance.
- Build consensus with peers for challenging discussions.
- Propose agenda adjustments for deeper ethical review.

These behind-the-scenes conversations often *prevent bad decisions before they happen*.

9.3.4.2 Mentoring Management on Ethics

Experienced IDs can mentor CXOs not by policing but by *coaching*:

- Advising on ethical grey zones.
- Encouraging transparent stakeholder communication.
- Promoting long-term over short-term thinking.

Ethics thrive when independent directors refuse to look away.

This builds a culture of trust and ethical maturity across the leadership chain.

9.3.5 Engaging with External Stakeholders

The ID's ethical responsibility extends beyond the boardroom. Transparency to shareholders, regulators, and the public is critical in building trust.

9.3.5.1 Shareholder Engagement

IDs can shape ethical tone by:

- Participating in Annual General Meetings (AGMs).
- Being accessible to institutional investors.
- Clarifying how the board upholds ESG goals and ethical risks.

9.3.5.2 Engagement with Regulators and the Media

While media interactions are generally the domain of the Chair or CEO, in cases of ethical crisis, IDs must support *accurate, timely, and honest* disclosures. Silence or evasion can deepen reputational damage.

In extreme cases, such as whistleblower allegations or fraud, IDs must ensure prompt engagement with regulators like SEBI, SFIO, or the Ministry of Corporate Affairs (MCA).

9.3.6 Ethical Tone in Family-Owned and Promoter-Driven Companies

India's corporate landscape is dominated by promoter-led companies. This introduces a unique complexity to the role of IDs. Here, setting the ethical tone becomes more sensitive and more essential.

A truly independent director doesn't just ask hard questions; they demand real answers.

9.3.6.1 Navigating Promoter Influence

Promoters often hold significant shareholding and control. IDs must:

- Maintain assertive independence without being antagonistic.
- Use *soft power* – persuasion, principle-based questioning, and collective alignment.
- Remind promoters that *ethics and longevity are interlinked.*

9.3.6.2 Encouraging Succession and Professionalisation

An ethical ID also supports:

- Transparent succession planning.
- Leadership transitions that reward integrity, not just loyalty.
- Separation of personal interest from company interest.

These actions reinforce ethical systems that outlast personalities.

9.4 Challenges to Ethical Oversight

9.4.1 Structural Impediments to Ethical Independence

Despite their critical role, IDs in India often find themselves disempowered by systemic constraints that undermine ethical oversight. These challenges are not merely incidental; they are structural, embedded in the very architecture of Indian corporate governance.

9.4.1.1 Board Capture by Promoters

Promoter-led companies dominate Indian business, and many boards function under implicit (or explicit) influence from founders or family owners. The presence of IDs does not always guarantee real independence when:

- The promoter selects IDs based on loyalty rather than competence.

Independent oversight is the seatbelt for ethical slippage.

- IDs feel beholden to the promoter for reappointment.
- Boardroom dissent is discouraged or subtly punished.

This creates a **chilling effect**, where IDs are reluctant to raise ethical red flags, especially if they involve promoter-related interests.

9.4.1.2 Limited Access to Information

IDs often rely on management for information. If the executive team controls what is shared or delays critical disclosures, ethical blind spots emerge. Common issues include:

- Agenda papers circulated late or in incomplete form
- Financial anomalies buried in voluminous documents
- Risk reports sanitised before presentation

Ethical vigilance requires **timely, transparent, and comprehensive** information access, something IDs must demand, not passively await.

9.4.1.3 Inadequate Time Commitment

Many IDs hold multiple board positions, especially in listed companies, where they are in demand due to SEBI's mandatory quota. However, time constraints can compromise effectiveness:

- Rushed preparation before meetings
- Superficial review of audit findings or CSR spending
- Inability to build a deep understanding of the company culture

Ethical oversight is not an occasional responsibility; it requires consistent engagement and curiosity.

Directors must lead with values, not just vote with consensus.

9.4.2 Cultural and Behavioural Barriers

Beyond structure, *culture* plays a significant role in shaping ID behaviour. The norms of Indian corporate life, respect for hierarchy, preference for consensus, and discomfort with confrontation, can dilute the assertiveness required to challenge unethical conduct.

9.4.2.1 Reluctance to Dissent

Many IDs avoid voicing dissent for fear of:

- Being seen as "troublemakers"
- Losing future board opportunities
- Being ostracised socially or professionally

This results in a troubling trend: conformity over conscience.

9.4.2.2 Boardroom Groupthink

Boardrooms are often echo chambers. If other directors are silent or supportive of unethical practices, it becomes harder for a lone ID to resist. Psychological research confirms that humans tend to conform in group settings, even against their better judgment.

9.4.2.3 Misplaced Loyalty to Management

In long-serving boards, some IDs develop personal rapport with senior management, making them less objective. They may:

- Rationalise questionable behaviour as "pragmatic".
- Excuse ethical lapses as "one-offs".
- Avoid hard questions to protect relationships.

True independence means loyalty to **principles**, not personalities.

The director who shrinks from scrutiny feeds the seeds of scandal.

9.4.3 Regulatory and Legal Ambiguities

Even though the legal framework for IDs has improved significantly over the past decade, gaps remain in enforcement and protection.

9.4.3.1 Ambiguity in Duties and Liabilities

While section 149(6) of the Companies Act 2013 lays out ID qualifications and duties, the practical scope of responsibility remains vague. Questions abound:

- What is the extent of diligence expected in detecting fraud?
- Can an ID be held liable for management's unethical actions?
- When does silence become complicity?

The answers are context-dependent, and that uncertainty breeds hesitation.

9.4.3.2 Fear of Legal Repercussions

Post high-profile cases (like IL&FS, Satyam, or National Stock Exchange), IDs face increasing scrutiny from regulators and law enforcement. Many fears:

- Being named in SEBI orders or SFIO probes.
- Arrests or interrogation without direct culpability.
- Costly legal battles with reputational damage.

This fear sometimes leads to excessive caution, where IDs disengage instead of confronting.

9.4.3.3 Lack of Regulatory Backing

Even when IDs report ethical violations, responses from authorities may be slow or ambiguous. Without timely and decisive regulatory support:

- IDs may feel isolated.

Governance fails not in ignorance, but in avoidance.

- Wrongdoers may escape consequences.
- Companies may avoid necessary reforms.

9.4.4 Personal and Psychological Constraints

Ethical decision-making is not just legal, it's deeply psychological. IDs are human beings, and their ability to resist pressure depends on personal factors:

9.4.4.1 Fear of Retaliation

In companies where the promoter holds significant control, IDs may fear:

- Non-renewal of tenure
- Loss of professional networks
- Direct or indirect threats (reputational or otherwise)

In private companies, such retaliation can be more covert but no less effective.

9.4.4.2 Lack of Moral Clarity

Not every ethical decision is black and white. Many dilemmas exist in grey zones. Without a strong moral compass or training, IDs may:

- Struggle to define the "right" course
- Defer to the majority
- Default to silence

Continuous ethical education and peer dialogue are essential to sharpen judgment.

The board's first duty is not to power but to principle.

9.4.4.3 Ethical Fatigue

Repeated exposure to ethical compromise without resolution can result in **moral burnout**. IDs may become resigned, cynical, or numb:

"It's not my fight. Nothing will change. Why risk it?"

This erosion of ethical will is perhaps the most insidious risk.

9.4.5 Case Snapshots of Ethical Paralysis

Let's look at a few illustrative snapshots (names anonymised for legal neutrality):

Snapshot	Description	Why	Result
The Marketing Mirage	In a mid-sized FMCG firm, the board discovered a misleading campaign about the health benefits of a product. Despite internal concerns, marketing was not paused. The IDs raised it once and never again.	The campaign had already boosted quarterly sales. Management subtly reminded IDs of "revenue impact" and "competitive pressure."	The product faced consumer backlash. Brand reputation collapsed six months later.
The Friendly Audit	An ID discovered that the statutory auditor had longstanding ties with the Chief Financial Officer. Despite raising this as a conflict of interest, the Audit Committee overruled. No formal note was made of the objection.	The auditor was seen as "efficient and cooperative." No one wanted to "rock the boat."	A future forensic audit revealed massive underreporting of vendor liabilities.

Trust begins where excuses end.

The CSR Diversion	In a healthcare company, a CSR fund was being routed to a trust indirectly controlled by the promoter's spouse. An ID raised the issue, but was reassured it was "approved by legal." The matter was not pursued further.	The ID felt outnumbered. Two other IDs expressed support for the promoter. .	NGO watchdog flagged the arrangement. Media scrutiny followed

9.4.6 Overcoming the Barriers: A Preview

While these challenges are real and complex, they are not insurmountable. The key lies in:

- Reforming structural flaws in board composition and access
- Strengthening regulatory and peer support for IDs
- Equipping IDs with legal, psychological, and professional skills to act ethically under pressure

In the next section, we explore what these **enablers of ethical courage** look like and how the system can evolve to better support ethical directorship.

9.5 Building Ethical Courage Tools, Allies, and Systems for Change

9.5.1 Redefining Independence: From Formality to Function

It is time to rethink independence not as a status but as a stance. Regulatory compliance may ensure that a board has the mandated number of IDs, but true independence is demonstrated in ethical action, not in designation.

A compromised board breeds a compromised company.

To encourage ethical courage, independence must be understood as:

- **Freedom of thought**: The ability to question dominant narratives
- **Freedom of speech**: The psychological safety to voice dissent
- **Freedom from fear**: Protection against retaliation or reputational damage

These freedoms must be embedded in boardroom structures and director training programs.

9.5.2 Tools for Ethical Decision-Making

IDs need not rely on gut instinct alone. Several frameworks can guide ethical reasoning under pressure.

9.5.2.1 The Ethics Triad: Legality, Impact, and Integrity

Every complex decision can be examined through three filters:

- **Is it legal?** (Compliant with applicable law)
- **Is it ethical?** (Fair to all stakeholders)
- **Is it aligned with our values?** (True to the company's stated purpose)

When all three are aligned, the decision is on firm ground. When they diverge, it is a cue for deeper reflection.

9.5.2.2 Stakeholder Mapping

Ethical IDs consider who is impacted:

- Employees, vendors, and consumers
- Local communities
- Investors and regulators
- The company's long-term reputation

Accountability isn't about catching the guilty; it's about guiding the honest.

They ask: Whose voice is missing from this decision? This simple question can reframe boardroom choices in powerful ways.

9.5.2.3 Decision Trees for Ethical Dilemmas

Structured questioning helps reduce ambiguity:

- What are the possible actions?
- What are the short- and long-term consequences?
- Who benefits and who might suffer?
- Would I be comfortable disclosing this publicly?

Frameworks like the "Mirror Test", "Newspaper Test", or "Role Reversal Test" help make ethics personal and concrete.

9.5.3 Boardroom Culture as a Safety Net

IDs are more likely to act ethically when the board culture encourages dissent and treats ethics as central, not peripheral.

9.5.3.1 Chairs Who Invite Challenge

The chair of the board plays a critical role in shaping tone. Ethical courage flourishes when the Chair:

- Welcomes diverse viewpoints
- Gives space for objections and critical questions
- Does not penalise uncomfortable truths

An independent-minded Chair is often the difference between compliance theatre and governance integrity.

Ethics without enforcement is theatre.

9.5.3.2 Safe Space for Dissent

Boards should create formal and informal spaces for ethical dialogue:

- Regular executive sessions (without management)
- Annual ethics off-sites or retreats
- Feedback loops that review how past dissent was handled

A board that learns from dissent strengthens its moral compass.

9.5.3.3 Shared Ethical Leadership

IDs should build informal alliances with other ethical directors to avoid isolation. Ethical courage is easier when it is *collective*, not *individual*.

9.5.4 The Role of Support Ecosystems

IDs need institutional and professional support—particularly when facing complex, high-stakes decisions.

9.5.4.1 Director Networks and Peer Circles

Membership in associations like:

- Institute of Directors (IOD) India
- The Indian Institute of Corporate Affairs (IICA)
- Confederation of Indian Industry (CII) forums for directors

9.5.4.2 Independent Legal Counsel

In high-risk ethical scenarios, IDs must have access to external legal counsel not just rely on the company's internal legal team.

The boardroom isn't just for compliance - it's for conscience.

This empowers IDs to:

- Validate legal exposure
- Understand protections under the Companies Act
- Prepare whistleblower disclosures, if necessary

Companies should not resist this it strengthens governance.

9.5.4.3 Ethics Officers and Ombudspersons

IDs should advocate for the appointment of a Chief Ethics Officer or Ethics Ombudsperson who is accessible, trusted, and empowered.

Such officers:

- Act as internal advisors for ethical issues
- Provide early warning signs of ethical drift
- Bridge gaps between boardroom and grassroots

9.5.5 Regulatory Enablers for Ethical Independence

The system must evolve to better protect and support IDs who take ethical stands.

9.5.5.1 Whistleblower Protection for Directors

The Companies Act, 2013, provides some protection for whistleblowers, but there is ambiguity around directors who raise concerns internally or externally.

SEBI and MCA should:

- Establish confidential director reporting channels
- Create non-retaliation protections for IDs
- Mandate prompt and transparent investigation processes

Directors must lead in the light, even when shadows are tempting.

9.5.5.2 Reappointment and Evaluation Reforms

Current reappointment practices often create a sense of dependency on promoters or boards. Solutions include:

- Shareholder-only reappointment for IDs
- External performance evaluations that include ethical judgment
- Term limits to prevent over-familiarity with management

IDs should be accountable to **stakeholders**, not just boards.

9.5.5.3 Legal Safe Harbours for Good Faith Actions

Clarifying liability standards for IDs acting in good faith is essential. Without this, fear of being dragged into litigation (even when innocent) will continue to stifle ethical boldness.

Proposed reforms include:

- Legal indemnity provisions built into ID contracts
- SEBI guidelines on *safe harbour* protections
- Rapid-response legal support via regulatory helplines

9.5.6 Developing the Ethical Reflex in Directors

Ethical courage is not a gift; it's a **discipline**. IDs must train themselves, just as athletes train for high-stress performance.

9.5.6.1 Scenario-Based Training

Board simulations using **ethical case studies** (e.g., whistleblowing, insider trading, supply chain labour abuse) allow IDs to practice responses in realistic settings.

What the board tolerates today, the company suffers tomorrow.

9.5.6.2 Ethics as a Continuing Education Requirement

Just as IDs must stay updated on financial regulations, they must also undertake:

- Annual ethics workshops
- Training on ESG-linked ethical issues
- Legal updates on director liability and whistleblower duties

Boards can embed this into **director development policies.**

9.5.6.3 Personal Reflection and Journaling

Encouraging directors to maintain **private reflection journals** of:

- Ethical decisions made
- Conflicts observed
- Lessons learned

9.5.7 A Cultural Reset: Moving from Compliance to Character

Ultimately, ethical governance must move beyond checkboxes. Culture – not regulation – is what shapes board behaviour in moments of tension.

To change culture, boards must:

- Talk about ethics **openly and frequently**
- Reward ethical behaviour, not just results
- Create rituals of reflection (e.g., an "Ethics Moment" at every board meeting)

Just as safety is non-negotiable in aviation, *ethics must be non-negotiable in the boardroom.*

Tone from the top demands integrity; corporate culture demands alignment.

9.6 The Future of Ethical Boardrooms: Vision 2030 for Independent Directors in India

9.6.1 Setting the Stage: Why 2030 Matters

The coming decade will be pivotal for Indian corporate governance. As India emerges as a global economic powerhouse, the expectations for transparency, accountability, and ethical leadership will soar.

IDs will no longer be optional compliance functions; they will be central architects of trust between companies, investors, regulators, and society.

9.6.2. Anticipated Governance Trends Impacting Ethics

9.6.2.1 Increasing ESG Integration

ESG factors will dominate board agendas. IDs must:

- Understand complex ESG risks and opportunities
- Ensure that sustainability claims are credible and verifiable
- Prevent "greenwashing" or superficial CSR efforts

Ethics and ESG will become inseparable, requiring new competencies and vigilance.

9.6.2.2 Digital Transformation and Ethical Risk

Technologies like AI, blockchain, and big data analytics will transform businesses but raise new ethical dilemmas:

- Data privacy and security
- Algorithmic bias and transparency
- Ethical use of automation impacting employment

IDs must be fluent in technology ethics to govern effectively.

Board integrity demands vigilance; organizational trust demands consistency.

9.6.2.3 Stakeholder Capitalism and Expanding Fiduciary Duties

There is a global shift from shareholder primacy to stakeholder capitalism. IDs will need to balance competing interests:

- Shareholders
- Employees
- Customers
- Communities
- Regulators

This complexity demands ethical frameworks that transcend narrow profit motives.

9.6.3 Vision for the Independent Director Role

By 2030, the ideal ID in India will be:

- **Ethically grounded:** Courageous, principled, and values driven.
- **Technologically savvy:** Comfortable engaging with digital governance risks.
- **Stakeholder-oriented:** Championing inclusive, sustainable value creation.
- **Culturally agile:** Able to navigate diverse corporate and regional cultures.
- **Continuously learning:** Committed to ongoing education and self-reflection.

This profile requires systemic changes in director recruitment, training, and evaluation.

Ethical leadership demands example; corporate culture demands reinforcement.

9.6.4 Strengthening Institutional Frameworks

To realise this vision, several institutional reforms are essential:

9.6.4.1 Enhanced Regulatory Mandates

- More rigorous selection criteria focusing on ethics and expertise
- Mandatory ESG and ethics disclosures in board reports
- Strengthened enforcement mechanisms for director accountability

9.6.4.2 Professionalisation of the Independent Director Role

- Establishment of a **National Institute for IDs** with a mandatory certification regime
- Continuous professional development programs, including ethics, technology, and ESG
- ID accreditation tied to performance and ethical standards

9.6.4.3 Robust Ethical Oversight Bodies

- Independent Ethics Committees within companies with clear powers
- Industry-wide ethics councils providing guidance and mediation
- Regulatory ethics audits parallel to financial audits

9.6.5 Leveraging Technology for Ethical Governance

Digital tools will increasingly assist IDs in ethical oversight:

- **Real-time risk dashboards** integrating ESG and compliance data.
- **AI-driven anomaly detection** for fraud or ethical breaches.
- **Secure whistleblower platforms** with anonymity guarantees.

Governance frameworks demand adherence; ethical standards demand courage.

- **Virtual boardrooms** enabling more frequent and flexible ethical deliberations.

Technology will not replace judgment but augment the ID's ability to act timely and informed.

9.6.6 Cultivating Ethical Leadership Ecosystems

Ethical governance requires a supportive ecosystem beyond the boardroom:

9.6.6.1 Shareholder Engagement

- Empowered institutional investors insisting on ethics as a key performance metric
- Shareholder activism supporting independent oversight and whistleblowers

9.6.6.2 Civil Society and Media

- Active watchdog NGOs providing independent ethical assessments
- Investigative journalism spotlighting ethical lapses and successes

9.6.6.3 Education and Academia

- Integration of corporate ethics and governance into business school curricula
- Research centres focused on governance innovation and ethical leadership

9.6.7 The Role of Culture and National Ethos

India's rich cultural heritage, emphasising dharma (duty), satya (truth), and ahimsa (non-violence), can inform a uniquely Indian approach to boardroom ethics.

Tone from the top demands alignment; boardroom behavior demands accountability.

By embedding these values into corporate governance norms, India can pioneer a model of ethical capitalism that resonates globally.

9.6.8 Addressing Emerging Ethical Challenges

As business models evolve, new ethical frontiers will arise:

- Gig economy worker rights and protections
- Climate change accountability and carbon footprint disclosures
- Artificial intelligence governance and human rights

IDs must be proactive, anticipating ethical dilemmas before crises emerge.

9.6.9 Measuring Ethical Impact

Future boards will need **metrics** beyond financial KPIs to assess ethical performance:

- Ethics audits
- Stakeholder satisfaction surveys
- ESG impact scores
- Incident and whistleblower resolution statistics

Such transparency will build trust and guide continuous improvement.

9.7 Final Thoughts: The Independent Director as Ethical Beacon

As we look ahead to the evolving landscape of corporate governance, the role of the ID is no longer confined to that of a passive monitor or mere compliance custodian. Instead, the ID of the future must stand as the unwavering ethical beacon illuminating the path for corporations to act with conscience, accountability, and long-term stewardship.

Leadership accountability demands initiative; corporate conscience demands guidance.

By the year 2030, the most resilient and respected boards will not be those that simply navigate regulations or deliver shareholder returns, but those that cultivate a deep-rooted culture of ethical leadership, purpose, and transparency. These are the boards that will command the trust of global investors, attract the brightest minds, retain loyal stakeholders, and remain relevant in a world where public scrutiny and societal expectations grow sharper by the day. In contrast, boards that fail to integrate this moral compass into their governance DNA will find themselves sidelined, outpaced by market forces and alienated by the communities they once served.

The tone from the top is not just a cultural cue; it is a societal covenant. IDs must be the voice of this covenant: a voice that speaks truth to power, asks difficult questions when silence is easier, and guards the soul of the corporation even when it is under siege. They are not just guardians of governance; they are architects of trust, stewards of stakeholder equity, and custodians of corporate integrity in its purest form.

"In the architecture of trust, Independent Directors are the foundation - because when the top leads with ethics, the organisation walks in integrity; but when the top wavers, the whole house trembles."

CHAPTER 10

Tech, Trust, and Transparency: The Digital Governance Challenge for Independent Directors

"A board that doesn't understand technology cannot govern its risks."

10.1 Introduction: A New Era of Boardroom Oversight

In a world where algorithms increasingly shape markets and data fuel every corporate decision, the role of Independent Directors (IDs) is no longer confined to financial oversight or legal compliance. Today's boardrooms are digital battlegrounds where cyber risk, Artificial Intelligence (AI) ethics, data privacy, and digital transformation demand not just literacy, but leadership.

As technology becomes the backbone of modern business, it also opens the door to new risks. A single cyberattack can wipe out shareholder value, shatter consumer trust, and damage a company's reputation overnight. Yet, many IDs remain on the sidelines unprepared to question tech decisions, oversee digital risks, or demand clarity in a world driven by algorithms and data. In the digital age, staying uninformed is no longer an option.

In the age of algorithms, directors must ask who writes the code and why.

This section explores the emerging mandate for IDs to become champions of tech literacy, trust stewardship, and transparent governance in the digital age. Because in the future of corporate governance, silence is not safety, and ignorance is not independence.

10.1.1 The Digital Tsunami and Its Boardroom Ripple Effects

In recent years, digital transformation has redefined every dimension of corporate existence from strategy and operations to customer engagement and supply chain orchestration. Technologies like AI, blockchain, cloud computing, and big data analytics are not just tools; they are tectonic forces altering the corporate terrain. For IDs, this shift is not peripheral; it's foundational. The traditional boundaries of oversight and control have blurred, with digital imperatives now interwoven into the fabric of risk, compliance, performance, and reputation. Boards are no longer judged merely on financial outcomes; they are now assessed on how responsibly they steer their companies through digital waters. Cybersecurity breaches, algorithmic biases, Environmental, Social, and Governance (ESG) data manipulation, and opaque digital platforms have placed technology governance firmly on the board agenda.

10.1.2 Independent Directors: Guardians of Governance in a Digital Age

IDs in India, mandated by the Securities Exchange Board of India (SEBI) and enshrined in company law, are envisioned as objective arbiters free from management influence, serving the interests of minority shareholders, and acting as watchdogs of ethical conduct and strategic prudence. But as companies increasingly embed technology into their business models, these directors are now expected to govern not just business strategy, but also digital architecture.

Their roles are evolving from financial auditors to digital stewards, from passive overseers to active interrogators of data ethics, cybersecurity

A boardroom that fears technology invites obsolescence by default.

resilience, and algorithmic transparency. Questions that were once the domain of the Chief Investment Officers (CIOs) or Chief Information Security Officers (CISOs), such as data governance, cyber risk posture, or AI explainability, are now boardroom concerns. For IDs, this is a daunting yet critical transformation.

10.1.3 From Governance to Digital Governance

The traditional governance triad strategy, risk, and compliance has been complicated by a digital layer that is fast, opaque, and frequently misunderstood. A company's competitive edge today may lie in its algorithms, data models, or digital platform elements that are difficult to audit through conventional governance frameworks.

Digital governance introduces new challenges:

- Who is responsible when an AI model discriminates?
- How should a board respond to a ransomware attack?
- Can a board verify that ESG data disclosed is not "greenwashed" by automated systems?
- What constitutes adequate digital diligence during mergers or acquisitions?

IDs are now at the forefront of such inquiries. Their ability to ask the right questions, understand the limitations of technology, and ensure management accountability defines the new frontier of boardroom oversight.

10.1.4 Trust and Transparency: The Twin Pillars of the Digital Boardroom

In the age of digital ecosystems and stakeholder capitalism, trust is currency. Whether it's a customer trusting a platform with personal data, an investor trusting disclosures, or regulators trusting compliance, trust

You cannot govern what you do not understand: especially in the digital age.

is increasingly mediated through code and algorithms. Yet, technology can both enable and erode trust.

Transparency, therefore, becomes the mechanism through which trust is built. For IDs, fostering digital trust means ensuring that systems are explainable, decisions are auditable, data is protected, and ethical boundaries are respected. It is no longer sufficient to review financial reports or compliance dashboards – today's board members must also interrogate AI black boxes and data pipelines.

10.1.5 The Road Ahead: A Call to Action

This section aims to chart the contours of this emerging terrain. It will unpack the specific digital challenges confronting IDs in India, assess the legal and ethical frameworks evolving around technology governance, and present actionable insights for directors seeking to become digitally literate, ethically grounded, and strategically agile.

We are entering an era where IDs must act as interpreters between technical complexity and ethical governance, between innovation and accountability. The future boardroom belongs not just to the financially astute but to the digitally vigilant.

10.2 The Digital Disruption of Governance Norms

10.2.1 The End of the Analogue Board

For decades, corporate governance operated within relatively stable norms of financial disclosures, physical meetings, regulatory filings, risk registers, and compliance checklists. These analogue foundations provided a sense of predictability, both in decision-making and in boardroom dynamics. However, digital disruption has rendered many of these models insufficient, if not obsolete.

The shift toward platform-based business models, remote workforces, digital customer journeys, and automated decision-making systems has upended the assumptions on which traditional governance rested.

Digital ignorance is the new breach of fiduciary duty.

Business moves faster, decisions are increasingly data-driven, and much of the value creation (and risk exposure) is embedded in intangible digital assets—code, data, algorithms, and intellectual property.

10.2.2 Traditional Oversight in a Tech-Centric World: A Mismatch

IDs, particularly those from non-technical backgrounds, often find themselves unequipped to meaningfully interrogate digital strategies. The boardroom's language, once dominated by EBITDA, ROCE, and P&L statements, must now accommodate terms like API integration, machine learning models, blockchain protocols, and cybersecurity architectures.

This mismatch manifests in several ways:

- **Lack of tech fluency**: Directors may rely excessively on management's interpretation of technical risks, leading to weak challenge or superficial understanding.
- **Invisibility of digital risk**: Unlike financial risks that leave a trail, digital risks such as data breaches, AI bias, or reputational harm from misinformation are harder to detect and quantify.
- **Compressed timelines**: Digital decisions often require real-time or near-real-time responses, whereas board governance is structured around quarterly deliberations.

The result is a widening governance gap a dangerous space where fast-moving digital risk escapes slow-moving board scrutiny.

10.2.3 Data is the New Asset and the New Liability

In the digital age, data is not just a competitive asset but also a regulatory and reputational landmine. Boards must grapple with fundamental questions:

- Is our data ethically sourced?
- Are we in compliance with data localisation laws?

When data becomes capital, privacy becomes governance.

- Do we have sufficient protection against data leaks and ransomware attacks?
- Can we vouch for the integrity of our ESG or impact data?

For IDs, data oversight is a multi-dimensional challenge. It requires balancing innovation and privacy, personalisation and consent, efficiency and fairness. Directors must ensure that the organisation's data practices not only meet legal obligations but also uphold stakeholder trust.

10.2.4 New Governance Terrain: Algorithms, Artificial Intelligence, and Black Boxes

Digital governance is no longer just about Information Technology (IT) strategy; it's about the governance of decision-making itself. Algorithms now influence everything from hiring decisions to credit scoring, product recommendations to fraud detection. But algorithms can also encode bias, reinforce inequality, or make decisions that even developers don't fully understand.

IDs must push for **algorithmic accountability,** the ability to explain, audit, and challenge decisions made by AI systems. This includes:

- Demanding explainability and transparency reports from management.
- Ensuring fairness, inclusivity, and bias mitigation in algorithm design.
- Overseeing governance frameworks for AI lifecycle management.

Failing to govern algorithms is tantamount to abdicating one's fiduciary duty in a world where software shapes reality.

10.2.5 Platform Governance and the Rise of Ecosystems

The shift from linear business models to digital platforms has introduced new governance challenges. In platform ecosystems like

Every click creates a trail; every trail is a liability.

marketplaces, ride-hailing apps, fintech networks, or SaaS businesses, the company doesn't control all the value chain components. Instead, it orchestrates interactions among users, developers, partners, and regulators.

In such environments, IDs must oversee not just internal governance, but **ecosystem governance**:

- How are third-party vendors and partners vetted and governed?
- What are the liabilities for user-generated content or algorithmic decisions?
- Is the platform being used in ways that violate human rights or local laws?

Directors must ensure that governance frameworks extend beyond organisational boundaries and into digital ecosystems.

10.2.6 The Evolving Regulatory Landscape

In response to digital disruption, regulators in India and globally are fast catching up. From SEBI's expectations around cyber resilience to the Reserve Bank of India's data localisation mandates and the upcoming Digital India Act, there is a growing legal infrastructure surrounding digital operations.

Boards must not only be reactive to regulatory compliance but also proactively anticipate legal and reputational risks emerging from the digital domain. IDs, in particular, must be the ones asking the tough questions:

- Is our digital business model legally sound?
- Are we prepared for audits under digital regulation?
- Are we being transparent with regulators, investors, and customers?

Cybersecurity is not IT's problem it's the board's problem.

10.3 Tech Fluency as a Boardroom Imperative

10.3.1 From Financial Acumen to Digital Dexterity

IDs have long been appointed for their financial acumen, legal knowledge, or regulatory experience. While these continue to be valuable, they are no longer sufficient. As technology reshapes the strategic core of businesses, directors must cultivate a working knowledge of digital tools, systems, and risks. This does not mean that every ID must be a coder or data scientist, but it does mean they must be able to engage meaningfully with technology leadership, ask relevant questions, and understand the implications of digital strategy on governance outcomes.

Tech fluency at the board level enables directors to decode technical jargon, challenge oversimplified explanations, and interpret the risks embedded in innovation. Without this fluency, directors are left to rely solely on management's framing of digital opportunities and threats, weakening their ability to provide effective oversight. In an age where business value and risk increasingly reside in the virtual realm, ignorance is no longer an option; it is a liability.

10.3.2 Demystifying the Digital Vocabulary

One of the biggest barriers to tech fluency is language. The digital world is filled with complex, often intimidating terminology terms like blockchain, API, zero-trust architecture, deep learning, and predictive analytics. Many IDs hesitate to engage in technology discussions for fear of revealing their lack of knowledge. This hesitation creates a silence that can be exploited by management, especially when digital initiatives are cloaked in buzzwords but lack depth, feasibility, or ethical safeguards.

Building confidence begins with demystifying the language of technology. Directors should prioritise understanding the foundational concepts behind the technologies that matter to their company's business model. Just as they have mastered financial statements or compliance frameworks over the years, directors can and must develop a similar working comfort with digital structures. Several board training programs, including those offered by IICA, SEBI, and global institutions, now provide modules on digital governance, cybersecurity, and emerging tech oversight specifically designed for non-technical board members.

10.3.3 The Risk of Overreliance on Management and Consultants

Many boards fall into the trap of outsourcing their digital thinking to consultants or internal executives, assuming that technology issues are best handled by the experts. While technical depth certainly resides within the organisation, strategic judgment belongs with the board. An overreliance on external presentations or glossy dashboards can lead to a false sense of security. Without the ability to probe deeper, directors may miss red flags, underestimate complexity, or approve high-risk digital strategies without due scrutiny.

IDs must remember that their mandate includes acting in the interest of shareholders and stakeholders, not simply trusting management's assurances. This requires the courage to ask "naive" questions, the persistence to unpack technical proposals, and the wisdom to know when outside advice should be challenged. Blind trust in management's digital claims is antithetical to the very idea of independent oversight.

10.3.4 Building Digital Fluency in the Boardroom

Boards must take a structured approach to building tech fluency among IDs. This can include regular training on emerging technologies, scenario workshops on cyberattacks and AI bias, peer learning with digitally savvy directors, and ongoing engagement with CIOs and Chief Data Officers. Some companies have introduced the concept of a "Tech Committee" within the board structure, mirroring audit or risk committees, to provide specialised attention to digital governance.

Artificial intelligence demands human accountability.

Others are appointing at least one director with a strong technology background to bring diversity of thought and digital insight. However, while such appointments are useful, they cannot replace the broader goal of equipping every director with the baseline ability to understand and interrogate digital matters. Technology is not a siloed function anymore; it is a cross-cutting concern that touches every aspect of business strategy, risk, compliance, reputation, and ethics.

10.3.5 From Literacy to Stewardship

The ultimate goal is not merely digital literacy but digital stewardship. IDs should evolve from passive recipients of technical updates to active shapers of digital direction. This includes participating in strategic debates around technology adoption, ensuring the alignment of digital initiatives with corporate values, monitoring the ethical implications of data use, and safeguarding the interests of customers, employees, and society.

Tech fluency is a precondition for digital leadership. Directors who understand the potential and pitfalls of technology can guide companies toward responsible innovation. They can steer boards through crises like data breaches, reputational attacks, or algorithmic failures. They can ask the hard questions about automation, surveillance, misinformation, or sustainability. In doing so, they fulfil their duty not only as governance professionals but as societal custodians of trust in the digital age.

10.4 Cybersecurity and Data Privacy – A Fiduciary Duty Reimagined

10.4.1 Cybersecurity as a Board-Level Concern

In an era marked by relentless cyberattacks, data leaks, ransomware incidents, and state-sponsored hacking, cybersecurity has emerged as one of the most urgent responsibilities for boards of directors. IDs, in particular, are expected to provide vigilant oversight over how companies protect their digital infrastructure and the sensitive data they hold. Gone are the days when cybersecurity could be relegated to the IT department. Today, it is a core governance concern with direct implications for financial stability, reputation, and legal liability.

When a breach occurs, whether it's the theft of intellectual property, the compromise of customer data, or the shutdown of operations due to ransomware, the board is held accountable for whether it exercised adequate diligence. Regulators, investors, and the media increasingly expect IDs to understand cyber risks, scrutinise incident response plans, and ensure that management is not just reacting to threats but preparing proactively.

10.4.2 The Expanding Fiduciary Responsibility of Directors

Traditionally, the fiduciary duties of IDs revolved around loyalty, care, and prudence in protecting shareholder value. However, with the digitisation of assets, operations, and stakeholder relationships, these duties now extend into digital terrain. Safeguarding data is not just a technical function; it is a matter of trust. Mishandling data can result in not only financial penalties but also loss of brand reputation, consumer confidence, and long-term market value.

Data privacy regulations around the world, from the European Union's General Data Protection Regulation (GDPR) to India's Digital Personal Data Protection Act (DPDPA), are increasing the legal expectations on boards. Directors must ensure that the company collects, stores, processes, and shares data in ways that are lawful, transparent, and aligned with stakeholder expectations. Failure to do so could expose them to regulatory action and even personal liability.

10.4.3 Understanding the Anatomy of Cyber Risk

Cyber risk is multifaceted. It includes external threats such as hackers, insider threats from employees or contractors, third-party vulnerabilities through vendors, and systemic risks across digital supply chains.

If your board doesn't understand the cloud, prepare for a storm.

For boards, this complexity makes oversight challenging but non-negotiable. IDs must understand the nature of the company's digital assets, what data is most sensitive, where it resides, who has access to it, and what protections are in place.

They must also probe deeper into the organisation's cyber strategy. Is there a clear cybersecurity governance framework? Are roles and responsibilities defined across the CISO, CIO, and legal teams? How frequently are risks reviewed and tested? Does the board receive regular briefings on threat intelligence, audit results, and incident simulations? These questions help directors go beyond surface-level assurances and demand substantive accountability.

10.4.4 Crisis Preparedness and Incident Response

Cybersecurity governance is not just about preventing breaches; it is also about responding effectively when they occur. IDs should be intimately familiar with the company's incident response protocols. This includes knowing whether there is a formal plan, who leads it, how communication with regulators and customers is handled, and whether cyber insurance coverage is in place.

Many boards now conduct tabletop exercises to simulate cyber crises and test their responsiveness. Directors should insist on being part of these exercises, both to understand the dynamics of decision-making under pressure and to identify weaknesses in coordination, disclosure, or legal preparedness. The ability to respond quickly, transparently, and ethically during a cyber event can preserve stakeholder trust and, in some cases, the company's very survival.

10.4.5 Data Privacy as a Moral and Strategic Issue

Beyond security, data privacy is emerging as a distinct concern, one that goes beyond regulatory compliance to touch on ethics and strategy. Customers, employees, and citizens are increasingly aware of how their data is used. Any perception of surveillance, manipulation, or

A line of code can break a company faster than a financial fraud.

exploitation can damage a brand irreparably. Directors must ask whether the company's data practices are not only legal but also fair. Is consent genuine? Are data minimisation principles followed? Are users informed about how their data fuels algorithmic decisions?

Moreover, in sectors like healthcare, finance, education, and e-commerce, data is not just a resource it's a source of strategic advantage. Companies that demonstrate high standards of data ethics and privacy are more likely to build long-term loyalty, reduce regulatory friction, and differentiate themselves in crowded markets. IDs have a critical role in setting the tone for such a privacy-first culture.

10.4.6 Personal Liability and Reputational Exposure

One of the most striking developments in recent years is the personal exposure of directors in the event of cyber failures. Global regulators, including SEBI in India, have signalled that boards cannot absolve themselves by delegating cyber duties. Directors who fail to demonstrate reasonable understanding and action may face penalties, disqualification, or reputational damage. Shareholders may also initiate lawsuits if breaches result in financial loss, especially when red flags were ignored.

To mitigate this, boards are increasingly adopting cybersecurity as a standing agenda item. Some are setting up Risk and IT Governance Committees with specialist advisors. Others are requiring cyber metrics in management performance reviews. Directors must also ensure that they are covered under adequate Directors and Officers (D&O) insurance policies with explicit cyber provisions.

10.4.7 The Path Forward: Building a Culture of Resilience

Ultimately, the role of IDs is to foster a culture where cybersecurity and data privacy are not compliance burdens but strategic priorities. This means pushing for investments in talent, systems, and training. It means challenging complacency and demanding transparency from the executive team. It also means embedding cyber and privacy considerations into every major boardroom decision, from acquisitions and partnerships to product launches and customer engagement.

Digital resilience is now a marker of good governance. Companies that are prepared, transparent, and ethical in handling cyber risks and data challenges will command greater trust and stability. IDs must see themselves not just as guardians of shareholder value—but as protectors of stakeholder trust in a digitally fragile world.

10.5 Artificial Intelligence, Automation, and Algorithmic Accountability

10.5.1 The Algorithmic Turn in Corporate Decision-Making

Across sectors, from finance and healthcare to logistics and marketing, companies are deploying AI and automation tools to make decisions faster, cheaper, and more efficiently. Algorithms are now recommending products, screening job candidates, managing inventories, predicting defaults, detecting fraud, and even driving vehicles. These systems are increasingly embedded in the DNA of corporate operations.

For boards and especially for IDs, this transformation presents a paradox. On one hand, AI promises innovation and competitive advantage. On the other hand, it introduces opacity, ethical complexity, and systemic risk. The use of algorithms is no longer limited to technical departments; it directly impacts customer experience, regulatory compliance, brand perception, and legal exposure. Governance must evolve to match this shift.

10.5.2 Understanding the Governance Gap in Artificial Intelligence and Automation

Most boards are still catching up to the implications of AI. Unlike financial models that can be audited and debated using established methods, many AI systems are black box complex, constantly evolving, and often trained on proprietary or opaque data sets. When an AI system produces an unfair outcome or makes an error, tracing accountability becomes a serious challenge.

This is where the governance gap emerges. Directors may not fully understand how these systems work, who designed them, what data was used, or how decisions are explained and audited. In the absence of structured oversight, algorithmic decisions can embed bias, produce unethical outcomes, or violate laws without human review. The challenge is not simply technical; it is deeply ethical and legal.

10.5.3 Bias, Fairness, and Inclusion in Algorithmic Systems

One of the most troubling risks in AI governance is bias. Algorithms trained on historical data often replicate existing inequalities, whether in hiring, lending, insurance, or policing. If left unchecked, such systems can discriminate against marginalised groups, create reputational crises, and lead to regulatory sanctions. IDs must therefore ask hard questions about fairness and inclusion.

They must probe how bias is detected, mitigated, and monitored in the company's AI systems. Are diverse datasets being used? Are there safeguards against gender, racial, or socio-economic discrimination? Is the AI reviewed by independent auditors? These are not academic concerns; they strike at the heart of a company's social license to operate. Directors must ensure that digital innovation does not come at the cost of ethical erosion.

10.5.4 The Explainability and Accountability Imperative

One of the central principles in emerging AI governance is explainability, the ability to understand, interpret, and communicate how an algorithm reaches a decision. This is especially crucial in sectors like banking, healthcare, and criminal justice, where opaque AI decisions can have life-altering consequences.

Boards must champion explainability as a non-negotiable standard. IDs should demand that management provide clear documentation of AI systems, their purposes, limitations, and risk profiles. They must also push for human-in-the-loop mechanisms where critical decisions can be reviewed or overridden by humans when necessary. A company that cannot explain its algorithmic decisions is vulnerable to public backlash and legal challenge.

10.5.5 Legal and Regulatory Pressures: Global and Indian Context

The regulatory environment around AI is tightening. The European Union's AI Act is pioneering a tiered risk-based approach, placing heavy obligations on companies using high-risk AI systems. In India, while AI-specific legislation is still nascent, concerns around data protection, consumer rights, and algorithmic discrimination are gaining traction. Courts, regulators, and civil society are beginning to hold companies accountable for automated decisions.

This evolving landscape demands proactive adaptation from boards. Directors should not wait for regulation to catch up; they should set internal governance frameworks that anticipate legal expectations. This includes setting up AI oversight mechanisms, commissioning regular audits, and integrating AI ethics into risk management and compliance systems.

10.5.6 The Rise of Algorithmic Ethics Committees and Internal Audits

Forward-looking companies are establishing internal AI governance bodies, sometimes called algorithmic ethics committees or digital oversight panels. These bodies bring together legal, technical, ethical, and operational perspectives to evaluate how AI is deployed and governed. Boards should be briefed regularly by these committees, and IDs should ensure they have sufficient visibility into their findings and recommendations.

Moreover, algorithmic audits are becoming a vital part of internal assurance. These audits assess whether the systems meet principles of fairness, accountability, transparency, and safety. IDs can play a key role in mandating and reviewing such audits, just as they do with financial or compliance audits. The same standards of due diligence must now apply to machines that make consequential decisions.

10.5.7 Artificial Intelligence and Automation in the Boardroom Itself

Ironically, AI is also beginning to reshape governance itself. Tools are emerging that assist directors with board intelligence curating reports, analysing risks, predicting compliance gaps, and even evaluating ESG performance. Chatbots, decision dashboards, and boardroom analytics platforms are being adopted by progressive boards.

While these tools enhance efficiency, they also raise questions about overreliance. Directors must ensure that their judgment remains primary, that AI serves the board, not the other way around. It is also essential that the use of such tools respects confidentiality, avoids undue automation of discretion, and is subjected to proper risk review.

10.6 The Surveillance Dilemma – Balancing Monitoring with Morality

10.6.1 Surveillance Capitalism in the Corporate Landscape

The digital era has ushered in unprecedented capabilities for data collection and behavioural tracking. Organisations now possess sophisticated tools to monitor employees, customers, vendors, and even board members. Whether it's through CCTV, keystroke tracking, location data, customer profiling, or algorithmic monitoring of emails and chats, the rise of surveillance has become normalised in corporate life. What was once a function of physical security has evolved into a pervasive system of digital oversight.

Companies argue that such monitoring enhances productivity, reduces fraud, strengthens compliance, and improves customer targeting. But these benefits come with costs, costs that are ethical, psychological, and reputational. Boards must now ask not just can we monitor, but should we monitor, and if so, how much, how transparently, and with what safeguards? IDs stand at the moral fulcrum of this debate.

10.6.2 The Board's Responsibility in a Surveillance Economy

IDs are not only stewards of financial value, but they are also protectors of institutional integrity. In the age of surveillance capitalism, where data is harvested and monetised as a commodity, this duty expands. Boards must understand how surveillance technologies are used in the organisation, whether policies are in place to prevent misuse, and if the rights of individual employees, customers, and even partners are being respected.

The risk of reputational damage is significant. News of covert surveillance or intrusive monitoring can spark outrage, legal battles, and employee attrition. Directors must therefore establish governance protocols that balance security and compliance with dignity and trust. It is not merely a data issue; it is a human issue.

10.6.3 Workplace Surveillance: Oversight or Overreach?

In the workplace, surveillance tools have multiplied. Organisations deploy screen monitoring, webcam snapshots, biometric tracking, location tracing, and productivity algorithms to assess employee performance. While these tools may deter misconduct or support remote work management, they also erode privacy and foster an atmosphere of distrust.

Boards must evaluate whether such practices align with the company's values. Are employees informed and consenting participants in surveillance? Is monitoring proportionate to the risks being managed? Are there safeguards against discrimination, false positives, or misuse of collected data? The answers to these questions define the ethical boundaries of workplace oversight.

When trust is the currency, transparency is the vault.

A responsible board may consider establishing a Workplace Technology Charter, which sets out principles such as:

- Transparency in what is being monitored and why.
- Minimalism – Collecting only data that is necessary and relevant.
- Oversight mechanisms to review surveillance practices regularly.
- Clear grievance redressal avenues for employees.
- Regular impact assessments on employee morale and autonomy.

Such frameworks ensure that oversight doesn't become overreach.

10.6.4 Surveillance of Customers and the Risk of Manipulation

Outside the organisation, companies gather immense volumes of customer data, often passively and invisibly. Online behaviour, search queries, voice commands, purchase patterns, and even emotions are mined to predict and influence behaviour. The line between personalisation and manipulation is razor-thin. Algorithms can nudge users toward specific choices, pricing tiers, or behaviours, often without their conscious knowledge.

Boards must interrogate these practices with clarity. Are customers being fairly informed about how their data is used? Are choices genuinely free, or are they being engineered? Are vulnerable populations such as children, elderly users, or financially insecure customers being targeted unfairly? IDs have an obligation to ensure that ethical marketing and responsible AI standards guide digital customer engagement.

10.6.5 Surveillance and Social License to Operate

In a digital society, public expectations around privacy are rising. People expect autonomy over their data, transparency from institutions, and recourse when harm occurs. Companies that overstep these boundaries risk losing their social license to operate, especially in sectors like education, healthcare, finance, and technology.

Boards should view surveillance not just as a privacy issue, but as a trust issue. Directors must ensure that company policies reflect the values of the society they operate in. This includes proactively disclosing monitoring practices, engaging with civil society concerns, and ensuring alignment with evolving global norms on digital rights.

10.6.6 The Emerging Legal Landscape

Globally, privacy and surveillance regulations are maturing. Europe's GDPR, India's DPDPA, and sectoral laws across jurisdictions are placing explicit limits on surveillance practices. They emphasise consent, data minimisation, user rights, and accountability. Directors who ignore these trends do so at their peril.

IDs must be familiar with the legal boundaries of surveillance, understand the company's compliance posture, and ensure regular legal reviews. They must also ensure that surveillance data is secure and not vulnerable to misuse or breach, which could multiply legal exposure.

10.6.7 Ethical Surveillance: A Governance Agenda

Rather than rejecting surveillance outright, boards must guide its responsible use. This means embedding privacy-by-design principles into technology deployments, using anonymised or aggregated data wherever possible, and resisting the urge to track every behaviour just because it is technically feasible.

The ethics of surveillance should become a standing part of boardroom dialogue. IDs can lead this agenda by:

- Demanding periodic surveillance audits and privacy impact assessments.
- Reviewing board-level dashboards on data collection practices.

A secure system is only as strong as its weakest ethical link.

- Insisting on cross-functional input from legal, ethics, human resources, and IT before approving surveillance systems.
- Encouraging whistleblower protections related to unethical data use.

By institutionalising this scrutiny, boards can ensure that monitoring serves legitimate interests without violating rights.

10.7 Digital Reputation and the Role of Independent Directors in Crisis Communication

10.7.1 The Fragility of Reputation in the Digital Age

In a hyperconnected world, reputations are no longer shaped slowly over decades; they can be dismantled in minutes. A single whistleblower tweet, a leaked email, an exposed algorithm, or a viral customer complaint can ignite a firestorm capable of upending investor confidence, market capitalisation, and public trust. Corporate missteps, whether ethical, legal, technological, or environmental, are instantly amplified through social media, and judgments are often rendered before companies have a chance to respond.

In this volatile ecosystem, digital reputation has become a form of currency and a fragile one at that. Boards, and particularly IDs, must view reputational resilience not as a public relations function but as a core component of corporate governance. Their fiduciary responsibilities now extend beyond financial oversight into the realm of trust, credibility, and institutional narrative.

10.7.2 The Expanded Role of the Board in Reputation Management

While Chief Executive Officers and communication heads may lead media relations during a crisis, boards are increasingly held accountable for the underlying failures that lead to reputational damage. Whether it's a data breach, ESG failure, regulatory penalty, or ethical lapse, stakeholders now expect that directors have either the foresight to prevent the crisis or the resolve to respond decisively.

Stakeholders trust boards that speak clearly, not just legally.

IDs, in particular, serve as the conscience of the boardroom. They are expected to ask difficult questions, surface early warning signs, and insist on transparency. Their independence is vital in assessing whether the company's story is aligned with its values, and whether crisis responses are sincere, swift, and stakeholder centred.

To be effective stewards of reputation, directors must adopt a proactive posture monitoring digital sentiment, overseeing ethical risk registers, and ensuring that communication strategies are not reactive, but readiness driven.

10.7.3 Anatomy of a Digital Crisis

A typical digital-era corporate crisis often follows a pattern: a triggering event (such as a leaked internal memo, a whistleblower allegation, or a technical failure) is followed by immediate social media outrage, regulatory attention, and media scrutiny. The speed and shape of the narrative are often dictated not by facts but by perception and the company's ability to correct, clarify, or counter that perception determines the damage curve.

Boards must therefore recognise that in many cases, the *first response* is the *last chance* to protect trust. The tone of the company's initial statement, the presence of accountability, the speed of disclosure, and the consistency of messaging across platforms all determine whether the company is seen as trustworthy or evasive.

IDs must ensure that the company has a well-practiced digital crisis response plan in place one that covers rapid escalation, multi-platform messaging, regulatory disclosure protocols, stakeholder engagement, and ethical response framing.

10.7.4 Boardroom Communication Strategy in the Age of Hashtags

One of the major governance challenges today is that public scrutiny is no longer reserved for the executive team; directors themselves are

Online reputation management begins offline in the boardroom.

named, scrutinised, and held accountable in public forums. Proxy advisors, activist investors, media outlets, and regulators increasingly examine board minutes, past decisions, and even individual director behaviour in public digital domains.

This means directors must be aware of how they are digitally perceived and how their actions or inactions may be interpreted. They must also demand communication strategies that reflect integrity rather than spin. In high-stakes moments, sincerity and accountability outweigh sophistication.

A modern crisis communication strategy overseen by the board should include:

- A clear spokesperson protocol (who speaks, when, and on what).
- Internal communication frameworks to keep employees informed and united.
- Real-time monitoring of digital channels for misinformation or escalations.
- Legal, ethical, and reputational filters applied to all public statements.
- Integration of ESG and stakeholder language, not just financial defence.

Boards that fail to prepare for digital crises often find themselves reacting with outdated tools to a radically new battlefield.

10.7.5 Lessons from High-Profile Failures

Across the globe, digital reputation failures have exposed weak governance. From algorithmic bias revelations to MeToo scandals, and from greenwashing exposés to cyber-leaks, the consequences have been swift and unforgiving. In many cases, the failure was not the initial error but the response: deflecting blame, denying facts, delaying transparency, or treating stakeholders with disdain.

In a hyperconnected world, silence is suspicious.

Boards that weathered such storms best were those that acted early, aligned messaging with ethics, and displayed courage to hold leadership accountable, even if it meant leadership change. IDs often served as the pivot, insisting on disclosure, pushing for a genuine apology, and authorising bold course corrections.

The lesson is clear: reputation is not protected by hiding the truth but by confronting it with maturity.

10.7.6 Independent Directors and the Culture of Transparency

Reputation is ultimately a reflection of corporate culture. A culture of silence, denial, or fear will always implode when tested. IDs can shape a different trajectory by championing transparency, psychological safety, and open internal dialogue.

Their position allows them to speak truth to power, to question dominant narratives, and to surface dissenting voices long before those voices reach the outside world. Directors should support whistleblower frameworks, endorse independent investigations, and ensure that grievance redressal systems are not only present but also trusted.

Digital reputation begins inside the boardroom, long before a crisis appears on Twitter.

10.7.7 Preparing the Board for the Next Digital Reputation Test

Preparedness is everything. Boards must conduct regular crisis simulations, including mock digital scenarios involving data breaches, social media firestorms, or ESG blowups. These simulations should involve communications teams, legal counsel, ethics officers, and technology experts.

IDs should also invest in personal readiness, understanding the basics of social media dynamics, regulatory disclosure norms in the digital

Digital footprints last longer than press releases.

context, and ethical frameworks for crisis response. They must be capable of identifying *when* the board needs to step in and *how* it should assert leadership over crisis response.

When the next crisis strikes and it will, it is not speed alone that will matter, but the *quality* of the response: its truthfulness, empathy, and accountability.

10.8 From Digital Ignorance to Digital Fluency – Building Tech-Savvy Boards

10.8.1 The Digital Blind Spot at the Board Level

Despite the increasing centrality of digital technology to business models, many boards continue to struggle with a critical shortfall: digital literacy. While companies are transforming through AI, automation, cloud platforms, cyber-risk frameworks, and digital-first customer models, boardrooms are often dominated by directors who are far more fluent in finance, law, or traditional operations than in emerging technologies.

This digital blind spot is not merely inconvenient, it is dangerous. Boards that lack a functional understanding of technology cannot adequately oversee digital transformation strategies, assess tech investments, or navigate risk landscapes that are increasingly driven by cyber threats and data governance issues. Worse still, they may rubber-stamp decisions or rely too heavily on management without the ability to challenge, interpret, or foresee technological consequences.

IDs, expected to bring impartial oversight and strategic questioning, are uniquely positioned to close this gap but only if they commit to developing digital fluency.

10.8.2 What Digital Fluency Means for a Board

Digital fluency does not mean turning every board member into a coder or systems architect. Rather, it means enabling directors to ask the right questions, interpret the implications of digital initiatives, and link technology choices to business strategy, ethical governance, and stakeholder impact.

A digitally fluent board understands:

- How data flows through the organisation and where it is vulnerable
- The basic logic behind AI systems, predictive analytics, and algorithmic bias
- The implications of automation for jobs, roles, and internal controls
- The competitive impact of digital platforms, ecosystem partnerships, and disruptive entrants
- The trade-offs between digital speed and security, personalisation and privacy, scalability and ethics

This fluency allows IDs to engage constructively in dialogue, interrogate digital Key Performance Indicators, and ensure that technology serves the company's purpose, not the other way around.

10.8.3 The Cost of Digital Ignorance

Several high-profile governance failures have been rooted in poor board-level understanding of technology. Whether in the form of data breaches, flawed algorithms, opaque AI decision-making, or failed IT overhauls, the common thread has been the board's inability to foresee or question the design, deployment, and risks of digital systems.

Regulators, investors, and the public are no longer tolerant of this ignorance. Directors are expected to demonstrate proactive engagement with cyber resilience, data protection, and ethical AI frameworks. Courts and compliance regimes are increasingly attributing accountability to boards for digital failures, particularly when harm to consumers, employees, or markets occurs.

If your users don't trust you, your products are irrelevant.

In this environment, digital illiteracy is not just a weakness, it is a liability.

10.8.4 Overcoming Resistance to Tech Learning in the Boardroom

One of the major barriers to digital fluency is cultural. Many board members, especially those from non-technical backgrounds or older generations, perceive technology as an operational detail rather than a strategic pillar. Some express open discomfort with digital language, while others view tech learning as optional or defer entirely to CIOs or digital officers.

Boards must confront and dismantle this mindset. Digital governance is no longer delegated; it is integrated. IDs must take responsibility for their own learning journeys and be willing to close knowledge gaps that impede their effectiveness.

Board chairs and nomination committees should create an environment where digital inquiry is encouraged, where jargon is translated, and where continuous learning is institutionalised. It is not a question of age or background; it is a matter of mindset.

10.8.5 Pathways to Digital Fluency for Independent Directors

To move from ignorance to fluency, IDs can pursue a mix of structured and experiential learning pathways. These include:

- **Onboarding programs focused on technology**: New director induction should include briefings on the company's digital architecture, data use policies, cybersecurity posture, and digital roadmap.
- **Board-level workshops and simulations**: Periodic deep-dives into emerging technologies (e.g., AI, blockchain, quantum

computing) help demystify new trends and encourage cross-functional awareness.

- **Peer learning and reverse mentoring**: Pairing senior board members with younger digital natives within the company can foster informal but impactful learning exchanges.
- **External certifications and executive programs**: Directors may benefit from courses offered by institutions like the Indian School of Business, IIMs, or global bodies such as NACD, INSEAD, or MIT Sloan in digital governance and cybersecurity.
- **Engagement with start-ups and innovation hubs**: Exposure to agile and tech-driven environments sharpens strategic insight and disruptor awareness.

Boards that embed such learning pathways into their calendar not just as one-off sessions, but as continuous routines build a digital muscle over time.

10.8.6 The Role of a Chief Digital Officer at the Board Table

Some companies have found value in having a Chief Digital Officer or Chief Technology Officer (CTO) regularly brief the board, not just on projects but on ecosystem shifts, customer digital behaviour, and strategic disruption risks. These officers act as translators between technological complexity and board-level decision-making.

IDs should not just passively listen; they must challenge assumptions, test the alignment of digital investments with corporate values, and ensure that tech leaders are thinking inclusively, ethically, and systemically.

Where possible, boards may also consider recruiting at least one ID with deep digital expertise, helping to anchor the board in technical realism and strategic foresight.

Ethics is the firewall trust depends on.

10.8.7 Creating a Digitally Enabled Governance Culture

The ultimate goal is not just individual learning, but collective transformation. A digitally fluent board operates differently: it integrates tech risks into enterprise risk discussions; it asks whether customer trust is being eroded by algorithmic opacity; it questions the diversity of data sets used in AI tools; and it aligns digital projects with long-term value creation.

Such boards are more likely to balance innovation with prudence, to steer digital transformation with integrity, and to detect early signs of ethical or reputational risk. They also inspire greater confidence in stakeholders' investors, employees, and regulators alike who increasingly demand that governance bodies understand the technologies shaping our future.

10.9 Data Governance and the New Fiduciary Duty

10.9.1 Data as a Strategic Asset and a Strategic Risk

In today's digital economy, data is no longer merely an operational by-product it is the bedrock of value creation, competitive differentiation, customer trust, and corporate identity. From consumer behaviour and supply chain analytics to employee productivity metrics and ESG performance indicators, data fuels nearly every strategic decision a company makes.

But this asset is also a double-edged sword. Poorly governed data unsecured, misused, biased, or non-compliant can lead to regulatory fines, reputational damage, customer exodus, and litigation. In many high-profile governance failures in recent years, data mishandling was the central issue: misuse of personal information, unauthorised surveillance, biased algorithms, opaque AI models, and breaches exposing millions of records.

In this environment, data governance is not just a technical issue it is a boardroom issue. And for IDs, it signals a fundamental shift in fiduciary responsibility.

In the digital era, trust is not a principle - it's infrastructure.

10.9.2 The Expanding Scope of Fiduciary Duty in the Digital Era

Traditionally, fiduciary duties of directors have centred around the duty of care, duty of loyalty, and duty of diligence, with a focus on protecting shareholder value, ensuring informed decision-making, and avoiding conflicts of interest. In the digital age, these duties are being reinterpreted to include the stewardship of data as a matter of both strategic insight and ethical obligation.

IDs are increasingly expected to:

- Understand how the company collects, stores, processes, and monetises data.
- Oversee how data is used in decision-making algorithms and automated processes.
- Ensure that data governance frameworks respect privacy rights and legal obligations.
- Monitor whether data practices align with the company's values, purpose, and ESG commitments.

This new fiduciary landscape demands that directors view data not just as a resource, but as a responsibility, one that must be governed with foresight, fairness, and accountability.

10.9.3 The Board's Role in Overseeing Data Governance Frameworks

A robust data governance framework ensures that data within the organisation is accurate, accessible, secure, and ethically used. While management is responsible for designing and implementing these frameworks, the board, particularly its IDs, must oversee and validate their integrity.

Transparency is no longer a virtue - it's a requirement.

This oversight involves asking strategic questions:

- What kinds of data are we collecting, and why?
- Who owns and has access to sensitive data?
- What safeguards are in place to prevent breaches or misuse?
- Are we transparent with customers and stakeholders about how we use their data?
- How are ethical considerations integrated into our AI and analytics models?

Boards should regularly review internal data governance policies, audit reports, data protection impact assessments, and privacy compliance metrics. In highly regulated industries like finance and healthcare, this scrutiny must be even more rigorous.

IDs should insist that data is treated with the same seriousness as financial capital: traceable, measurable, audited, and accountable.

10.9.4 Data Privacy, Consent, and Stakeholder Trust

Privacy is at the heart of the data governance conversation. The rise of global regulations such as the EU's GDPR, India's DPDPA, and other regional frameworks has elevated privacy compliance from a legal matter to a governance imperative.

Yet beyond legal compliance lies a more human question: *Do our stakeholders trust us with their data?*

Boards must ensure that the organisation has not only secured lawful consent but also earned societal legitimacy in its data practices. This means minimising data extraction, maximising transparency, and designing consent in ways that are meaningful and user-friendly, not buried in legal jargon or click-through traps.

IDs should also examine whether data monetisation strategies align with the company's values. Is the company profiting from personal data in ways that could undermine public trust or create long-term reputational risk? These are not just commercial questions, they are governance questions.

10.9.5 Algorithmic Accountability and Ethical Oversight

As companies increasingly rely on data-driven algorithms to make decisions from pricing and hiring to loan approvals and content curation, the risks of bias, discrimination, and opacity multiply. Many algorithms reflect hidden prejudices in their training data, reinforcing inequality or marginalisation without human oversight.

IDs have a critical role to play in demanding algorithmic transparency and fairness. They should:

- Ensure that AI governance frameworks are in place and board approved.
- Push for diversity in datasets and in the team's building of these models.
- Advocate for explainability, where decisions made by algorithms can be understood, questioned, and justified.
- Review cases where algorithmic decisions have harmed stakeholders or raised ethical concerns.

A board that fails to oversee AI ethics is a board that risks regulatory sanction and social backlash. IDs must be the voice that asks: *Just because we can automate this decision, should we?*

10.9.6 Cybersecurity: The Frontline of Data Governance

Cyber threats represent one of the most immediate and material data-related risks facing corporations today. Ransomware, phishing, insider breaches, and nation-state attacks can cripple systems, destroy data, and erode years of trust in a single incident.

The best way to stay ahead of a crisis is to be ahead of disclosure.

Cybersecurity is no longer just the CIO's concern; it is a board-level risk that demands constant vigilance. IDs must:

- Review cybersecurity preparedness and incident response plans.
- Insist on third-party penetration testing and vulnerability assessments.
- Demand regular board briefings on threat landscapes and remediation actions.
- Verify whether cyber insurance coverage is appropriate to the organisation's risk profile.

When cyberattacks happen, and they will, the board's prior engagement (or lack thereof) becomes a matter of public and legal scrutiny. Directors must treat cyber risk as a constant, evolving battlefield and stay engaged in the defence.

10.9.7 Toward a Data-Conscious Board Culture

To be effective in data governance, IDs must help foster a boardroom culture where data is viewed holistically: as a strategic, operational, ethical, legal, and reputational concern. Data literacy must be part of the board's DNA, not an occasional agenda item.

Boards may consider establishing a dedicated Data Ethics or Technology Risk committee or strengthening the mandate of existing Risk or Audit Committees to explicitly cover data governance. The language of data usage, lineage, bias, and breach must be normalised in boardroom discussions.

Directors should also advocate for clear accountability structures within the organisation: appointing CDO, empowering Data Protection Officers, and ensuring that the first, second, and third lines of defence are well-resourced and coordinated.

Sunlight is the best antivirus for bad governance.

10.10 Cybersecurity and Digital Risk – A Board-Level Priority

10.10.1 The Escalating Threat Landscape

In the digital age, cybersecurity is no longer an IT issue confined to firewalls and antivirus software; it is a fundamental business risk that threatens every facet of an organisation. Cyberattacks have grown in frequency, sophistication, and impact, targeting everything from intellectual property and customer data to operational infrastructure and financial systems.

IDs must recognise that cyber risk is a strategic threat, capable of inflicting severe financial loss, regulatory penalties, operational disruption, and lasting reputational damage. Recent ransomware incidents, supply chain breaches, and data leaks affecting major corporations globally have shown how vulnerable even the most sophisticated organisations are.

Given the pervasive nature of digital risk, boards cannot afford to treat cybersecurity as a technical sidebar. Instead, it must be integrated into enterprise risk management and overseen at the highest levels.

10.10.2 Understanding Cyber Risk Beyond the Technical

Cybersecurity encompasses much more than technology defences; it is a complex risk landscape involving human behaviour, governance processes, legal compliance, third-party exposures, and crisis preparedness.

IDs should develop a holistic understanding of cyber risk, including:

- How human error or insider threats can expose vulnerabilities.
- The role of vendor and supply chain security in the organisation's risk profile,
- The regulatory environment governing data protection and breach notifications.

A transparent boardroom prevents opaque decisions.

- Crisis management capabilities for rapid detection, response, and recovery.
- The interplay between cybersecurity and business continuity planning.

Such a broad perspective equips the board to challenge management on readiness, resource allocation, and culture.

10.10.3 The Board's Cybersecurity Oversight Role

Effective board oversight requires moving beyond check-the-box attitudes and superficial discussions. IDs must:

- Regularly receive clear, jargon-free reports on cyber threats, incident trends, and mitigation efforts.
- Verify that cybersecurity risk is integrated into the overall risk appetite and strategy of the company.
- Ensure that a qualified CISO or equivalent is in place with direct access to the board.
- Confirm that regular independent audits, penetration tests, and vulnerability assessments are conducted and acted upon.
- Scrutinise cybersecurity budgets to confirm adequate resourcing

Such oversight demonstrates seriousness to regulators, investors, and stakeholders.

10.10.4 Board Composition and Expertise in Cybersecurity

Given the specialised nature of cyber risk, many boards have added members with deep experience in cybersecurity, IT risk, or information governance. IDs without a technology background can still elevate board effectiveness by actively learning and engaging with cyber topics.

Accountability is easier when transparency is constant.

Peer learning, external advisory sessions, and executive education focused on cyber risk can equip directors with the confidence to ask probing questions and interpret technical reports. Boards should strive to balance technical expertise with diverse perspectives to avoid "tech siloing" and ensure cybersecurity is linked to broader business strategy.

10.10.5 Cybersecurity Culture: The Human Firewall

Technology alone cannot eliminate cyber risk; human behaviour remains the weakest link. Phishing attacks, poor password hygiene, and social engineering exploits often bypass advanced defences.

IDs must champion a culture of cybersecurity awareness across the organisation. This involves:

- Encouraging regular employee training and simulated attack drills
- Promoting accountability for cyber hygiene from top executives down to frontline staff
- Supporting clear policies on data handling, device usage, and remote work security
- Advocating for transparency in reporting near misses and incidents without fear of reprisal

A resilient "human firewall" complements technical controls and reduces risk.

10.10.6 Incident Response and Crisis Management

No organisation is completely immune to cyber incidents. What differentiates leaders from laggards is the ability to respond swiftly and effectively.

IDs should ensure that:

- A well-documented and tested incident response plan exists.
- Roles and responsibilities for crisis management are clearly defined.

Dark data leads to blind governance.

- Communication plans cover internal stakeholders, customers, regulators, and the media.
- Post-incident reviews lead to tangible improvements in controls and policies.

Board engagement during a cyber crisis sends a strong signal to the organisation and external audiences that cybersecurity is a top priority.

10.10.7 Cyber Insurance and Risk Transfer

Given the potentially catastrophic financial impact of cyber events, many organisations turn to cyber insurance as part of their risk management strategy.

Boards should critically evaluate:

- The scope and limits of cyber insurance coverage.
- Policy exclusions and conditions that may affect claims.
- Alignment of insurance with the organisation's overall risk profile and mitigation controls.

Insurance is not a substitute for robust cybersecurity, but it can provide valuable financial resilience.

10.10.8 Regulatory and Legal Implications

Cybersecurity is an increasingly regulated domain. Non-compliance with data protection laws, failure to notify breaches timely manner, or inadequate risk management can result in severe fines, legal action, and loss of license.

IDs must stay abreast of evolving regulatory requirements relevant to their industry and geography. They should also monitor emerging legal precedents that hold boards personally accountable for cybersecurity failures.

Digital oversight demands vigilance; data integrity demands rigor.

10.11 Digital Ethics and Responsible Innovation

10.11.1 The Rise of Ethical Questions in Digital Transformation

Digital technologies AI, machine learning, big data analytics, blockchain, and automation, are reshaping industries at an unprecedented speed. While these innovations promise operational efficiency, enhanced customer experiences, and new business models, they also raise profound ethical questions that go beyond compliance or risk management.

For IDs, digital ethics represents a new frontier of governance responsibility. It challenges boards to look beyond what companies *can* do with technology and focus on what they *should* do in alignment with values, societal norms, and human rights.

10.11.2 Defining Digital Ethics in the Corporate Context

Digital ethics concerns itself with the moral principles guiding the development, deployment, and impact of digital technologies. Core themes include:

- Fairness and non-discrimination in algorithmic decision-making
- Privacy and data rights protection
- Transparency and explainability of AI systems
- Accountability for unintended consequences and harm
- Respect for human dignity and autonomy

IDs must ensure that their companies' technology strategies incorporate these principles and do not sacrifice ethics for short-term gains.

10.11.3 Responsible Innovation: Balancing Speed with Caution

In the race to innovate, companies often prioritise speed to market and competitive advantage. However, responsible innovation calls for a balance that encourages experimentation while carefully evaluating risks and societal impacts.

Transparency demands disclosure; digital trust demands consistency.

Boards should guide management to adopt frameworks such as "ethics by design," where ethical considerations are embedded from the earliest stages of product and system development. This includes:

- Conducting ethical impact assessments.
- Engaging diverse stakeholders in design processes.
- Establishing clear escalation channels for ethical concerns.

Responsible innovation mitigates risk, builds trust, and supports sustainable value creation.

10.11.4 The Board's Role in Digital Ethics Oversight

IDs must:

- Promote a culture of ethical awareness around technology use.
- Require regular updates on digital ethics initiatives and challenges.
- Encourage cross-functional collaboration among technology, legal, compliance, and sustainability teams.
- Engage with external experts, ethicists, and civil society to broaden perspectives.
- Incorporate digital ethics into risk management and corporate social responsibility (CSR) frameworks.

By elevating digital ethics as a board agenda item, directors signal its strategic importance.

10.11.5 Transparency and Stakeholder Communication

Transparency is foundational to ethical governance. Boards must ensure that companies communicate openly with stakeholders about their digital practices, including:

- How data is collected, used, and shared.

- Measures taken to ensure fairness and privacy.
- Challenges encountered and steps to address them.

Clear communication fosters trust and accountability in an era of scepticism toward technology.

10.11.6 Aligning Digital Ethics with Environmental, Social, and Governance and Corporate Purpose

Digital ethics intersects with ESG priorities, amplifying the company's social license to operate. Boards should integrate digital ethics into broader ESG strategies, linking technology governance to corporate purpose, stakeholder engagement, and sustainable development goals.

Such alignment enhances reputation, attracts ethical investors, and supports long-term resilience.

10.11.7 Building Board Competence in Digital Ethics

To govern digital ethics effectively, IDs need ongoing education and exposure to evolving ethical debates, technological trends, and regulatory developments.

Training programs, workshops with ethicists, participation in multi-stakeholder forums, and collaboration with academic institutions can enhance directors' understanding and ability to challenge management constructively.

10.12 The Future of Boardrooms – Embracing Digital Governance

10.12.1 The Digital Imperative for Modern Boards

The rapid evolution of digital technologies is reshaping how companies operate, compete, and create value. For boards, especially IDs, this shift demands a fundamental rethinking of governance. The boardroom of

Decision-making demands accuracy; digital accountability demands scrutiny.

the future must move beyond traditional oversight of financial and operational risks to become a hub for strategic digital governance.

This transformation requires embracing new skill sets, tools, mindsets, and structures that can keep pace with technological change and its cascading impact on business models, stakeholders, and society.

10.12.2 Evolving Board Roles and Responsibilities

Digital governance redefines the scope of board responsibility in several ways:

- **Strategic foresight:** Boards must anticipate digital disruptions and guide long-term digital strategy, balancing innovation with risk.
- **Risk oversight:** Cybersecurity, data privacy, and technology risks are no longer peripheral; they must be core components of enterprise risk management.
- **Ethical stewardship:** Boards have a duty to ensure technologies are deployed responsibly, upholding corporate values and societal expectations.
- **Talent and culture:** The digital era demands diverse boards with digital literacy and the ability to foster a culture of agility and learning.

IDs play a critical role as objective voices that challenge management assumptions and hold the organisation accountable in this evolving landscape.

10.12.3 Building Digital Literacy at the Board Level

Digital literacy is no longer optional. Directors must understand the fundamentals of emerging technologies, their strategic implications, and associated governance challenges.

Information security demands vigilance; operational integrity demands resilience.

Boards can enhance digital literacy through:

- Regular education sessions and workshops tailored to board members.
- Engagement with external experts, technologists, and ethicists.
- Hands-on exposure to digital tools and data dashboards.
- Participation in industry forums and peer learning groups.

This knowledge foundation empowers directors to engage confidently, ask informed questions, and provide meaningful oversight.

10.12.4 Integrating Digital Governance into Board Processes

To embed digital governance, boards should consider:

- Incorporating digital risk and strategy explicitly into board agendas.
- Creating or strengthening board committees focused on technology, data, and innovation.
- Establishing clear reporting lines from CDOs, CISOs, and Data Protection Officers to the board.
- Using real-time digital dashboards and analytics for timely insights and decision-making.
- Setting measurable digital governance KPIs aligned with corporate objectives.

Such integration ensures digital issues receive sustained attention rather than ad hoc consideration.

Digital transformation demands courage; governance frameworks demand structure.

10.12.5 The Role of Independent Directors as Digital Guardians

IDs serve as guardians of good governance, impartiality, and stakeholder interests. In digital governance, they are uniquely positioned to:

- Advocate for transparency in technology deployment and data use.
- Monitor management's adherence to ethical standards and regulatory requirements.
- Ensure that digital investments align with long-term value creation.
- Champion diversity and inclusion in digital teams and governance structures.
- Push for resilience and adaptability in the face of technological change.

Their independent perspective is essential to balance enthusiasm for innovation with prudent risk management.

10.12.6 Navigating Challenges in Digital Governance

Despite the urgency, boards face challenges in digital governance, including:

- Rapid technology change that outpaces board understanding.
- Difficulty recruiting directors with digital expertise without compromising diversity.
- Balancing confidentiality with the need for open discussion and learning.
- Managing potential conflicts of interest with technology vendors or advisors.
- Aligning digital governance with global and local regulatory requirements.

Addressing these challenges requires intentional board development, clear policies, and a culture that values continuous learning and candid dialogue.

Tech strategy demands insight; organizational trust demands protection.

10.12.7 Looking Ahead: Boardrooms of Tomorrow

The future boardroom will be a digital-ready, agile, and purpose-driven space where technology and governance intersect seamlessly. Innovations such as AI-assisted decision-making, blockchain-based transparency, and virtual board meetings will become standard.

Boards that proactively embrace this future will not only safeguard their organisations against digital risks but also unlock new avenues for growth, stakeholder engagement, and sustainable impact.

10.12.8 Conclusion: Seizing the Digital Governance Opportunity

The digital revolution offers both immense opportunity and unprecedented governance complexity. IDs stand at a crossroads where their leadership can define the trajectory of corporate trust, resilience, and innovation.

By embracing digital governance wholeheartedly, developing new competencies, and fostering ethical, transparent cultures, boards can steer their organisations confidently into the digital age, ensuring technology serves as a catalyst for long-term value and societal good.

The journey through *Tech, Trust, and Transparency* reveals a profound transformation in the role of IDs amid the digital revolution. Across twelve comprehensive sections, we have seen how technology is no longer a backdrop but a central axis shaping corporate governance, risk, ethics, and strategy.

IDs face a multifaceted challenge: to build trust in an era of rapid technological change, ensure transparency where complexity threatens clarity, and uphold ethical standards as digital innovation tests societal norms. From understanding cybersecurity risks to championing responsible AI, from fostering digital literacy to embedding ethics at the core of innovation, the mandate for boards is clear and urgent.

Data governance demands standards; digital culture demands reinforcement.

The future of governance hinges on the ability of IDs to evolve to become agile learners, strategic digital stewards, and courageous ethical leaders. Embracing digital governance is not merely about managing risk; it is about unlocking new avenues for sustainable value creation and stakeholder confidence.

As organisations navigate the complex interplay of technology, trust, and transparency, IDs are uniquely positioned to guide this transformation with insight, independence, and integrity. Their leadership will define how businesses not only survive but thrive in the digital age, safeguarding reputations, empowering people, and contributing meaningfully to society.

In this digital governance era, the call to action is unmistakable: lead boldly, govern wisely, and champion a future where technology serves as a force for good, anchored in trust and illuminated by transparency.

"When machines outpace minds, wisdom must lead. In tomorrow's boardrooms, trust will outweigh code. Transparency is the new firewall, and the Independent Director - its vigilant guardian."

CHAPTER 11

Guardians of Tomorrow: Building a Talent Pipeline for India's Independent Director Revolution

"From mentorship to mastery: cultivating independent directors equipped for modern governance."

11.1 Introduction: The Coming Governance Inflexion Point

In a world redefined by pandemics, climate emergencies, artificial intelligence (AI), and the expectations of an increasingly conscious public, boardrooms can no longer remain bastions of status quo thinking. The corporate director of the 20th century – often selected through opaque networks and judged by tenure more than talent – is no longer fit for the complexities of the 21st century. Today's enterprises demand stewards who are agile, digitally fluent, Environmental, Social, and Governance (ESG)-conscious, and unafraid to ask difficult questions.

India, poised to become the world's third-largest economy by the end of this decade, finds itself at a governance crossroads. Regulatory bodies like the Securities and Exchange Board of India (SEBI) have mandated independent oversight, but a deeper question remains: where will the next generation of truly IDs come from?

A boardroom without succession is a fortress without a gate.

The challenge is not merely regulatory; it is cultural and strategic. The average Independent Director (ID) in India is over 60, often drawn from a narrow pool of bureaucrats, ex-Chief Executive Officers (CEOs), and industry veterans. While experience is invaluable, it cannot substitute for diversity of thought, digital insight, or social sensibility. Generational refresh is not a luxury – it is a governance necessity.

This section lays out a bold, multi-pronged roadmap to build a structured talent pipeline for India's next generation IDs. These "Guardians of Tomorrow" must be cultivated, not found by chance, to uphold the integrity, innovation, and inclusivity that the future demands.

11.1.1 Why a Talent Pipeline is the Need of the Hour

11.1.1.1 Boardrooms are Ageing, But Challenges are Young

As of 2024, the average age of IDs on the boards of India's top 200 companies is approximately 64.1 years, aligning with global averages but highlighting a significant generational gap in corporate leadership. This demographic trend is further underscored by the fact that nearly 60% of IDs in National Stock Exchange (NSE)-listed companies have tenures exceeding six years, with some serving for over a decade.

In contrast, India's demographic landscape presents a stark contrast. The country boasts a "youth dividend," with over 65% of its population under the age of 35. This youthful majority is notably absent from the decision-making tables of corporate India, leading to a disconnect between boardroom strategies and the aspirations of the younger populace. This generational mismatch poses challenges in addressing contemporary issues such as digital transformation, climate change, and evolving consumer behaviours. Younger professionals bring fresh perspectives, technological acumen, and a deeper understanding of emerging trends, all of which are crucial for steering companies through the complexities of the modern business environment.

Tomorrow's governance is built by those we train today, not those we remember yesterday.

Recognising this gap, there has been a concerted effort to rejuvenate boards with younger talent. For instance, as of March 31, 2024, there were 745 IDs under the age of 40 across all NSE-listed companies, marking a 456% increase from a decade earlier. This shift reflects a growing acknowledgement of the need for diverse age representation in boardrooms.

However, while these numbers are promising, they still constitute a minority. The challenge lies not just in increasing numbers but in integrating younger voices into strategic decision-making processes. Boards must evolve to become more inclusive, ensuring that the perspectives of the majority demographic are adequately represented.

In conclusion, while India's boardrooms are ageing, the challenges they face are decidedly young. To remain relevant and effective, corporate India must embrace a more dynamic approach to governance, one that values the insights and contributions of its younger members.

11.2 The Risks of a Closed Circle

Board appointments in India have historically been shaped by informal networks and personal referrals, a "recycling" of elite professionals who rotate across multiple directorships. While this club-like system provides familiarity and continuity, it comes at a significant cost: it constrains diversity of thought, background, and perspective. Highly qualified candidates - especially women, professionals from Tier-2 and Tier-3 cities, socially conscious entrepreneurs, and emerging domain experts in technology, ESG, and data analytics – are frequently excluded.

This gatekeeping is not merely an issue of fairness; it is a strategic vulnerability. Homogenous boards are prone to groupthink, less likely to challenge entrenched assumptions, and may fail to anticipate blind spots in strategy, risk management, or governance. In a rapidly evolving business environment – where consumer expectations, digital disruptions, climate risks, and regulatory pressures intersect, such narrow-mindedness can have real consequences. Boards disconnected from the broader societal, generational, and technological context risk making decisions that are out of step with market realities, eroding both competitiveness and trust.

The absence of diversity also diminishes the board's ability to connect with younger employees and consumers, a critical oversight in a country where over 65% of the population is under 35. Without fresh perspectives, boards may misread shifting trends, overlook emerging risks, and fail to innovate - ultimately jeopardising long-term value creation. In essence, a closed-circle board is not just insular; it is fragile, ill-equipped to navigate the complexities of 21st-century corporate governance.

11.3 Global Comparisons: The Missing Indian Leap

Globally, forward-looking economies are actively building structured pathways to cultivate the next generation of corporate directors. In the United Kingdom (UK), programs such as board apprentice place young professionals – often under 40 into board observer roles, providing hands-on exposure to governance while preserving fiduciary safeguards. Similarly, Singapore's Future Directors Scheme embeds high-potential talent in corporate boards through structured mentorships, training modules, and phased responsibility, ensuring that leadership continuity and diversity are systematically nurtured. These programs are not experimental – they reflect a recognition that board effectiveness depends on generational renewal, diversity of thought, and early immersion in decision-making.

India, despite being home to over 1.4 million registered companies and a robust ecosystem of business schools and professional networks, has no comparable national initiative. Less than 15% of board positions in NSE-listed companies are held by directors under 50, and women constitute only about 12-14% of IDs. There is no formal "talent-to-board" pipeline to mentor, train, and gradually induct young professionals into governance roles. Consequently, boards remain dominated by senior executives and retired bureaucrats, often lacking exposure to emerging technologies, ESG imperatives, and evolving stakeholder expectations.

Legacy is not age - it is foresight turned into mentorship.

Without structured programs, India risks a generational disconnect. Boards are slow to respond to digital disruption, climate risks, and evolving regulatory landscapes, and younger professionals are denied the experiential learning necessary to become effective future directors. To leapfrog global benchmarks, India must institutionalise talent pipelines that combine mentorship, practical exposure, and phased governance responsibility, ensuring that the next generation of IDs is not discovered by chance but systematically cultivated.

11.4 Market Trends Require New Skill Sets

The Indian boardroom is facing an unprecedented confluence of challenges that demand capabilities far beyond traditional financial acumen. Rapid technological evolution, regulatory expectations, and shifting stakeholder priorities mean that boards must now be equipped to handle complex, multidimensional risks:

- **Artificial intelligence and cybersecurity:** As AI-driven decision-making and digital ecosystems become integral to business strategy, boards must understand algorithmic risks, data ethics, and cybersecurity threats. According to a 2024 NASSCOM report, over 70% of Indian enterprises face cybersecurity gaps at the board level, highlighting a critical knowledge deficit.
- **Environmental, social, and governance compliance and sustainability strategy:** ESG metrics are no longer optional disclosures; they directly affect investor decisions, access to capital, and reputational risk. The SEBI ESG reporting guidelines (2023) mandate robust ESG frameworks for the top 1,000 listed companies, yet many boards struggle to translate regulatory compliance into meaningful strategy.
- **Diversity, equity, and inclusion:** Investors increasingly demand diverse boards that reflect broader societal perspectives. Gender, regional, and cognitive diversity are linked not only to innovation

The true mark of an Independent Director is not their tenure, but their ability to shape the next.

but also to improved governance outcomes, yet India's boards remain largely homogenous.

- **Strategic sustainability beyond corporate social responsibility:** Sustainability today is about embedding long-term value creation across operations, supply chains, and product strategy - not just fulfilling Corporate Social Responsibility (CSR) quotas. Boards must be able to critically assess sustainable business models and align them with evolving global standards.

The average director in India today, often above 60 years of age, may lack lived experience with these rapidly evolving challenges. By contrast, a younger generation – digitally fluent, globally aware, and socially conscious- can bring an intrinsic understanding of these domains. But awareness alone is insufficient; structured mentorship, exposure, and formal induction into board responsibilities are critical to harnessing this potential. Only by preparing the next generation can boards transform from reactive overseers into proactive stewards of long-term value.

11.4 Regulation alone is not Enough

SEBI's rules on board independence, evaluation, and diversity are necessary - but not sufficient. Too often, they encourage box-ticking rather than true independence, where compliance replaces courage and formalities overshadow substance.

A strategic pipeline approach reframes the question: it is not only "Do we have enough IDs?" but more importantly, "Are we developing the right leaders to steer tomorrow's boards?"

11.5 Defining the Future – Ready Independent Director

The ID of tomorrow cannot merely be a custodian of compliance. They must be a strategic conscience equipped with sharp judgment, grounded ethics, and the foresight to steer companies through both turbulence and transformation. So, what exactly defines a "future-ready" ID?

If the roots are never watered, the forest of governance will one day wither.

11.6 Digital Fluency is Non-Negotiable

As businesses increasingly operate in a digital-first world, IDs must develop a working understanding of:

- **Artificial intelligence and machine learning** – Their operational, ethical, and strategic implications.
- **Cybersecurity risks and data governance** – Risks that extend far beyond Information technology (IT) and impact the organisation's resilience and reputation.
- **Platform and ecosystem business models** – From gig economy dynamics to digital monopolies shaping competitive landscapes.

While every ID need not be a technical expert, they must be capable of asking the right questions and providing informed oversight in technology-driven boardroom discussions.

"When the algorithm fails, it's the director's insight that must prevail."

11.7 Environmental, Social, and Governance Literacy is Core, Not Peripheral

ESG issues are no longer peripheral – they are central to strategic decision-making. They influence:

- **Long-term reputation and brand trust** - the intangible assets that define market resilience.
- **Investor confidence** - particularly for global funds increasingly guided by sustainability mandates.
- **Risk exposure** - from compliance fines to activist campaigns and potential market exits.

A future-ready ID understands:

- **Climate disclosures and carbon targets** – Can evaluate their credibility and impact.

Nurturing boardroom talent is like planting trees we must invest long before we need the shade.

- **Human rights due diligence** – Ensuring ethical practices across global supply chains.
- **Diversity, Equity, Inclusion** – Not merely as a quota but as a driver of innovation, culture, and performance.

11.8 Ethical Resilience and Moral Courage

Future boardrooms will increasingly confront ethical Grey zones – from AI bias and data misuse to whistleblower retaliation and complex stakeholder pressures. In these situations, compliance alone is insufficient; conscience must lead.

The modern ID must embody:

- **Moral clarity** – The ability to dissent respectfully and substantively.
- **Courage** – The readiness to step away when ethical red lines are crossed.
- **Integrity** – The fortitude to challenge the CEO, promoters, or prevailing groupthink, even when unpopular.

"In a time of digital acceleration, the director's inner compass becomes the true firewall."

11.9 Stakeholder Empathy and Generational Intelligence

Corporate decisions today ripple far beyond shareholders - they shape the lives of employees, communities, customers, and ecosystems. The future-ready ID must cultivate:

- **Empathy for multiple stakeholders** – Balancing profit with purpose.
- **Intergenerational awareness** – Understanding the implications of board decisions on both Gen Z employees and long-term retirees.

The Independent Director of tomorrow is defined not by title, but by trustworthiness, insight, and ethical courage.

- **Long-term vision** – Seeing beyond quarterly earnings to measure societal, environmental, and cultural impact.

11.10 Boardroom Agility and Adaptive Thinking

Boards frequently face crises and ambiguity, as COVID-19 starkly demonstrated, revealing vulnerabilities even in the most established companies. The next generation ID must embody:

- **Scenario thinking and contingency planning** – Anticipating challenges before they arise.
- **Data-driven decision agility** – Making swift, informed choices under pressure.
- **Continuous learning and strategic humility** – Adapting to evolving business, technological, and societal landscapes.

"In turbulent times, it is not experience alone but adaptability that keeps the board steady."

11.11 Emotional Intelligence and Collaborative Spirit

The boardroom is not a battlefield; it is a collective space for complex dialogue. Future IDs need:

- **High EQ** to manage egos, conflicts, and stakeholder tension.
- The **ability to build alliances** with promoters, auditors, legal counsel, and external regulators.
- A sense of **self-awareness and boardroom etiquette**.

11.12 Personal Brand of Trustworthiness

In an era of heightened transparency, IDs are increasingly public figures, and their reputation directly affects investor confidence and institutional credibility. The next-generation ID must:

Seeds of integrity bloom only in soil tilled by intention and inclusion.

- **Cultivate thought leadership** – Actively share insights and perspectives while building a credible digital presence.
- **Uphold ethical boundaries** – Maintain integrity and discretion, particularly in social media and public commentary.
- **Demonstrate independence of mind and action** – Consistently align decisions with principles rather than pressures.

In short, the ID of tomorrow is not defined by age or designation, but by a **distinctive set of mindsets and capabilities**. They are ethically anchored, digitally aware, stakeholder-savvy, and relentlessly curious.

11.13 Building Blocks of a Talent Pipeline

Creating a steady, scalable supply of future-ready IDs cannot be left to chance. It requires deliberate architecture – a structured pipeline that educates, exposes, mentors, certifies, and empowers emerging professionals to join and thrive on corporate boards. This section outlines the key pillars of that talent pipeline, adapted to India's unique regulatory, educational, and corporate context.

11.13.1 Education and Awareness: Seeding the Idea Early

Many talented professionals remain unaware that Independent Directorship is a viable and prestigious career path. Early exposure is crucial to cultivating curiosity, capability, and aspiration.

11.13.1.1 Integrate Governance into B-Schools

- Make boardroom governance a **core subject**, not an elective.
- Embed **ethics, corporate law, ESG, and digital risk management** into the curriculum.
- Use **real-world simulations** such as mock board meetings, crisis scenarios, and case studies from Indian and global companies

The pipeline to the boardroom is not a ladder it is a bridge we must build.

11.13.1.2 Undergraduate Exposure

- Introduce **short-term workshops** on corporate governance in law, commerce, economics, and technology programs.
- Launch "Introduction to corporate boards" modules at premier institutions such as IIMs, NLS, IITs, and other B-Schools to familiarise students early with governance responsibilities.

11.13.1.3. Public Campaigns

- Harness digital media and social platforms to promote Independent Directorship as a purposeful career path.
- Spotlight inspiring stories of young IDs, especially women and professionals from Tier-2/3 cities, to demonstrate accessibility and inclusivity.

11.13.2 Certification and Structured Learning

While experience cannot be shortcut, structured learning can accelerate preparedness and build confidence for future board roles.

11.13.2.1 Expand Existing Programs

- Scale up the Indian Institute of Corporate Affairs (IICA's) **Certificate Course on Independent Directorship**, making it more accessible to early-career professionals.
- Encourage NSE, Bombay Stock Exchange, Institute of Chartered Accountants of India, Institute of Company Secretaries of India, and SEBI to co-create a **National Director Curriculum** focused on:
    - Governance frameworks and global best practices.
    - Boardroom behaviour and effective deliberation.
    - Legal liabilities, fiduciary duties, and ethics.
    - Cybersecurity, ESG and emerging risk management.

A boardroom that mirrors only the past cannot govern the future.

11.13.2.2 Tiered Certification Model

- **Level 1 - Foundation:** Core governance principles, ethics, and fiduciary duties (targeted at early professionals).
- **Level 2 - Sector-specific exposure:** Industry-specific insights for banking, technology, manufacturing, and other key sectors.
- **Level 3 - Boardroom readiness**: Practical simulations, mentorship, and evaluation to create a pre-qualified placement pool for boards.

"A pipeline without training is just a hope. A pipeline with certification becomes a strategy."

11.13.3 Mentorship and Reverse Mentorship Models

A future-ready pipeline thrives on intergenerational wisdom exchange, where experience meets fresh perspective.

11.13.3.1 Veteran-Led Mentorship

- SEBI or industry bodies (CII, FICCI) can establish a **National Mentorship Registry**, pairing retired board leaders with high-potential mentees.
- Structured mentoring milestones may include:
    - o Ethics roundtables and governance discussions.
    - o Boardroom shadowing to observe decision-making in real time.
    - o Decision-analysis exercises and case-study evaluations.

11.13.3.2 Reverse Mentorship

- Young professionals' mentor experienced boards on emerging challenges such as:
    - o Technology trends and digital transformation.

Diversity is not a checkbox it is the spark that prevents groupthink.

- o Social impact expectations and ESG initiatives.
- o Youth engagement, brand positioning, and generational insight.

This mutual exchange cultivates humility, trust, and innovation, preparing both mentors and mentees for the evolving demands of modern boardrooms.

11.13.4 Internship and Observer Ship Opportunities

Directorship cannot be learned solely in classrooms – it must be witnessed and practised.

11.13.4.1 Shadow Board Programs

- Emerging directors attend real board meetings as non-voting observers.
- Structured learning includes pre-briefs on agenda and context, post-meeting debriefs and discussion of key decisions, and Ethics notes highlighting dilemmas and best practices.

11.13.4.2 Board Apprenticeships

- Companies, especially Private sector units and large private firms, can offer 1-year board apprenticeships to certified future directors under regulatory oversight.
- Apprentices gain hands-on experience in decision-making, committee participation, and risk review.

11.13.4.3 Startup Board Labs

- Partner with incubators (e.g., T-Hub, NSRCEL) to allow young professionals to act as governance advisors for startups.
- Focus areas include balancing risk, innovation, and structure, while mentoring founders on ESG, compliance, and strategic governance.

Generational diversity is not a threat to experience - it is its strongest ally.

11.13.5 A National Platform for Independent Director Talent Discovery

To cultivate the next generation of IDs, India needs a centralised, digital hub where trained and vetted professionals can be discovered by companies seeking board talent.

11.13.5.1 SEBI-Backed ID Talent Exchange

- Envision a LinkedIn-meets-Naukri platform for governance talent.
- Profiles include verified credentials, certifications, sector expertise, and availability.
- Promotes merit-based, diverse, and transparent board placements.

11.13.5.2 Transparent Board Appointment Panels

- Encourage companies, especially initial public offer-bound and large-cap firms, to select directors via independent panels drawing from the talent exchange.
- Ensures fairness, accountability, and alignment with the skills and diversity needs of modern boards.

These building blocks together form a **structured pipeline,** one that identifies high-potential individuals, educates them, mentors them, gives them real exposure, and connects them with board opportunities in a fair and credible manner.

11.14 Enabling Institutions: Who Must Lead the Change

Building a robust, future-ready talent pipeline for IDs cannot be left to chance. It requires coordinated action across multiple institutions, regulators, educational bodies, corporate stakeholders, industry associations, and governance professionals must work in tandem to cultivate, certify, and mentor the next generation of board leaders.

The silence of new voices is the loudest risk in any boardroom.

11.14.1 Regulators: Driving Policy-Level Change

11.14.1.1 Securities and Exchange Board of India (SEBI)

- Mandate structured board mentorship programs within listed companies, allowing young professionals to observe and learn from experienced directors.
- Introduce regulatory flexibility for the appointment of young, certified IDs under a controlled framework.
- Require listed companies to publicly disclose board diversity initiatives, with an emphasis on generational and skill diversity.

11.14.1.2 Ministry of Corporate Affairs (MCA)

- Incentivise board observer programs and early-career exposure through governance ratings, awards, or formal recognition.
- Support a national framework for ID training, including cross-sectoral, digital, and ESG-focused modules.
- Facilitate a centralised ID registry, integrated with the MCA21 platform, to streamline discovery, appointments, and tracking of talent.

11.14.1.3 Indian Institute of Corporate Affairs (IICA)

- Expand its capacity to offer structured certification programs and continuous refresher courses for aspiring and incumbent directors.
- Collaborate with industry to design sector-specific governance modules, ensuring directors are prepared for challenges across banking, technology, manufacturing, and emerging sectors.

An empty chair for youth today is a hollow board tomorrow.

11.14.2 Educational Institutions: Early Identification and Training

Developing next-generation IDs begins at the educational stage, identifying talent early and equipping them with both governance knowledge and practical exposure.

11.14.2.1 Business Schools (e.g., IIMs, ISB, XLRI)

- Integrate corporate governance, ethics, and ESG as core curriculum components across management and leadership programs.
- Collaborate with SEBI, NSE, and leading corporate boards for capstone projects and governance simulations, providing hands-on exposure to real-world board decision-making.
- Promote boardroom shadowing programs for high-performing students, giving early experience in committee deliberations and risk discussions.

11.14.2.2 Law Schools and Public Policy Institutions

- Offer specialised electives on corporate law, regulatory frameworks, fiduciary duties, and board accountability.
- Provide research fellowships and policy labs focused on emerging trends in corporate governance, transparency, and board effectiveness.
- Encourage interdisciplinary programs combining law, business, and ethics to create well-rounded future directors.

11.14.2.3 Technical and Engineering Institutions

- Introduce modules on digital governance, intellectual property ethics, cybersecurity, and technology oversight, preparing students to serve as tech-savvy IDs.

Mentorship is the governance glue between experience and promise.

- Facilitate industry partnerships and internships with tech-driven companies and startups, bridging the gap between technical expertise and governance responsibilities.

11.14.3 Corporates and Boards: Implementing Talent Practices

Corporate boards play a pivotal role in translating policy and training into practical boardroom experience. By actively shaping talent pipelines, they ensure that the next generation of IDs is prepared, diverse, and impactful.

11.14.3.1 Board Nomination and Remuneration Committees (NRCs)

- Broaden selection pools to include certified professionals under traditional age thresholds, ensuring generational diversity.
- Formalise mentorship programs within the board and committees, pairing veteran directors with emerging talent for structured knowledge transfer.
- Allocate training budgets for onboarding and continuous development, covering governance frameworks, ESG, digital literacy, and ethical decision-making.

11.14.3.2 Startups and Unicorns

- Function as early-stage governance incubators, providing hands-on experience through advisory boards and non-executive roles.
- Enable emerging directors to navigate high-growth, risk-intensive environments, building agility and strategic foresight from the ground up.

A great director is not just one who governs well, but one who teaches others to govern wisely.

11.14.3.3 Public Sector Undertakings (PSUs)

- Pilot structured board apprenticeships and observer roles, offering young professionals' exposure to governance in a public-interest and regulatory-sensitive context.
- Provide cross-sector learning opportunities, bridging public accountability and corporate best practices.

11.14.4 Industry Associations and Governance Bodies

Industry associations and professional bodies act as catalysts in shaping a next-generation talent ecosystem for IDs. Their role extends beyond advocacy to capacity building, recognition, and mentorship.

11.14.4.1 Confederation of Indian Industry (CII), FICCI, ASSOCHAM

- Advocate voluntary boardroom renewal charters incorporating generational, skill-based, and gender diversity metrics.
- Create peer forums and knowledge-sharing platforms where aspiring directors engage with seasoned board leaders, learning governance, risk oversight, and ethical decision-making in practice.

11.14.4.2 Institute of Company Secretaries of India and Institute of Chartered Accountants of India

- Offer Continuing Professional Education (CPE) focused on advanced boardroom leadership, ESG stewardship, and ethical governance.
- Collaborate on co-certification frameworks with SEBI and IICA to provide structured accreditation that ensures readiness for board responsibilities.

Boards are only as strong as the directors they cultivate.

11.15 Civil Society and Think Tanks

Civil society organisations and think tanks play a pivotal role in strengthening boardroom governance by acting as independent watchdogs and thought leaders:

- *Research and dialogue*: Conduct in-depth studies on emerging governance risks, ethical standards, and evolving stakeholder expectations, shaping informed discourse for boards and regulators.
- *Transparency and benchmarking*: Publicly report on generational, gender, and skill-based diversity metrics across boards, creating accountability and encouraging best practices.

11.16 International Partnerships

Global collaboration is essential to elevate Indian boardroom standards and nurture the next generation of IDs:

- **Adapting global frameworks**: Partner with institutions like the OECD, IFC, and World Economic Forum (WEF) to contextualise best-practice governance frameworks for Indian boards.
- **Boardroom exchange programs**: Facilitate international exchange initiatives that expose young Indian professionals to diverse governance models, strategic decision-making, and cross-cultural boardroom practices.

11.17 Case Studies and Models: Learning from Practice

To transform vision into action, India can draw insights from both global initiatives and domestic innovations that have successfully prepared next-generation board talent. These models provide practical blueprints to strengthen governance and ensure a sustainable pipeline of skilled IDs.

Training today ensures governance tomorrow.

11.17.1 The United Kingdom's Board Apprentice Program

Overview:

Launched in 2014, Board Apprentice places diverse, high-potential individuals as non-voting observers on corporate boards for a period of 12 to 18 months.

Key Features:

- Apprentices attend all board and subcommittee meetings.
- Receive mentorship and guidance from a sitting director.
- Gain hands-on experience in corporate governance, strategic decision-making, and compliance oversight.

Impact:

- Significantly increased board diversity across FTSE-listed companies.
- Enhanced visibility and professional development opportunities for underrepresented talent.
- Supported by multiple FTSE 100 companies and global nonprofit organisations.

Lesson for India:

India can implement a structured national observer ship scheme, particularly targeting NSE-listed companies and large family-run businesses seeking generational renewal and broader skill representation on boards.

11.17.2 Singapore's Future Directors Initiative

Overview:

Spearheaded by the Singapore Institute of Directors (SID), the Future Directors Initiative targets high-potential professionals under the age of

Youth without guidance is raw energy; with direction, it is transformative.

40, equipping them with training, mentorship, and practical board exposure.

Key Features:

- Collaborates with corporates to provide real-time board exposure through observer and mentorship programs.
- Curriculum includes digital governance, AI ethics, ESG regulations, and cross-sectoral risk management.
- Emphasises diversity across industries, gender, and professional backgrounds to foster holistic governance perspectives.

Impact:

- Significantly expanded the pool of certified, board-ready professionals across the Association of Southeast Asian Nations.
- Encouraged a long-term cultural shift toward inclusive, generationally diverse governance.
- Increased awareness of ethical, technological, and sustainability challenges among emerging directors.

Lesson for India:

India can adopt a cross-sector talent identification ecosystem in collaboration with SEBI, MCA, premier B-schools, and industry bodies to systematically nurture young professionals ready for board roles.

11.17.3 Infosys' Internal Shadow Board Model (India)

Overview:

Infosys, a flagship IT company, pioneered an innovative "shadow board" comprising young employees tasked with simulating decision-making processes of the main board and proposing strategic initiatives.

Key Features:

- Young leaders participate in structured mock board deliberations, mirroring real governance scenarios.
- Exposure to top leadership decision frameworks, including strategic, financial, and risk evaluation.
- Recommendations from the shadow board are considered seriously, with several ideas implemented by senior executives.

Impact:

- Cultivated a pipeline of future leaders equipped with board-level thinking.
- Provided the main board with fresh, next-generation perspectives on technology, market trends, and organisational culture.
- Strengthened alignment between corporate strategy and emerging workforce expectations.

Lesson for India:

Large Indian corporations can institutionalise shadow boards to create a safe, practical training environment for future directors, fostering intergenerational dialogue and innovation in governance.

11.17.4 The World Economic Forum's Young Global Leaders in Governance

Overview:

The WEF identifies and grooms exceptional individuals under 40 through its Young Global Leaders (YGL) program, emphasising ethics, systems thinking, and advanced corporate governance principles.

Key Features:

- Mentorship by senior global leaders across industries and geographies.

If we do not teach the language of governance, the next generation will inherit silence.

- Participation in high-level policy forums and strategic board discussions.
- Exposure to multi-sectoral challenges, including technology, climate change, health, and global business trends.

Impact:

- Many alumni have advanced to serve on multinational corporate boards, public institutions, and advisory councils.
- Demonstrated a scalable, cross-border model for cultivating values-driven leadership and board readiness.

Lesson for India:

India can establish a Young Directors Forum, modelled on WEF's YGL program and anchored by IICA, CII, or SEBI. This platform can mentor, certify, and prepare high-potential governance professionals for board roles in both corporate and public sectors, bridging generational and skill gaps.

11.17.5 Women on Boards Initiatives (Australia, Canada)

Overview:

Countries such as Australia and Canada have introduced structured initiatives to accelerate gender diversity on corporate boards. These programs not only identify talented women for board service but also provide the training, mentorship, and visibility necessary to succeed in complex governance roles.

Key Features:

- Centralised public databases of board-ready women directors.
- Skill-building programs covering governance, finance, ESG, and leadership.

Leadership demands foresight; boardroom talent demands cultivation.

- Partnerships with regulators, institutional investors, and industry associations to ensure visibility and placement opportunities.

Impact:

- Marked increase in women's representation on corporate boards over the past decade.
- Empirical evidence shows boards with diverse compositions exhibit stronger ESG oversight, enhanced innovation, and more balanced strategic decision-making.

Lesson for India:

India can replicate and expand these initiatives through inclusive director registries that go beyond gender to include age diversity, regional representation, professional backgrounds, and sector-specific expertise. Such a platform can support merit-based, transparent, and future-ready board appointments.

11.18 Challenges and Resistance: What's Holding Us Back?

While the case for cultivating a new generation of IDs is clear and compelling, the journey is fraught with obstacles, cultural, structural, and psychological that require candid acknowledgement and strategic solutions.

11.18.1 Ageism in Reverse: The "Experience Bias"

Despite growing enthusiasm for youth in entrepreneurship, innovation, and digital leadership, a pervasive scepticism persists toward younger professionals assuming governance roles. Common refrains include:

"Too young to understand risk."
"Not enough grey hair to command respect."
"Let them gain 20 years of experience first."

This mindset overlooks the reality that contemporary boardroom challenges – cybersecurity threats, climate transitions, ESG compliance, and stakeholder activism – demand skills, intuition, and adaptability often more pronounced in younger professionals.

Rigid notions equating age with wisdom must give way to a more nuanced approach: **age + structured training + mentorship = boardroom readiness**. Recognising this is the first step in dismantling barriers to generational renewal in India's corporate governance landscape.

11.18.2 Elite Capture and Boardroom Gatekeeping

India's boardrooms remain, in many cases, closed ecosystems, dominated by familiar surnames, former bureaucrats, retired CEOs, or individuals with promoter affiliations. Even with regulatory safeguards on tenure, interlocks, and director limits, appointments often prioritise personal connections over demonstrated competence or a fresh perspective.

For young, first-generation professionals, particularly those from Tier-2/3 cities, non-traditional sectors, or marginalised backgrounds, this creates formidable entry barriers. Many talented individuals remain unaware of pathways into board roles, while others struggle to gain recognition in networks that operate largely on informal referrals.

If India is to foster a truly future-ready cadre of IDs, this gatekeeping must be actively dismantled. Transparent nomination processes, blind screening of candidates, and digital discovery platforms, as discussed earlier, are essential levers to democratise access, diversify perspectives, and inject fresh talent into corporate governance.

11.18.3 Perceived Risk of Youth: Boldness or Liability?

Among promoters and incumbent boards, there exists a subtle, often unspoken apprehension:

- "Will this young director ask too many questions?"
- "Will they report us to the regulators if something goes wrong?"

Talent identification demands vision; board readiness demands preparation.

Young IDs are sometimes perceived as unpredictable reformers, bringing dissent, digital disruption, or regulatory vigilance. This perception can create resistance to their inclusion in boards that prioritise compliance over challenge.

Yet, this fear is often overstated. A well-trained, ethically grounded, and mentored young ID can be both independent and constructive, offering fresh perspectives and innovative problem-solving without antagonism. The true risk lies not in youth, but in boards that resist scrutiny and avoid challenge altogether.

11.18.4 Structural Gaps in Regulation and Policy

Despite SEBI's mandates on board evaluations, diversity, and director rotation, India's regulatory framework lacks mechanisms to actively promote generational renewal. There are no incentives for companies to groom first-time IDs, nor is there a public registry of aspiring board professionals. Key gaps include:

- No provision for board observer-ships under the Companies Act.
- Absence of tax or regulatory incentives for structured mentorship programs.
- No formal protections for young IDs who raise red flags or exercise dissent.

This regulatory silence sends a clear signal: "Experience counts. Fresh perspectives, not so much."

Meaningful policy reform is needed not to lower the standard of governance, but to broaden the entry pathway, ensuring boards are equipped with diverse, capable, and forward-looking talent.

11.18.5 Cultural Norms and Psychological Inertia

Beyond structural and regulatory barriers, cultural attitudes create significant resistance to younger directors. In India, deference to age and hierarchy is deeply ingrained across family-run businesses, PSUs, and corporates. The idea of a 30-year-old providing strategic counsel to a 70-year-old founder still challenges conventional norms.

Addressing this requires:

- A cultural shift in how leadership, expertise, and wisdom are perceived.
- Showcasing success stories of young directors to normalise their presence and contributions.
- Leadership from company chairs and regulators who champion principle-driven governance, not just rule-based compliance.

Changing this mindset will require:

- A cultural shift in how we perceive leadership and wisdom.
- Narratives of successful young directors to normalise the idea.
- Company chairs and regulators who champion the principle, not just the rule.

11.18.6 Risk of Tokenism

Merely adding young IDs to satisfy regulatory mandates risks creating symbolic appointments - boards with presence but no real influence. Tokenism undermines both the development of next-gen talent and the credibility of governance reform.

To avoid this:

- Assign meaningful committee responsibilities (e.g., CSR, Technology Risk, ESG Oversight) to young directors.
- Track and publish participation metrics, focusing on engagement and contribution, not just board presence.
- Avoid placing emerging professionals solely in companies with weak governance as a "sandbox" for experimentation."

Governance literacy demands education; leadership potential demands recognition.

Overcoming these barriers requires a coalition of will: reform-minded regulators, visionary promoters, open-minded veteran directors, and fearless young professionals who prioritise integrity over inertia. Only then can the promise of a next-generation board become reality.

11.19 Conclusion – The Guardians Must Rise

The journey to build a thriving, diverse, and future-ready corps of IDs is not simply a regulatory exercise – it is an ethical and national imperative. In an age of accelerating uncertainty, shifting stakeholder demands, and complex social challenges, corporate governance must evolve from a gatekeeper function to a guardian mission.

The next generation of IDs is not just a demographic statistic – they are the guardians of India's economic integrity, social equity, and sustainable future. They will be called upon to safeguard not just shareholder interests, but the rights of employees, communities, consumers, and the environment.

This is the time to:

- **Invest boldly** in education, mentorship, and structured pipelines that prepare young talent to lead.
- **Reimagine boardrooms** as inclusive, dynamic forums were age diversity fuels innovation and resilience.
- **Enact policy reforms** that open doors without lowering standards – balancing experience with fresh perspectives.
- **Celebrate stories** of young IDs who bring courage, wisdom, and digital savvy to governance.
- **Hold ourselves accountable** as a society, regulator, and corporate citizen to make governance a beacon of integrity for generations to come.

Boardroom acumen demands practice; succession readiness demands foresight.

"The boardrooms of tomorrow are being shaped today in classrooms, co-working spaces, ESG rallies, and coding bootcamps. It is time India recognises this silent revolution and begins to build the scaffolding for a new kind of stewardship."

The call to action is clear: **The Guardians Must Rise.** It is our collective responsibility to cultivate them, empower them, and entrust them with the profound task of guiding India's corporate future with wisdom, courage, and unwavering independence.

Satyam

IL&FS

YES BANK

KINGFISHER

Lessons from the Boardroom

Ten Corporate Case Studies on Governance and Independent Directors

CHAPTER 12

Lessons from the Boardroom: Ten Corporate Case Studies on Governance and Independent Directors

12.1 Introduction: Why Case Studies Matter

The corporate boardroom is a crucible where strategy, ethics, and governance converge. Decisions made behind closed doors can drive innovation, protect stakeholders, and safeguard shareholder value or, if mishandled, trigger catastrophic collapse. For Independent Directors (IDs), a board seat is not merely a position of privilege; it is a mantle of public trust, requiring vigilance, discernment, and courage.

In India, the role of IDs has undergone a profound evolution, shaped by landmark governance failures and regulatory reforms. From high-profile corporate scandals like Satyam and IL&FS to crises in the banking sector, such as Yes Bank, the stakes have never been higher. These events underscore that the presence of IDs alone does not guarantee effective governance; it is their action – or inaction – that determines outcomes.

Case studies offer a unique lens to understand the dynamics of board decision-making, the interplay between promoters, management, and IDs, and the subtle pressures that can erode oversight. They illuminate

Every scandal begins with a silence in the boardroom.

both exemplary practices and cautionary tales, providing a roadmap for emerging directors, policymakers, and corporate leaders alike.

This chapter presents ten instructive case studies, each chosen for its lessons in ethical stewardship, risk management, and boardroom effectiveness. Through these stories, readers will explore the consequences of oversight lapses, the transformative potential of principled resistance, and the urgent need for boardroom reform. Beyond historical recounting, these cases serve as a learning platform, demonstrating how IDs can uphold integrity, navigate crises, and act as guardians of long-term corporate sustainability in India's complex business landscape.

12.2 Case Studies: One by One

12.2.1 Case Study 1: Infosys – Resignation of Independent Director Over Governance Concerns

Summary:

In 2017, Infosys experienced a governance crisis when the then-CEO Vishal Sikka resigned, citing a continuous campaign to undermine him. This was followed by the resignation of ID Prof. Jeffrey Lehman. The situation revealed a rift between the board and the company's promoters, especially co-founder Narayana Murthy, over strategic decisions, and corporate culture.

Governance Issues:

- Promoter interference in board matters.
- Differences over vision and performance evaluation.
- Poor boardroom communication and public airing of disputes.

Role of Independent Directors:

- Attempted to balance the interests of executive management and promoters.

Independent thinking must never be an agenda item it must be a habit.

- Supported a formal inquiry into CEO performance.
- Resigned in protest when boardroom decorum broke down.

Outcome:

- Infosys revamped its board and introduced stronger governance protocols.
- A new CEO was appointed with a clearer mandate.
- Set a precedent for IDs to voice dissent against promoter overreach.

Lessons for Independent Directors:

- Independence means standing for process integrity.
- IDs must ensure healthy board dynamics.
- Sometimes, resignation is the most ethical stand.

12.2.2 Case Study 2: ICICI Bank – Conflict of Interest and the Chanda Kochhar Loan Scandal

Summary:

Chanda Kochhar, then CEO of ICICI Bank, was accused of approving loans to the Videocon Group, which had business ties with her husband. The board initially defended her but later changed its stance under media and regulatory scrutiny, initiating an independent inquiry.

Governance Issues:

- Conflict of interest and lack of disclosure.
- Board's initial passive response.
- Failure of oversight on large credit decisions.

Crisis exposes what complacency conceals.

Role of Independent Directors:

- Initially rubber-stamped CEO decisions.
- Reluctantly agreed to a third-party probe.
- Accused of failing to act proactively.

Outcome:

- The CEO was terminated with retrospective effect.
- Bank governance practices came under regulatory scanner.
- Strengthened norms for related party transactions and board evaluation.

Lessons for Independent Directors:

- Independence requires early scrutiny of red flags.
- Allegiance is to the company, not the executive.
- IDs must demand transparency and probe when in doubt.

12.2.3 Case Study 3: Tata Sons – Removal of Cyrus Mistry and Boardroom Turbulence

Summary:

In 2016, the Tata Sons board suddenly removed Executive Chairman Cyrus Mistry, leading to a legal battle. Several group companies' boards and their IDs expressed support for Mistry, sparking debates on the autonomy of IDs versus promoter control.

Governance Issues:

- Ambiguous division of power between Chairman, Board, and Promoters.
- Lack of due process in Mistry's removal.
- Boardroom capture by majority shareholders.

The first duty of oversight is to look beyond what's shown.

Role of Independent Directors:

- Some IDs backed Mistry, citing governance principles.
- Exposed to intense pressure, and some resigned.
- Highlighted the need for clear board charters.

Outcome:

- Supreme Court upheld Tata's decision legally but emphasised governance clarity.
- Institutional investors demanded better governance disclosures.
- Reinforced the need for IDs to protect minority interests.

Lessons for Independent Directors:

- Balance independence with legal clarity on roles.
- IDs must challenge governance irregularities.
- Resilience is key when confronting promoter dominance.

12.2.4 Case Study 4: IL&FS – Collapse of Oversight and Systemic Risk

Summary:

In 2018, IL&FS defaulted on several debt obligations, triggering a liquidity crisis in India's NBFC sector. Despite multiple committees and high-profile IDs, the board failed to detect or prevent mounting financial risks.

Governance Issues:

- Poor risk management and debt structuring.
- Internal audit failures.
- Passive board oversight.

Governance without grit is performance without purpose.

Role of Independent Directors:

- Failed to raise alarms despite deteriorating financials.
- Did not probe asset-liability mismatches.
- Seen as complicit through inaction.

Outcome:

- The government replaced the entire board.
- Probes revealed serious lapses and misgovernance.
- Led to governance reform in NBFCs.

Lessons for Independent Directors:

- Active participation in financial committees is crucial.
- IDs must demand stress testing and scenario analysis.
- Passive approval is not a defence in governance failure.

12.2.5 Case Study 5: Fortis Healthcare – Related Party Transactions and Boardroom Cleanup

Summary:

Promoters of Fortis Healthcare diverted funds to entities they controlled. Whistleblowers raised concerns, and IDs initiated forensic audits and supported a change in ownership structure.

Governance Issues:

- Diversion of funds via related party transactions.
- Lack of transparency in board approvals.
- Management override of internal controls.

Role of Independent Directors:

- Supported whistleblower complaints.
- Initiated and acted upon forensic audits.
- Helped restructure board and promoter ownership.

Outcome:

- Promoters ousted; new ownership by IHH Healthcare.
- Investor confidence restored.
- Improved transparency and board effectiveness.

Lessons for Independent Directors:

- Always scrutinise related-party dealings.
- Support and protect whistleblowers.
- Use audits and disclosures as corrective tools.

12.2.6 Case Study 6: Satyam – The Corporate Governance Earthquake

Summary:

In 2009, Satyam's chairman Ramalinga Raju confessed to inflating profits by over Rs. 7,000 crores. The board, despite having qualified IDs, failed to detect the fraud, particularly the fake bank balances.

Governance Issues:

- Massive financial fraud.
- Weak audit oversight.
- Board complicity through inaction.

Role of Independent Directors:

- Approved Maytas acquisition without diligence.
- Failed to probe unusual margins and cash positions.
- Did not question the auditor rigorously.

Outcome:

- Government reconstituted the board.
- Triggered corporate governance reforms.
- NFRA and revised Clause 49 norms followed.

Lessons for Independent Directors:

- Always verify financials and audit trails.
- Demand detailed explanations for acquisitions.
- Audit Committees must act assertively.

12.2.7 Case Study 7: Yes Bank – Lending, Governance, and Collapse of Confidence

Summary:

Yes Bank accumulated toxic assets under founder-CEO Rana Kapoor. Governance concerns and asset quality issues came to light too late, leading to regulatory intervention by Reserve Bank of India.

Governance Issues:

- Reckless lending and asset quality cover-ups.
- Poor governance disclosures.
- Dominant CEO unchecked by board.

In every scandal, the costliest failure is the one the board didn't see coming.

Role of Independent Directors:

- Did not question loan exposure concentration.
- Failed to act on early signs of governance failure.
- Supported CEO tenure extensions without performance audit.

Outcome:

- RBI imposed a moratorium.
- SBI-led rescue package.
- Arrest of Kapoor and new management team.

Lessons for Independent Directors:

- CEOs must be evaluated impartially.
- Risk committee participation is vital.
- Board independence must be exercised, not just declared.

12.2.8 Case Study 8: Sahara Group – SEBI Dispute and Lack of Transparency

Summary:

Sahara raised over Rs. 24,000 crores through OFCDs without SEBI approval. The company failed to provide investor details. The Supreme Court ordered a refund and asset seizure.

Governance Issues:

- Unauthorised fundraising.
- Non-compliance with SEBI regulations.
- Board in the dark or deliberately uninformed.

No director ever regrets speaking too early only too late.

Role of Independent Directors:

- Did not question large-scale fundraising mechanisms.
- No efforts to ensure investor protection.
- Enabled opaque promoter control.

Outcome:

- SEBI seized assets; Subrata Roy arrested.
- Investors not fully refunded due to lack of data.
- Regulatory tightening for public fundraising.

Lessons for Independent Directors:

- Understand regulatory boundaries.
- Always demand investor protection mechanisms.
- IDs must not remain silent spectators.

12.2.9 Case Study 9: Cognizant India – Bribery Allegations and Board Accountability

Summary:

Cognizant admitted to paying bribes in India to obtain building permits. The United States authorities fined the company under the FCPA, and several top executives faced investigation.

Governance Issues:

- Corruption in vendor and permit dealings.
- Ethics and compliance breakdown.
- Disjointed oversight between parent and subsidiary.

When the promoter is the storm, the board must be the anchor.

Role of Independent Directors (India):

- Had limited visibility into corruption risks.
- Compliance reports were not discussed in detail.
- Lacked access to real-time operational data.

Outcome:

- Fines and reputational damage.
- Strengthened global compliance frameworks.
- Renewed focus on ethics training and vendor scrutiny.

Lessons for Independent Directors:

- Demand detailed compliance updates.
- Ensure anti-corruption controls in operations.
- Whistleblower mechanisms must be actively tested.

12.2.10 Case Study 10: Kingfisher Airlines – Debt, Defaults, and Director Dilemmas

Summary:

Kingfisher Airlines defaulted on over Rs. 9,000 crores in bank loans. Despite poor financials, the board continued to approve management decisions without proper accountability.

Governance Issues:

- High debt and misallocation of funds.
- No viable turnaround strategy.
- Board complicity in continued lending.

Role of Independent Directors:

- Failed to raise objections on high leverage.
- Approved lavish spending amidst losses.
- Some resigned only after regulatory scrutiny began.

Outcome:

- Airline grounded; promoter fled India.
- Banks marked loans as NPAs.
- Debate on wilful default and board accountability ensued.

Lessons for Independent Directors:

- Question business models that rely on unsustainable debt.
- Walk away when governance is consistently ignored.
- Directors are accountable for enabling financial mismanagement.

Don't wait for the regulator to ask what you should have asked first.

12.3 Comparative Matrix of Governance Failures and Independent Director Responses (Part 1 of 2)

Company name	Infosys	ICICI Bank	Tata Sons	IL&FS	Fortis
Year	2017	2018	2016	2018	2018
Sector	IT Services	Banking	Conglomerate	Infrastructure/ Finance	Healthcare
Governance issue	Boardroom conflict, promoter interference	Conflict of interest, related-party loans	Board-chairman role conflict	Debt-fuelled collapse, risk failures	Diversion of funds via RPTs
Scale of failure	Strategic crisis, resignations	Rs. 3,000 crores in NPAs linked to scandal	Legal-political crisis, national headlines	Rs. 90,000+ crore in liabilities, systemic risk	Rs. 450 crores in misappropriation
Primary board failure	Unable to check promoter dominance	Delayed action on the CEO conflict	No clear role definition, power imbalance	Weak risk and audit oversight	Allowed RPTs, poor whistleblower support
Independent director response	Some IDs resigned, citing decorum breakdown	Initially supported the CEO, later changed stance	Split- some backed Mistry, others resigned	Passive and ineffective	Proactive -commissioned audits, supported change
Whistleblower involvement	No	Yes (external + media)	No	No	Yes (internal)

Company name	Infosys	ICICI Bank	Tata Sons	IL&FS	Fortis
Regulatory action	Board reconstituted	The CEO was dismissed, and penalties were imposed by SEBI	Legal battle to the Supreme Court	Board superseded by the Government	New promoters, audit reforms
Impact on reputation	Temporary crisis, restored	Major image hit, public inquiry	Long-standing trust shaken	Deep systemic distrust	Improved after clean-up
Reform triggered	Board decorum and promoter interference	Strengthened conflict-of-interest norms	Minority rights & board clarity	Risk oversight reforms	Strengthened RPT scrutiny
Role of Audit Committee	Not proactive	Did not raise red flags early	Not highlighted	Ineffective and dormant	Worked post-whistleblower report
Risk oversight effectiveness	Weak in strategic matters	Poor on credit exposure	Overpowered by promoters	Total failure	Improved post-crisis
Financial literacy of independent directors	High but not assertive	Strong but passive	Mixed	Strong on paper, weak in practice	Strong, later assertive
Ethical clarity of independent directors	Mixed – some upheld independence	Delayed but later realigned	High among a few	Poor – complicit by inaction	Strong post-whistleblower
Outcome for promoters/ executives	Co-founder criticism, public apologies	The CEO was removed, prosecuted	Chairman retained, successor removed	Senior executives charged	Promoters exited
Long-term lessons for independent directors	Stand firm under pressure	Do not delay probing conflicts	Legal clarity + courage	Engage deeply in financials	Forensics + whistleblowers = impact

12.4 Comparative Matrix of Governance Failures and Independent Director Responses (Part 2 of 2)

Company name	Satyam	Yes Bank	Sahara	Cognizant	Kingfisher
Year	2009	2020	2012–2020	2019	2012
Sector	IT Services	Banking	Financial services	IT (MNC)	Aviation
Governance issue	Accounting fraud	Poor asset quality, promoter dominance	Unregulated public fundraising	Bribery & compliance lapses	Debt default, poor financial planning
Scale of failure	Rs. 7,000 crore fraud	Rs. 20,000+ crore NPAs, liquidity collapse	Rs. 24,000+ crore collected illegally	USD 25 million penalty	Rs. 9,000+ crore loan defaults
Primary board failure	Ignored red flags, no forensic diligence	Rubber-stamped loans, weak risk governance	No due diligence on fundraising	Low visibility into compliance risks	Approved unsustainable financials
Independent directors response	Passive, failed to question	Ineffective oversight, delayed resignations	Passive and silent	Limited influence, lacked visibility	Rubber-stamped, late resignations
Whistleblower involvement	No	Yes	No	No	No

Company name	Satyam	Yes Bank	Sahara	Cognizant	Kingfisher
Regulatory action	Board reconstituted, NFRA created	Moratorium, rescue by SBI	Asset seizure, SC refund orders	U.S. SEC & DOJ actions	Banks classify as a wilful defaulter
Impact on reputation	India's Enron moment	Loss of investor confidence	Lasting stigma	Global ethical scrutiny	Reputational collapse
Reform triggered	Audit reforms (Clause 49, NFRA)	RBI scrutiny on boards	SEBI scrutiny on unlisted companies	Ethics compliance in multi-national Companies	Lending accountability
Role of Audit Committee	Ineffective oversight	Weak loan portfolio review	Non-functional	Ineffective at the India level	No evident challenge to management
Risk oversight effectiveness	Failed to detect red flags	Ineffective	Ignored	Not prioritised	Ignored asset-liability mismatch
Financial literacy of independent directors	Strong but unused	Strong but dormant	Poor	Poor board access	Weak relative to sector needs
Ethical clarity of independent directors	Low	Very low	Low	Moderate (due to structural limits)	Weak, resigned late
Outcome for promoters/executives	Founder jailed	CEO arrested	Promoter jailed	Executives investigated	Promoter fled the country
Long-term lessons for independent directors	Never trust numbers blindly	Demand accountability	IDs must be gatekeepers	Know compliance liability	Glamour ≠ governance

12.5 Thematic Takeaways

12.5.1 Promoter Dominance Undermines True Independence

In cases like **Satyam, Kingfisher, and Tata Sons**, the dominance of a promoter or founding family eroded the effectiveness of board independence. IDs often deferred to founder authority, sometimes out of loyalty, sometimes out of fear, and often due to board capture.

Takeaway: Independence must be structural, cultural, and psychological. IDs must cultivate the courage to challenge powerful promoters, especially in founder-led companies.

12.5.2 Red Flags are Always There - If You're Willing to See Them

In **IL&FS, Yes Bank, and Fortis**, signs of stress and misconduct were visible early. In most cases, financial irregularities, inter-group exposures, or whistleblower complaints were either ignored or downplayed.

Takeaway: IDs must treat early warnings, no matter how small, as potential entry points to deeper problems. Diligent follow-up, forensic questioning, and board-level escalation are essential.

12.5.3 Passive Resignation is not Accountability

Several IDs chose to resign silently during governance breakdowns (**Kingfisher, Yes Bank, ICICI Bank**), often to avoid reputational fallout. Yet, none went on record or raised institutional concerns that might have led to earlier reforms.

Takeaway: Silent exits help no one. If resignation is warranted, it must be accompanied by reasoned disclosures to regulators or shareholders. Ethical dissent is part of fiduciary responsibility.

A director who doesn't read the audit notes is reading the obituary.

12.5.4 Whistleblower Mechanisms Need Independent Director Protection

The **Infosys and ICICI Bank** cases show contrasting ID responses to whistleblowers. While Infosys conducted a transparent investigation, ICICI initially ignored internal concerns. Boards that ignore whistleblowers often lose both trust and time.

Takeaway: IDs should champion protected channels for internal complaints and ensure every concern is reviewed independently. Audit Committees and NRCs must include whistleblower tracking as part of quarterly reviews.

12.5.5 Committee Participation Without Diligence is Dangerous

In **IL&FS** and **ICICI**, IDs were members of the key board committees but failed to intervene. Being part of an Audit Committee or Risk Committee comes with responsibility, not symbolic presence.

Takeaway: Committee membership demands competence, preparation, and a willingness to speak up. IDs must demand adequate data, engage external experts when necessary, and document dissent in minutes.

12.5.6 Regulatory Literacy is Essential

In Sahara and Cognizant, regulatory frameworks (SEBI, FCPA) were either misunderstood or neglected. IDs failed to question non-compliance or understand the legal exposure.

Takeaway: IDs must invest in continuous legal and regulatory education. They must understand sectoral norms and jurisdictional differences, especially in global or listed entities.

Decision-making demands foresight; past mistakes demand remembrance.

12.5.7 Independence is Tested Most in Internal Conflicts

The Tata Sons and Fortis cases illustrate that real independence is tested not in routine decisions, but in moments of internal conflict between promoter and professional, between founder and governance, or between short-term and long-term interests.

Takeaway: IDs must remember their fiduciary duty is to the company and its stakeholders, not to any individual or group. Voting against the majority is not insubordination; it is integrity in action.

12.5.8 Crisis is the Worst Time to Start Leading

In almost every case reviewed, by the time the IDs began raising concerns, the damage was already done. This reactive approach reduces their relevance and power.

Takeaway: Governance is a proactive endeavour. Effective IDs engage meaningfully from Day 1, understanding business models, examining strategy, asking questions, and setting an ethical tone at the top.

12.5.9 Reputation is Earned in Silence, Lost in Crisis

Many IDs with impeccable careers found their reputations questioned due to their association with failing companies. The lesson is simple: the boardroom is no place for complacency.

Takeaway: Vigilance is the price of trust. IDs must remember that their role is a public trust, not just a boardroom credential.

12.5.10 Courage is the Most Important Qualification

Degrees, designations, and networks matter, but what defines the best IDs is their courage to act when it matters. Whether it is confronting a promoter, supporting a whistleblower, or resigning publicly, courage is the trait that separates good directors from great ones.

Takeaway: Independent Directorship is not for the timid. It demands moral clarity, emotional intelligence, and an unwavering commitment to fiduciary responsibility.

12.6 Conclusion: From Passive Participants to Active Stewards

The stories in this chapter paint a sobering yet instructive picture of boardroom dynamics in India. IDs are not mere advisors; they are guardians of corporate integrity. When they fail to ask questions, challenge assumptions, or act on early warnings, the consequences can be systemic.

Yet, there are also examples of courage where IDs resisted pressure, demanded accountability, or resigned in protest. These are the models that the future of Indian corporate governance must embrace. Because in every boardroom, the real test of independence is not structure but action.

"Every boardroom leaves behind a legacy some as cautionary tales, others as models of integrity; and in each, the role of the Independent Director determines whether the story ends in collapse or in credibility."

Annexure

Board Oversight Toolkit and Key Questions

Committee	Focus Area	Key Questions for Management	Purpose / Oversight Objective (and Red Flags)	When to Probe Deeper / Investigation Trigger	Frequency of Review / Discussion	Evidence / Supporting Documents	Risk / Criticality	Notes / Observations / Follow-up	Case Study / Example
Audit Committee	**Financial Reporting & Controls**	1. Are there significant changes in accounting policies or assumptions this period?	Ensure transparency; sudden policy shifts may mask earnings manipulation.	If changes occur near year-end or significantly alter profit/assets.	Quarterly	Financial statements, audit reports	High	Track trends and explanations; follow-up on discrepancies	Satyam: Aggressive accounting policies hid financial misstatements
		2. Are there any unusual, complex, or off-balance-sheet transactions?	Safeguard against hidden liabilities or creative accounting.	If material transactions lack clear business rationale or are repetitive.	Quarterly	Transaction reports, board minutes	High	Investigate rationale and approvals	Cognizant: Off-balance-sheet exposures overlooked in risk assessment
		3. Have internal audits revealed control weaknesses? What remedial actions have been taken?	Evaluate financial discipline; repeated issues signal systemic failure.	If recurring weaknesses are unresolved across consecutive periods.	Quarterly	Internal audit reports, action plans	High	Ensure remedial actions are tracked and closed	Yes Bank: Weak internal controls contributed to financial instability
		4. Are subsidiary and joint venture controls independently verified?	Verify group-level integrity; missing oversight can conceal exposure.	If audit reports for subsidiaries show repeated gaps or no independent review.	Quarterly	Audit reports, JV statements	High	Follow-up on corrective actions and reporting gaps	Kingfisher Airlines: Lack of oversight in subsidiaries led to financial exposure
		5. Are management override controls effective?	Prevent manipulation of financial reporting.	If override events occur frequently or without documentation.	Quarterly	Audit logs, management reports	High	Monitor for patterns of override	Enron: Management override led to fraudulent financial reporting

Committee	Focus Area	Key Questions for Management	Purpose / Oversight Objective (and Red Flags)	When to Probe Deeper / Investigation Trigger	Frequency of Review / Discussion	Evidence / Supporting Documents	Risk / Criticality	Notes / Observations / Follow-up	Case Study / Example
	Compliance & Regulatory	6. Are we fully compliant with SEBI, Companies Act, and other regulations?	Reinforce legal accountability; non-compliance can trigger penalties.	If repeated regulatory notices, fines, or late filings occur.	Quarterly	Compliance certificates, board reports	High	Track regulatory correspondence	Sahara case: Non-compliance with regulatory filings attracted penalties
		7. How are whistleblower complaints tracked and resolved?	Uphold ethical governance; unresolved cases suggest cultural breakdown.	If complaints remain unresolved >90 days or trend upward.	Quarterly	Whistleblower logs, HR reports	High	Review resolution timelines and patterns	Satyam whistleblower ignored warnings of financial irregularities
		8. Are regulatory inspections or audits reported timely to the board?	Ensure early corrective actions.	If inspections reveal repeated issues or are not escalated.	Quarterly	Inspection reports, management memos	High	Ensure timely escalation and action	Cognizant: Delayed reporting of compliance issues impacted risk oversight
	Risk & Fraud	9. Have any incidents of fraud or financial irregularity been reported?	Demand transparency; delayed reporting is a red flag.	If "no fraud" is reported despite prior audit or control gaps.	Quarterly	Fraud register, audit reports	High	Validate reports against audit and control findings	Satyam: Concealed fraud due to weak reporting mechanisms
		10. Are audit findings independently validated?	Confirm auditor independence; management influence compromises credibility.	If management overrides or delays auditor recommendations.	Quarterly	External auditor reports	High	Track external verification and discrepancies	Yes Bank: Auditor independence questioned during governance review

Committee	Focus Area	Key Questions for Management	Purpose / Oversight Objective (and Red Flags)	When to Probe Deeper / Investigation Trigger	Frequency of Review / Discussion	Evidence / Supporting Documents	Risk / Criticality	Notes / Observations / Follow-up	Case Study / Example
		11. Is there a fraud risk assessment and monitoring mechanism in place?	Detect early warning signs of financial misconduct.	If fraud risk assessment is outdated or not conducted annually.	Annually	Fraud risk assessment reports	High	Ensure updates are conducted annually	Cognizant: Cyber and financial fraud risk assessments not updated annually
		12. Are there significant deviations in actual vs budgeted results?	Identify potential manipulation or operational issues.	If deviations exceed threshold limits without valid explanations.	Quarterly	Financial reports, variance analysis	High	Investigate explanations for deviations	Kingfisher Airlines: Budget deviations not adequately explained
Nomination & Remuneration Committee (NRC)	**Board Composition & Governance**	1. Does the board have the right mix of skills, diversity, and experience?	Ensure strategic balance; over-representation of insiders dilutes oversight.	If board composition hasn't changed for >3 years or lacks critical skills.	Annually	Board skill matrix, CVs	High	Review skill gaps and diversity metrics	FMCG example: Board diversity improved decision-making outcomes
		2. Are director evaluation processes robust and evidence-based?	Maintain accountability and performance orientation.	If evaluations are qualitative only or not linked to performance improvements.	Annually	Evaluation reports	High	Track follow-up on evaluation results	Infosys: Director evaluation tied to business KPIs enhanced governance
		3. Are director onboarding and training programs sufficient?	Build informed, competent directors.	If training records show incomplete induction or refresher programs.	Annually	Training records	Medium	Monitor training completion	Tata Consultancy: Robust onboarding programs improved board readiness

Committee	Focus Area	Key Questions for Management	Purpose / Oversight Objective (and Red Flags)	When to Probe Deeper / Investigation Trigger	Frequency of Review / Discussion	Evidence / Supporting Documents	Risk / Criticality	Notes / Observations / Follow-up	Case Study / Example
	Executive Remuneration	4.Are remuneration policies aligned with long-term value creation and ESG goals?	Prevent short-termism; misaligned incentives drive excessive risk-taking.	If variable pay rises despite poor long-term performance or ESG metrics.	Annually	Remuneration policy documents	High	Ensure ESG and long-term metrics incorporated	Infosys: Incentives linked to sustainability and long-term growth metrics
		5. Are performance metrics measurable and transparent?	Foster fairness; opaque metrics conceal bias.	If KPI targets are unclear, inconsistent, or subjective.	Annually	Performance evaluation reports	High	Track clarity and alignment of KPIs	FMCG example: Transparent KPIs reduced bias in executive evaluation
		6. How is remuneration benchmarked against industry peers?	Ensure competitive but fair pay structures.	If pay exceeds peer median significantly without justification.	Annually	Compensation surveys, benchmarking reports	Medium	Review benchmarking rationale	Tata Motors: Benchmarking ensured fair executive compensation
	Succession Planning	7. Is there a clear, regularly reviewed succession plan for the CEO and key executives?	Guarantee leadership continuity; absence of successors signals vulnerability.	If no documented succession plan exists or last review >12 months ago.	Annually	Succession plans	High	Track updates and readiness assessments	Infosys succession planning maintained business continuity during leadership change

Committee	Focus Area	Key Questions for Management	Purpose / Oversight Objective (and Red Flags)	When to Probe Deeper / Investigation Trigger	Frequency of Review / Discussion	Evidence / Supporting Documents	Risk / Criticality	Notes / Observations / Follow-up	Case Study / Example
		8. How are potential leaders groomed and assessed for readiness?	Build resilience and future capability.	If training or mentoring programs are inconsistent or incomplete.	Annually	Development plans, mentoring reports	Medium	Ensure mentoring is effective	HDFC Bank: Grooming internal talent ensured smooth CEO transition
		9. Are emergency succession plans in place for unforeseen CEO exits?	Protect business continuity.	If plans are absent or untested.	Annually	Board-approved emergency plans	High	Test emergency procedures	Wipro: Emergency plans tested for unforeseen leadership changes
		10. Are high-potential internal candidates periodically reviewed for readiness?	Ensure bench strength.	If internal talent pipelines are stagnant or unassessed.	Semi-Annually	Talent review reports	Medium	Track follow-up and talent development	Tata Steel: Regular review strengthened internal succession pool
Risk Management Committee	**Enterprise Risk Strategy**	23. What are the top strategic, financial, operational, and ESG risks today?	Maintain risk visibility; unmanaged concentration is a warning sign.	If high-risk areas lack mitigation plans or risk registers are outdated.	Quarterly	Risk registers, board reports	High	Ensure mitigation plans exist	Cognizant: Failure to monitor emerging risks impacted operations
		24. How are emerging risks (cyber, geopolitical, climate) monitored?	Stay proactive; ignorance of emerging risks leads to shocks.	If emerging risks are absent from reports or unaddressed in strategy discussions.	Quarterly	Risk monitoring reports	High	Track emerging risk identification	Infosys: Cyber risk monitoring improved early threat detection

Committee	Focus Area	Key Questions for Management	Purpose / Oversight Objective (and Red Flags)	When to Probe Deeper / Investigation Trigger	Frequency of Review / Discussion	Evidence / Supporting Documents	Risk / Criticality	Notes / Observations / Follow-up	Case Study / Example
	Risk Appetite & Monitoring	25. Are the defined risk appetite still appropriate given current conditions?	Align strategy with tolerance; disconnects imply mismanagement.	If risk breaches occur repeatedly without adjustment to appetite.	Quarterly	Risk appetite statements	High	Ensure risk limits are updated	Kingfisher Airlines: Unchecked risk exposure caused financial stress
		26. What KRIs are being tracked and how often?	Ensure data-driven oversight; outdated indicators create blind spots.	If KRIs are outdated, missing, or unmonitored for >1 quarter.	Quarterly	KRI reports, dashboards	High	Track KRI effectiveness	HDFC Bank: KRIs helped detect operational risks early
	Crisis Preparedness	27. Are crisis and business continuity plans tested regularly?	Test organizational resilience; untested plans indicate false security.	If last tests >12 months ago or plans not updated after incidents.	Annually	BC/DR test reports	High	Ensure plans are updated	Wipro: Regular drills improved disaster preparedness
		28. How are learnings from past crises applied?	Embed continuous improvement; repetition of errors shows governance fatigue.	If similar operational failures recur or lessons are not documented.	Annually				
Stakeholders Relationship Committee	**Investor Relations**	29. How efficiently are shareholder grievances handled?	Protect investor confidence; recurring complaints indicate poor transparency.	If complaints remain unresolved beyond SLA or increase in volume.	Quarterly	Grievance logs, board minutes	High	Track resolution timelines	Satyam: Shareholder complaints ignored until exposed by whistleblower

Committee	Focus Area	Key Questions for Management	Purpose / Oversight Objective (and Red Flags)	When to Probe Deeper / Investigation Trigger	Frequency of Review / Discussion	Evidence / Supporting Documents	Risk / Criticality	Notes / Observations / Follow-up	Case Study / Example
		30. Are institutional investors' concerns reflected in board deliberations?	Strengthen trust and responsiveness.	If investor feedback is ignored or not addressed in minutes.	Quarterly	Investor meeting notes, emails	High	Ensure follow-up actions taken	Infosys: Investor feedback influenced strategic priorities
	Stakeholder Engagement	31. Are communications with regulators, communities, and employees open and timely?	Build stakeholder goodwill; delayed disclosure breeds distrust.	If key communications are delayed, incomplete, or reactive.	Quarterly	Communication logs, emails, reports	Medium	Track timeliness and accuracy	Tata Steel: Timely disclosure enhanced community trust
		32. How are social media and public perception risks monitored?	Manage reputation proactively.	If negative media/ social sentiment rises unaddressed.	Monthly	Social monitoring reports	Medium	Document corrective actions	HDFC Bank: Social monitoring mitigated reputational risk
		33. Are employee engagement surveys conducted and acted upon?	Promote organizational alignment.	If participation is low or corrective actions are absent.	Semi-Annually	Survey reports, action plans	Medium	Track completion and follow-up	Wipro: Survey-driven initiatives improved morale

Committee	Focus Area	Key Questions for Management	Purpose / Oversight Objective (and Red Flags)	When to Probe Deeper / Investigation Trigger	Frequency of Review / Discussion	Evidence / Supporting Documents	Risk / Criticality	Notes / Observations / Follow-up	Case Study / Example
CSR Committee	Strategy & Alignment	34. Are CSR projects aligned with corporate purpose and national priorities?	Link social investment to business purpose; tokenism undermines credibility.	If projects lack measurable outcomes or alignment.	Annually	Project plans, reports	Medium	Track alignment and impact	Tata Power: CSR aligned with renewable energy goals
		35. How is project impact measured and verified?	Ensure real outcomes; absence of impact metrics suggests box-ticking.	If no third-party assessment is conducted for >2 years.	Annually	Impact assessments, audits	Medium	Verify third-party validation	Infosys Foundation: Impact audits ensured social effectiveness
	Compliance & Reporting	36. Are CSR expenditures compliant with Section 135 and disclosed transparently?	Maintain statutory integrity; misreporting attracts legal risk.	If annual CSR report is delayed, incomplete, or inconsistent.	Annually	CSR reports, approvals	High	Check for regulatory compliance	Sahara: CSR misreporting led to scrutiny
		37. Are CSR vendors/NGOs evaluated for performance?	Ensure funds are used effectively.	If same partners are used without evaluation.	Annually	Vendor performance reports	Medium	Document evaluation outcomes	Reliance Foundation: Regular evaluations improved efficiency
		38. Are local community feedback mechanisms in place?	Ensure social license to operate.	If complaints/ grievances are unresolved.	Annually	Feedback logs, reports	Medium	Track and resolve issues	Tata Chemicals: Community feedback drove CSR improvements

Committee	Focus Area	Key Questions for Management	Purpose / Oversight Objective (and Red Flags)	When to Probe Deeper / Investigation Trigger	Frequency of Review / Discussion	Evidence / Supporting Documents	Risk / Criticality	Notes / Observations / Follow-up	Case Study / Example
Sustainability / ESG Committee	**Environmental Stewardship**	39. What are our carbon, water, and waste reduction targets?	Align with global standards; stagnant metrics imply greenwashing.	If targets remain unchanged >1 year or actual performance lags targets.	Quarterly	ESG reports, dashboards	High	Track progress and gaps	Infosys: ESG targets reduced environmental footprint
		40. How is climate risk integrated into financial planning?	Embed resilience; neglect exposes long-term valuation risk.	If climate risk is absent from scenario planning.	Annually	Financial planning documents	High	Assess risk integration	Wipro: Climate risk assessment embedded in budgeting
	Social Responsibility	41. Are workforce diversity and wellbeing metrics improving?	Track social license; stagnation signals cultural inertia.	If attrition spikes in underrepresented groups or metrics are static.	Semi-Annually	HR dashboards, reports	Medium	Monitor trends	HDFC Life: Diversity initiatives reduced attrition
		42. How are community and supply-chain impacts managed?	Reinforce holistic ESG accountability.	If supply-chain audits or community assessments are missing >1 year.	Annually	Audit reports, impact reports	Medium	Track corrective measures	Tata Motors: Supplier audits enhanced ESG compliance
	Governance Integration	43. Are ESG goals tied to executive KPIs and board reviews?	Drive accountability; lack of linkage weakens impact.	If ESG reported separately or not reviewed by board.	Annually	KPI dashboards, board minutes	High	Ensure linkage with performance	Infosys: ESG-linked incentives improved outcomes

Committee	Focus Area	Key Questions for Management	Purpose / Oversight Objective (and Red Flags)	When to Probe Deeper / Investigation Trigger	Frequency of Review / Discussion	Evidence / Supporting Documents	Risk / Criticality	Notes / Observations / Follow-up	Case Study / Example
		44. Are ESG disclosures aligned with TCFD / GRI / SASB frameworks?	Ensure global transparency standards.	If reporting does not meet framework expectations or is incomplete.	Annually	ESG disclosures	High	Verify completeness	Wipro: ESG disclosure aligned with TCFD guidelines
Related Party Transactions (RPT)	**Fairness & Transparency**	45. Are all material RPTs disclosed and reviewed by independent directors?	Ensure arm's-length fairness; opacity signals self-dealing.	If RPTs exceed thresholds or involve promoters repeatedly.	Quarterly	RPT registers, approvals	High	Investigate unusual or repetitive RPTs	Satyam: Undisclosed RPTs led to governance failure
		46. Are recurring RPTs periodically re-evaluated for necessity?	Prevent complacency and conflicts.	If recurring RPTs continue >2 years without review.	Annually	RPT review reports	Medium	Track re-evaluations	Kingfisher Airlines: Recurrent RPTs ignored risk
		47. Are RPT approvals aligned with board and regulatory guidelines?	Ensure governance compliance.	If approvals are delegated too widely or inconsistently documented.	Quarterly	Board approvals, policies	High	Review approval compliance	Cognizant: Non-compliant approvals raised audit flags
		48. Is there a documented rationale for each RPT?	Prevent insider benefit or favoritism.	If justifications are missing or inconsistent with policy.	Quarterly	RPT documentation	High	Validate rationale	Satyam: Lack of RPT rationale led to misreporting

Committee	Focus Area	Key Questions for Management	Purpose / Oversight Objective (and Red Flags)	When to Probe Deeper / Investigation Trigger	Frequency of Review / Discussion	Evidence / Supporting Documents	Risk / Criticality	Notes / Observations / Follow-up	Case Study / Example
Technology / Digital Transformation Committee	**Strategy & Innovation**	49. Is the technology roadmap aligned with growth and efficiency goals?	Ensure digital investments support value creation; ad-hoc projects waste capital.	If projects are delayed, over-budget, or misaligned with priorities.	Quarterly	IT roadmap, board reports	High	Monitor project delivery	Infosys: Roadmap alignment improved ROI on digital investments
		50. How are AI, automation, and digital ethics managed?	Maintain compliance and reputation in emerging tech use.	If AI deployments lack governance, ethical review, or KPIs.	Quarterly	AI governance reports	High	Review ethical framework	Wipro: Ethical AI framework reduced reputational risks
	Cybersecurity & Data Privacy	51. What are our most significant cyber risks and mitigation plans?	Protect assets and reputation; absence of testing is a red flag.	If security incidents increase or mitigation plans not tested.	Quarterly	Cyber risk assessments, DR plans	High	Track incident trends	HDFC Bank: Cyber mitigation prevented data breaches
		52. Are employees trained and systems stress-tested regularly?	Reinforce human-tech resilience.	If training completion <90% or systems untested >12 months.	Semi-Annually	Training logs, test reports	High	Track completion and effectiveness	Tata Consultancy: Regular drills improved resilience
		53. How is data privacy compliance (GDPR, PDPA) ensured?	Avoid legal penalties and reputational loss.	If audits reveal non-compliance or breaches.	Annually	Compliance audits	High	Ensure remediation of gaps	Infosys: Privacy compliance audits strengthened controls

Committee	Focus Area	Key Questions for Management	Purpose / Oversight Objective (and Red Flags)	When to Probe Deeper / Investigation Trigger	Frequency of Review / Discussion	Evidence / Supporting Documents	Risk / Criticality	Notes / Observations / Follow-up	Case Study / Example
General Board Oversight	**Strategy & Performance**	54. Are strategic objectives realistic and linked to measurable KPIs?	Align ambition with execution; vague goals hide underperformance.	If KPIs are unclear or results repeatedly fall short.	Quarterly	Strategy documents, KPI dashboards	High	Validate alignment	Kingfisher Airlines: Poor KPI alignment contributed to decline
		55. Is management's performance evaluated against risk-adjusted returns?	Promote disciplined decision-making.	If performance ignores risk-adjusted outcomes or benchmarks.	Quarterly	Performance reports	High	Compare returns vs risk	Yes Bank: Lack of risk-adjusted evaluation impacted oversight
	Culture & Ethics	56. Does the tone from the top reflect integrity and accountability?	Shape organizational behavior; tolerance of ethical lapses signals moral drift.	If whistleblower cases rise or senior management turnover is high.	Quarterly	HR and audit reports	High	Track ethical incidents	Satyam: Top-level moral lapses facilitated fraud
	Stakeholder Value	57. How are we ensuring sustainable long-term stakeholder value creation?	Anchor governance in stewardship; excessive short-term focus erodes trust.	If strategy emphasizes short-term gains over long-term metrics.	Quarterly	Financial and ESG reports	High	Monitor strategic alignment	Infosys: Long-term value focus strengthened governance
		58. Are stakeholder expectations and risks regularly assessed?	Align board priorities with stakeholder needs.	If feedback mechanisms are weak or absent.	Annually	Stakeholder surveys, reports	Medium	Track changes in stakeholder sentiment	Tata Power: Risk assessment improved stakeholder trust

Committee	Focus Area	Key Questions for Management	Purpose / Oversight Objective (and Red Flags)	When to Probe Deeper / Investigation Trigger	Frequency of Review / Discussion	Evidence / Supporting Documents	Risk / Criticality	Notes / Observations / Follow-up	Case Study / Example
		59. Are board decisions communicated transparently to stakeholders?	Maintain trust and credibility.	If communication is delayed, inconsistent, or selective.	Quarterly	Board communication logs	Medium	Validate timeliness and accuracy	Wipro: Transparent reporting enhanced reputation
		60. Are lessons from past governance failures integrated into board practices?	Embed continuous improvement; prevent repetition of errors.	If recurring governance gaps persist.	Annually	Board minutes, audit reports	High	Track implementation of lessons learned	Satyam: Lessons learned post-scandal improved board oversight